D1534993

Lukács, Marx and the Sources of Critical Theory

PHILOSOPHY AND SOCIETY SERIES

General Editor: Marshall Cohen

Lukács, Marx and the Sources of Critical Theory

ANDREW FEENBERG

ROWMAN AND LITTLEFIELD
Totowa, New Jersey

First published in the United States 1981 by
Rowman and Littlefield, 81 Adams Drive, Totowa, New Jersey 07512.

LIBRARY OF CONGRESS CATALOGING IN PUBLICATION DATA

Feenberg, Andrew.
    Lukács, Marx and the sources of critical theory.

    (Philosophy and society)
    Includes bibliographical references and index.
    1. Lukács, György, 1885–1971.   2. Marx, Karl,
1818–1883.   3. Frankfurt school of sociology—
History.   4. Dialectical materialism—History.
I. Title.   II. Series.
B4815.L84F43   335.4′1   80–22747
ISBN 0–8476–6272–1

Printed in the United States of America

For Anne-Marie

Contents

Preface

In recent years two books have come to be recognized as the most challenging contributions of Marxism to philosophy. They are Marx's *Economic and Philosophical Manuscripts,* and Georg Lukács' *History and Class Consciousness.* These books played a major role in the breakdown of the Stalinist interpretation of Marxism and the consequent revival of interest in Marxist thought among literary scholars, philosophers and sociologists. Yet despite the growing concern with the early works of Marx and Lukács, no one has attempted a comparative evaluation of these two most important texts of "unorthodox" Marxism. The main purpose of this book is to offer such an evaluation.

It is one of the great ironies of intellectual history that Marx and Lukács themselves failed to appreciate the significance of their own early works. Marx's *Manuscripts* were written in 1844 but had to wait nearly 100 years to see the light of day. Since its publication this unfinished early work has come to rival *Capital* as the text of reference for Marxists in the West. During the first half century after the publication of *History and Class Consciousness,* Lukács' book became an underground classic, rejected by its author and known only to a few European scholars. The seminal importance of this early work has only been widely recognized in the last decade.

The long eclipse of these books, left to what Engels once called "the nibbling of the mice," can be explained by their transitional position in the intellectual biographies of their authors. Both were trained as philosophers and steeped in a romantic revolutionism they eventually rejected in favor of "scientific socialism." Marx's *Manuscripts* and Lukács' *History and Class Consciousness* were written at similar turning points in their authors' spiritual trajectories, at times when they felt the need to move beyond these intellectual origins and believed they could do so without violent rupture through acts of dialectical transcendence. Later, they judged this transcendence inadequate, still internal to positions they uncompromisingly rejected in elaborating their mature outlook. There is little doubt that after the break their judgment on their early work was too harsh, that it contains more of value and had more influence on the later work than the authors were willing to concede.

The romantic influence is undoubtedly present in these early writings. By romanticism is usually meant that trend in modern culture which exalts subjectivity against objectivity, life against rationality, concreteness against abstraction. Certainly the antagonism of Marx and Lukács toward the oppressive formalism of capitalist social life, analyzed and condemned in parallel critiques of "alienation" and "reification," is to some degree tributary of that trend. And yet it would grossly distort the theories of alienation and reification to reduce them to a romantic protest against reason as is frequently suggested by contemporary critics.

It is true that Marx and Lukács were influenced by the romantic critique of capitalism, but they were still more profoundly influenced by the Hegelian critique of that critique. For Hegel, as for a number of other major figures in modern thought, romanticism has the value of a transcended moment, playing a propaedeutic role in the development of a rational outlook on the world that is not merely philistine and complacent but critical and rich in inwardness. It was Hegel who first systematically elaborated this characteristic modern response to the romantic revolt, the "post-romantic" reconciliation with rational necessity and human finitude that is defining for the "mature" personality of modern men and women.

The difficult and ambiguous program of the early Marx and Lukács involved preserving the moment of revolt in romanticism without recapitulating the subjectivistic errors so effectively criticized by Hegel. I will show that they are only partially successful in this task, but also that the task itself was well chosen and indeed still an obligatory one for a critical theory which rejects the facile pretensions to science of the so-called Marxist orthodoxy. Marx and Lukács approached this task with a similar method, which I will call "cultural" because of its orientation toward the most general patterns of meaning and purpose of entire societies. Just such a pattern is signified by the concepts of alienation and reification which they employ to analyze capitalist society. At the same time, these concepts are derived from reflection on the philosophical tradition and function in the context of the authors' discussion of philosophical problems. This unity of cultural and philosophical concerns is the distinctive trait of their early method.

For Marx and Lukács, philosophy is the discipline in which the operative horizon of everyday life is raised to consciousness and subjected to rational criticism. On this basis they argue that the conceptual dilemmas or "antinomies" of philosophy are symptomatic of deep cultural contradictions of the philosopher's society. Their most challenging conclusion is the idea of a "transcendence" of philosophy as such through the practical resolution of these contradictions in social life. This is perhaps the least well understood aspect of the early "philosophy of praxis" of Marx and Lukács, and the study of it will be the major theme uniting the various investigations which make up this book.

My method of approach in this study is that of a philosopher in the Continental tradition, specifically, the tradition founded on the early writings of Marx and Lukács. Because I believe the paradigms and problems of that tradition are still very much alive, this book is opened onto the future as well as the past, and is in fact less a work of intellectual history than an attempt at showing the continuing value of Marxism for social theory. To accomplish this purpose, I have selected among the themes and texts of my authors with an eye to contemporary concerns. As a result, much that is of primarily historical interests has been left by the wayside, however what remains is the larger and certainly the most interesting part of the whole.

I have devoted more space to the discussion of Lukács than to Marx, as the less well known of the two. Although Lukács was unaware of the existence of Marx's *Manuscripts* when he wrote *History and Class Consciousness*, his interpretation of *Capital* suggests a theory of the continuity of Marx's intellectual development which I elaborate in a specifically Lukácsian interpretation of the early Marx.

Lukács himself I approach from the standpoint of the two major schools of Marxist thought on which his early work had a profound influence. The Frankfurt School of Adorno, Horkheimer and Marcuse seized on Lukács' concept reification which, in combination with other sources, became the basis of its critique of positivism and its dialectical reformulation of Marxist theory. This influence is frequently acknowledged, but it has yet to be traced out in detail. While I do not accomplish that historiographic task here, one aim of this book is to expose some of the important links between Lukács and the Frankfurt School.

Somewhat later, in the period after World War II, French Marxism came under the influence of the early Lukács as a whole generation of social theorists sought radical alternatives to the dominant Stalinist orthodoxy. The most famous text of this trend is Maurice Merleau-Ponty's *Adventures of the Dialectic* which first introduced the term "Western Marxism" to describe the tradition stemming from *History and Class Consciousness*. The French were primarily interested in Lukács' theory of class consciousness which, along with reification, is the other major theme of the book. They saw in this theory an alternative to the official Marxist dogma of the party as surrogate subject of the revolution. With Lukács they reaffirmed the primacy of working class "praxis," articulated ideologically by the party but not replaced by it.

I had the good fortune to study with representatives of both these schools of thought, with Herbert Marcuse and Lucien Goldmann. Starting out from the disparate traditions and emphases they represent, I propose a new interpretation designed to reestablish the unity of Lukács' early Marxism. This background may help to explain the difference between my approach to Lukács and that of English and American scholars such as Gareth Stedman Jones and George Lichtheim, who condemn the theory of reification as ir-rationalist and find Stalinist implications in the theory of class consciousness. I believe it is time to reconsider these very negative evaluations which square neither with the content nor the intellectual impact of Lukács' text.

When Lukács is compared, not with Bergson or Stalin, but with Marx's early philosophical works, a very different picture emerges. Like the early Marx, the early Marxist Lukács is a critic of what Kolakowski has called the "alienation of reason" in modern capitalist society. But that critique is by no means irrationalist; rather, its aim is the establishment of a dialectical paradigm of rationality suited to the task of social self-understanding and human liberation. Such a dialectical paradigm of rationality can be of no service to authoritarian regimes, but only to a socialist culture of self-rule. Not the least important dimension of the early Marx and Lukács is the contribution they make to defining the broad outlines of such a culture.

* * *

The writing of this book has placed me in the debt of many people. Lucien Goldmann and Herbert Marcuse introduced me to Marxist philosophy and to the work of Lukács. My wife,

Anne-Marie Feenberg, and Jerry Doppelt read chapter after chapter and frequently convinced me to make changes for the better. Many others read portions of the manuscript and offered criticism and encouragement. I recall with pleasure long and often fruitful exchanges with Al Gouldner, Stanley Aronowitz, Doug Kellner, Bill Leiss, Stanley Rosen, and Mark Poster. I have also learned a great deal from others writing on Lukács, especially István Mészáros, Paul Breines, Andrew Arato, and Michael Löwy. Authors ask for a great deal of moral support and patience from those with whom they are in daily contact. For exemplary performance in this regard, I want to thank my colleagues in the philosophy department of San Diego State University and, once again, my wife.

1

The Philosophy of Praxis

MARX AND LUKÁCS

In the course of this first chapter, I will sketch a preliminary analysis of the philosophical enterprise in which the early Marx and Lukács were engaged. Because the methods of their early works are so similar, it is useful to clarify the one through the other. In this chapter and the next, I will discuss the philosophy of the early Marx from a Lukácsian perspective, as a background to the exposition of Lukács' own parallel attempt to resolve the problems first posed by Marx. There are, of course, considerable differences between these authors, and there is always the risk that in comparing them in this manner the identity of the one will be submerged in that of the other. I will naturally do my best to avoid an artificial identification of the two positions where they do actually differ; however, I will argue that in spite of real differences we are dealing here with a specific philosophical doctrine, which might be called "philosophy of praxis," and which is shared by a number of thinkers.[1] The identification of such doctrines, which ultimately are defined in ideal-types such as "empiricism" or "idealism," is an important, even if necessarily inconclusive contribution of philosophy to the history of ideas.

The method of Marx and Lukács in their early philosophical works is very different from the "scientific socialism" erected later on the basis of historical observation and economic theory. In 1843 and 1844 Marx developed a philosophy of revolution which at the time he seems to have intended as a foundation for empirical studies of economics such as those he presented in his later works. From 1919 to 1923 Lukács, similarly, elaborated a Marxist philosophical theory that is independent of Marxist economics in significant dimensions. For both the early Marx and Lukács, such central Marxist concepts as the proletariat and socialism were not first developed through empirical research. Instead, as philosophers they set out from a critical discussion of the philosophical tradition, in the course of which they *deduced* the characteristic historical concepts of Marxism. Included in this deduction is the concept of revolution, which plays a pivotal methodological role in the philosophies of Marx and Lukács.

In interpreting Marx's *Economic and Philosophical Manuscripts* as a philosophy of praxis, I have been obliged to choose positions in some of the numerous debates over this early work. It will be useful at the outset to make these positions explicit by situating this interpretation with respect to some others. I will not review the enormous literature on the *Manuscripts;* only two facets of it are relevant here, the debates over the *ontological* and the *normative* character of social categories in the *Manuscripts.*[2] At issue is more than a matter of textual exegesis. The larger question that depends on the interpretation given the text concerns whether the *Manuscripts* are a philosophy of praxis, as I am engaged in defining that term, or, on the contrary, a far less ambitious methodological preliminary or ethical complement to economic research within the framework of the traditional concept of reason.

I have done my best to show the former, that Marx founds a new concept of reason in revolution through an *ontological* treatment of *social* categories. This approach brings to the fore all that links the project of the early Marx to that of Lukács in a later period. In 1923 Lukács was of course unaware of the existence of Marx's *Manuscripts*, which had not yet been published when he wrote *History and Class Consciousness*. The similarities I will identify are all the more significant as indicating the inner connection of the philosophy of praxis with Marxism.

This matter of the similarity between the early Marxist work of Marx and Lukács requires further comment, because of the unwitting tendency of some commentators to treat *History and Class Consciousness* as though, like the *Manuscripts*, it had been written before Marx's *Capital*. Thus Lukács is sometimes blamed for assuming without proof theses which he and contemporary Marxist readers regarded as adequately established by *Capital;* sometimes Lukács is also blamed for having substituted philosophy for economics, regressing behind the level of scientificity achieved by Marxism, as though no philosophical problems might arise from or be resolved on the basis of the mature thought of Marx.

In fact, *Capital* is the basis of Lukács' philosophy of praxis and not the early work of Marx, much of which was still unpublished when Lukács began to write as a Marxist. Now *Capital* is a quite self-consciously unphilosophical work, in spite of Marx's prefatory acknowledgement of Hegel's influence. In it Marx is careful to minimize the use of philosophical terminology and to avoid the exploration of properly philosophical problems. Yet we now know on the basis of extensive textual evidence, as the early Lukács could not, just how complex were the philosophical considerations behind *Capital*. The link between the *Manuscripts* and the published writings of Marx's maturity is supplied by his own draft of *Capital;* but the publication of this text, the so-called *Grundrisse*, was delayed until the Second World War.[3] These textual absences, combined with the image Marx wished to project of his work in *Capital*, seemed to authorize a scientistic interpretation of Marx's later doctrine which Lukács first challenged from a dialectical perspective.

Lukács made the connection between Marxism and philosophy (that is to say, between Marx and Hegel), primarily through a reflection on Marx's methodology in his economic writings, and only secondarily on the basis of those of Marx's comments on philosophical matters with which he was acquainted. This is possible because, as Ernest Mandel remarks, "the concept of alienation . . . is part of the mature Marx's *instrumentarium.*"[4] Lukács was in fact the first to show this, to notice and explain not merely the influence of Hegel on Marx's early political essays, or on the general Marxian "worldview," but on the concepts and method of *Capital*. He reevaluated Marx's famous "coquetting" with Hegel, and showed that in that work, "a whole series of categories of central importance and in constant use stem directly from Hegel's *Logic.*"[5]

Lukács reconstructed a philosophy of praxis from the methodological traces of Marx's own philosophical position visible in his economic writings. The result of this effort is not identical with the position of either the *Manuscripts* or the *Grundrisse;* nevertheless, it is impressive to what extent Lukács' somewhat speculative extrapolations from Marx's published work can find support in these unpublished ones. Most important, Lukács' philosophy of praxis has remarkable structural similarities to that of Marx, notably insofar as Lukács develops an original critique of philosophy paralleling Marx's own. A large part of the reason for this convergence of the early Marx and the early Marxist Lukács may be biographical. Like Marx, Lukács was deeply schooled in Hegelian dialectics and so when he sought to develop a Marxist philosophy, he returned precisely to the Hegelian doctrine from which Marx set out. Yet this biographical coincidence does not quite explain the similarity of the transformation undergone by Hegel's dialectic at the hands of Marx and

Lukács. It is this link, mediated by the supposedly "scientific" work *Capital*, which bespeaks an affinity of Marxism for philosophy of praxis.

THE ANTINOMIES

The defining trait of philosophy of praxis, as I will use the term, is the attempt to show that the "antinomies" of philosophy can be resolved only in history. The concept of "antinomy" employed here is derived from Hegel, for whom it signifies the ever widening gap between subject and object in modern culture. Ever since Descartes distinguished the two substances, philosophy and life had become more and more sharply sundered in accordance with this distinction. Rich and complex theories of the subjective dimension of being pondered the meaning of freedom, value, political ideals, while equally powerful and encompassing theories of the objective dimension of being explained the laws of necessity in nature and history in totally incompatible terms. From his earliest to his last works, Hegel saw his task as cataloguing the resulting contradictions in modern culture and transcending them in a dialectical conception of being which would take into account both its subjective and objective dimensions.

For Hegel the transcendence of the antinomies was a theoretical task, although he did believe that the theory could only be brought to perfection under specific historical conditions which happened to be those under which he lived. Philosophy of praxis begins with a critique of the conservative implications of this approach to resolving the antinomies. Marx argued that because Hegel could not conceive of really radical changes in modern culture, he tended to rationalize temporary historical conditions as though they were eternal necessities. Social revolution and not philosophical speculation was required to transcend the antinomies.

Had Marx confined himself to arguing this position in

relation to the antinomies of moral and political life, he would have arrived at a new philosophy of value based on the demand for social change. This new philosophy would have been compatible with some traditional ontology and might have been formulated as a "left" variant of Hegel's philosophy. Marx's startling innovation was to include *all* the antinomies, those relating to epistemology and ontology as well as the moral and political ones, in denouncing Hegel's purely theoretical approach. Marx thus arrived at the astounding proposition that social change could not only accomplish such goals as reconciling individual and society, moral responsibility and self-interest, but that social change could also unite subject and object, thought and being, man and nature.

This proposition has a number of paradoxical corollaries from which we must not shrink in interpreting the early Marx. As we will see, Lukács too shares this same approach. When philosophy of praxis contends that human action is philosophically pertinent not just in ethics or politics but in all domains generally, it is asserting a wholly original *ontological* position. For this philosophy, human action touches the substratum of being as such, and not simply those special domains we usually conceive as affected by our activities. In somewhat different terms, essentially this same requirement can be formulated as the transcendence of the antinomy of value and fact, "Ought" and "Is." For, if human action can affect being, then values do not confront reality as a normless and humanly indifferent sphere, but rather as its highest potentialities.

The philosophy of praxis is thus opposed to both naturalism, for which human being is only a marginal and ontologically insignificant facet of reality, and also to ethical idealism, for which values stand impotently opposed to a reality defined at the outset as indifferent to value. Hence Marx writes that "nature too, taken abstractly, for itself, and rigidly separated from man, is *nothing* for man."[6] And Lukács argues that "the unmediated juxtaposition of natural laws and ethical imperatives is the logical expression of immediate societal existence in bourgeois society."[7]

This position is a coherent one only where the being of being generally is interpreted through a special sphere of being in which human being is actually able to transform the objects on which it acts. Then the apparently humanly indifferent spheres, such as nature, can be ontologically subordinated to those spheres within which human being can affect the substratum of reality. The attempt to understand being in general through human being is called philosophical anthropology. Marx and Lukács share this approach with philosophers such as Feuerbach and Heidegger, with this difference: the latter conceive human being metaphysically, and so construct speculative philosophies with moralistic overtones. For Marx and Lukács, on the contrary, history is the "paradigmatic order" for the interpretation of being generally.[8]

Because of this historical orientation, the philosophy of praxis is not a speculative doctrine, but is based on the (social) scientific study of reality. But, for this philosophy, "reality" is history, and history itself is to be understood as in essence an object of human practice. The ontologically significant relation between human being and being in general is now social action because history is constituted in such action. As Lukács puts it, "We have . . . made our own history and if we are able to regard the whole of reality [*Wirklichkeit*] as history (i.e. as *our* history, for there is no other), we shall have raised ourselves in fact to the position from which reality can be understood as our 'action.' "[9]

Because the philosophy of praxis conceives being as history and history as the product of human action, it can *mutatis mutandis* conceive of human action as pertinent to being. Then it can be shown that such philosophical antinomies as that of subject and object, value and fact can be transcended in history. Such transcending action takes on a universal significance, going beyond the merely human world to affect being as such. For philosophy of praxis, history *is* ontology, the becoming of the human species is the privileged domain within which the problems of the theory of being can finally be resolved. As Marcuse writes in an early essay on Marx's *Manuscripts:* "The history of man is at the same time the process of 'the whole of nature'; his history is the 'production and reproduction' of the whole of nature, furtherance of what exists objectively through once again transcending its current form."[10]

Throughout this book, I will be concerned with the implications of this remarkable proposition. These implications can be considered under two main headings. First, there is the dimension of philosophy of praxis concerned with the resolution of social antinomies through the disalienation or de-reification of social life. The discussion of this social dimension of the theory will occupy the major portion of this book. As I have argued above, the philosophical ambition of Marx and Lukacs goes beyond social theory, for they claim that all objectivity can be disalienated starting out from the disalienation of society. This wider claim indicates a second dimension of the theory concerned with the ontological generalization of results of the analysis of society. This most daring dimension of the philosophy of praxis will be treated separately in the concluding chapters of this book. There I will consider serious objections to the philosophy of praxis and attempt to formulate an original response drawing on the resources of philosophy of praxis itself. Before returning now to the social issues that will be the concern of the larger portion of this book, I would like to consider briefly some of the objections to viewing Marx's philosophy of praxis as a contribution to ontology.

ONTOLOGY OR HISTORY

The interpretation of Marx's *Manuscripts* as a philosophy of praxis in my sense is contested by an important tradition of Marx scholarship, the Frankfurt School. Alfred Schmidt's careful study of Marx's concept of nature attempts to situate the *Manuscripts* at an equal distance from a materialist ontology and a radical historicism such as that described above. Jürgen Habermas also rejects the interpretation of Marx's *Manuscripts* as a philosophy of praxis. Habermas argues that the early Marx distinguishes between nature as such, and nature as it enters the historical sphere through labor, and which therefore has a social character. This would restrict Marx's conclusions to society, in the larger framework of some traditional ontology in which being is in essence independent of man. Within this same tradition, however, it is customary to interpret Lukács' early Marxism critically as a philosophy of praxis. Thus the common traits I attempt to identify in these two basic sources of Marxist philosophy are here denied.

It is interesting to note that the other highly influential contemporary school of Marxist thought, that founded by Louis Althusser, makes no such distinction. Rejecting equally the early Marxist thought of both Marx and Lukács, the Althusserians see in them both a romantic refusal of scientific objectivity and the independence of nature. There is thus a certain unwitting convergence of Frankfurt School and Althusserian interpretations in that both emphasize the autonomy of nature as against philosophy of praxis and condemn as idealistic any doctrine that attempts to understand nature through history. I cannot consider these convergent critiques in detail. Here I would like simply to sketch the Frankfurt School's attempt to "save" the early Marx from historicism.

In *Knowledge and Human Interests*, Habermas does admit that Marx's text is ambiguous on this score. He claims that the ambiguities have given rise to a "phenomenological strain of Marxism" which overlooks Marx's naturalism and for which, therefore, "the category of labor then acquires unawares the meaning of world-constituting life activity in general."[11] Although Habermas includes Marcuse in this phenomenological tendency, only some of Marcuse's early essays truly belong to it. His later *Reason and Revolution* in fact belongs to the opposed tendency for which Habermas speaks.

There Marcuse formulates a position close to Schmidt's and

Habermas' in denying the ontological status of social categories. Marcuse too notes the ambiguities of Marx's text; he writes of it: "All this has an obvious resemblance to Hegel's idea of reason. Marx even goes so far as to describe the self-realization of man in terms of the unity of thought and being."[12] But, in fact, "Marx . . . detached dialectic from this ontological base. In his work, the negativity of reality becomes a *historical* condition which cannot be hypostasized as a metaphysical state of affairs."[13] And so for Marx, "The idea of reason has been superseded by the idea of happiness."[14]

Such an interpretation may explain Marx's later Marxism but it does not account for the *Manuscripts*. It is particularly significant that in the formulations of Habermas and Marcuse, all the antinomies Marx attempted to transcend reappear as alternatives between which he is supposed to have chosen: naturalism *or* humanism, history *or* ontology, happiness *or* reason. But Marx himself writes:

Communism as a fully developed naturalism is humanism, and as a fully developed humanism is naturalism. It is the *definitive* resolution of the antagonism between man and nature, and between man and man. It is the true solution of the conflict between existence and essence, between objectification and self-affirmation, between freedom and necessity, between individual and species. It is the solution of the riddle of history and knows itself to be this solution.[15]

Marx himself would not have defined his own advance over Hegel as the demonstration that alienation is a historical category rather than an ontological one. Rather, his advance was to show that all ontology is historical in essence and that the dichotomy between being and history is therefore false. The idea that history, properly understood, has ontological significance is the main philosophical claim of philosophy of praxis. Marx did not choose between an ontological and a historical interpretation of the social categories; he chose both. Only such an understanding of the text can make sense of Marx's most striking utterances, such as the one just quoted, or the following: "Society is the accomplished union of man and nature, the veritable resurrection of nature, the realized naturalism of man and the realized humanism of nature."[16]

THE NORMATIVE DIMENSION

The interpretation of the *Manuscripts* as a philosophy of praxis contributes to clarifying the debate concerning the "ethical" moment in Marx's early work. Marx's concept of the "human essence" which is "alienated" under capitalism is frequently interpreted as an ethical ideal opposed to a normless reality. Others see in the *Manuscripts* an attempt to transcend the opposition of value and fact implied in such an ethical conception. The debate over the *Manuscripts* is of course related to the larger debate over Marxism and ethics.[17] Considered as a philosophy of praxis, Marx's theory is unquestionably normative in some sense, but I argue that it is not based on an ethical conception.

What is at stake here is the dialectical character of Marx's theory, hence also his relation to Hegel. Were Marx to accept the dichotomy of value and fact, ethical and social reality, he would regress behind Hegel to a utopian-moralistic position like that of Bruno Bauer, Moses Hess and the other Left Hegelians. In his discussion of Hess, Lukács has shown that this philosophical tendency attempted to recover revolution-ary possibilities by positing ethical values as the basis for knowledge of the future, in opposition to Hegel's concrete analysis of and reconciliation with the present moment. But in the process, these thinkers lost Hegel's great advance over Kant and Fichte, his concept of being as continuous becoming. As Marcuse explains it, "Every state of existence has to be surpassed; it is something negative, which things, driven by their inner potentialities, desert for another state, which again reveals itself as negative, as limit."[18] It is through this conception that Hegel relativized the ethical ideal as a moment in the real process of becoming of what is, and so went beyond utopian moralism. This Hegelian conception of development is also the philosophical basis of the Marxian idea of a "transition" to socialism, in contrast with utopian schemes of reform.

Lukács discovers in this Hegelian dialectic of "Ought" and "Is" the basis of the Marxian critique of political economy as revolutionary science. He writes that,

In contrast to Fichte with his revolutionary Utopia, Hegel developed very early on in his work the tendency to "understand what is," a tendency which originally pointed energetically in the direction of the future. His concern to comprehend the present as at once become and becoming is . . . the germ of a true historical dialectics (the dialectics of history translated into thought). For it is precisely in the present that all forms of objectivity can be revealed quite concretely as processes, since it is the present which shows most clearly the unity of result and starting point of the process. Given that, the rejection of all "Oughts" and futuristic utopian thinking, the concentration of philosophy on knowledge of the present (grasped dialectically) emerges precisely as the only possible epistemological method of knowing what is really knowable about the future, the tendencies within the present which impel it really and concretely towards the future.[19]

On these terms, were Marx to posit the "human essence" as an ethical ideal, Hegelian philosophy would already have transcended it in thought through the demonstration of the relative rationality of what is. Alienation might, like the police courts Hegel deduces from the Idea, remain as an unpleasant fact of practical life. But then so are fleas and measles. The indifference of philosophical reason to such matters, essentially to human happiness and fulfillment, is not arbitrary but expresses the actual limits of the social world. The demand for the abstract ideal is already presupposed by this philosophy as a moment of romantic negation necessarily frustrated by an objectivity which transcends it, that is to say, by reason itself.

This philosophy is not overcome by the renewed positing of the ideal, but rather anticipates the latter and refutes it in advance.

Hegel's critique of Kant and of abstract ethical idealism in general, influenced Marx to seek a basis for revolutionary theory in the tendencies of social reality, in a dialectic of ideal and real in history. In his early writings, Marx attempts to transfer the ideal concepts of political philosophy from the domain of pure thought to the domain of reality, where they can be treated as potentialities awaiting realization. The contradictions between philosophy and reality are reformulated as immanent contradictions in reality itself. The new method is neither speculative nor empirical, but synthesizes these contrary approaches in a reflective ideology-critique. This ideology-critique relativizes what is and what ought to be as contradictory tendencies actually inhabiting the real-in-process.

Thus Marx does not set out from a philosophically elaborated concept of the state, that might be immediately contrasted with the institutions he wishes to criticize. In fact, he dismisses this method contemptuously in a letter to Ruge: "Until now the philosophers had the solution to all riddles in their desks, and the stupid outside world simply had to open its mouth so that the roasted pigeons of absolute science might fly into it."[20] Instead, the philosophical deduction of what ought to be must proceed from actual social struggles in which the living contradiction of ideal and real appears. The appropriate role for the new philosopher consists in "explaining to the world its own acts, "showing that actual struggles contain a transcending content that can be linked to the concept of a rational social life. "The critic," Marx writes, "therefore can start with any form of theoretical and practical consciousness and develop the true actuality out of the forms inherent in existing actuality as its ought-to-be and goal."[21]

In these earliest "Marxist" writings, Marx can be seen struggling to release new grounds for revolution from the conservative Hegelian formulation of political philosophy. A generation later Engels summarized Marx's conclusion with admirable simplicity. Where Hegel had claimed that "All that is real is rational; and all that is rational is real," for Marx:

The Hegelian proposition turns into its opposite through Hegelian dialectics itself: All that is real in the sphere of human history becomes irrational in the process of time, is therefore irrational by its very destination, is tainted beforehand with irrationality; and everything which is rational in the minds of men is destined to become real, however much it may contradict existing apparent reality. In accordance with all the rules of the Hegelian method of thought, the proposition of the rationality of everything which is real resolves itself into the other proposition: All that exists deserves to perish.[22]

In sum, the only way *beyond* Hegel is *through* him. This passage Marx makes in the *Manuscripts*, where he is finally able to "develop the true actuality out of the forms inherent in existing actuality as its ought-to-be and goal." There Marx identifies reason (true actuality) with the historically and socially mediated process of satisfying human needs and on that basis developing human individuality. Then the "existing actuality," alienated capitalist society, is shown to be reason's "unreasonable form," which must be further mediated and overcome through revolution. The critique of political economy, which begins already in the *Manuscripts*, appears here as the derivation of socialist potentialities from the contradictions of the given capitalist forms. The "ought-to-be and goal" emerges from the dialectic of existence and essence as a demand of reason, a methodological precondition of rationality, and not as an ethical ideal.

As a philosopher of praxis, Marx attempts to reconstruct the concept of reason so that capitalist alienation appears as reason's essential problem, a problem to be resolved through historical action. Marx takes what for Hegel and earlier philosophy is a mere social contingency, human suffering, and dignifies it with ontological status, not in order to attribute it to the human condition generally, but rather the better to comprehend the presuppositions of its historical transcendence. These presuppositions are preserved ideally in philosophy, in the concept of reason, and therefore Marx insists, against the reformers of the "practical political party," that "You cannot abolish philosophy without realizing it."[23]

The concept of an *"Aufhebung"* of philosophy also has a methodological side, with which we will be focally concerned in this book. Once again, it is by reference to the Frankfurt School that I will attempt to clarify the project of the early Marx and Lukács.

META-THEORY AS IDEOLOGY-CRITIQUE

The terms "meta-theory" and "meta-critique" have entered Marxist discourse through the Frankfurt School. They have achieved wide currency lately through Habermas' use of them to refer to the study of the various forms of theory in the light of their intrinsic dependence on specific "knowledge-constitutive interests."[24] These interests Habermas distinguishes from those of everyday practical affairs by their enormous generality, which makes of them transcendental conditions of possible objectivity for the spheres of knowledge they determine. Thus, for Habermas scientific knowledge is not really value-free, but is based on an interest in technical control that first generates for human thought the type of object studied by science.

Habermas' innovation is admittedly based on the Marxist theory of ideology, which also attempts to identify, through reflection on the larger context of beliefs, hidden interests which these beliefs rationalize or serve. Habermas is nevertheless justified in abandoning the traditional concept of "ideology" to introduce a newer terminology, given the historical accretion of often contradictory meanings that have rendered the traditional concept almost useless without a definitional effort quite as large as that required by a neologism. Most importantly, I believe, with the term "meta-theory" Habermas emphasizes the reflective side of the concept of "ideology," while completely avoiding the reductionist implications of that concept in most current usages.

The term "meta-theory" in this sense bears a useful resemblance to the method of Lukács and Marx in certain of their studies of the philosophical tradition. The philosophy of praxis approaches this tradition critically while avoiding sociological reductionism. Marx and Lukács are less concerned with deriving the categories of bourgeois philosophy from the conditions of capitalist society than with uncovering the "rational kernel within the mystical shell" of this philosophy. They attempt, in other words, to discover what retains validity in the tradition in spite of its socially relative limitations, which they also identify. The methodological approach they employ is a reflective one, focussed on the hidden connection of theory to a background of involvements from which one cannot successfully abstract, but which one can change.

There is, however, a considerable difference between what I will call the "meta-theoretical" approach of Marx and Lukács and the approach of Habermas. Habermas' knowledge-constitutive interests are anthropological in their generality. The (relative) truth of knowledge is conserved in contact with these interests by reason of their very generality. Reductionism is thus avoided at the high price of a loss in sociological concreteness. Marx and Lukács, I believe, offer no such theory of general anthropological interests. Instead, the meta-theory moves in an opposite direction, toward a domain of concreteness which is claimed to be founding for the theoretical abstractions constructed on its basis. We might better compare this approach with that recommended by Whitehead in a different context:

I hold that philosophy is the critic of abstractions. Its function is the double one, first of harmonising them by assigning to them their relative status as abstractions, and secondly of completing them by direct comparison with more concrete intuitions of the universe, and thereby promoting the formation of more complete schemes of thought.[25]

In Marx and Lukács, of course, the aim of such criticism of abstractions is not to found a speculative metaphysics, but rather to achieve what might be called a *sociological desublimation* of the concepts of philosophy.

To some extent this difference in orientation, as compared with Habermas, may be due to the fact that the latter is primarily concerned to refute a supposedly value-free positivism, while Marx and Lukács reflect on social theory in a cultural climate deeply imbued by Kantianism. In Kantian philosophy the formal properties of rationality are abstracted as completely as possible from the particular contents on which the faculty of reason exercises itself. The Kantian system consists in the derivation of these formal properties as they relate to epistemology, ethics and aesthetics, as general preconditions for any and all knowledge and action in the corresponding domains of real life. But, as Lukács notes, Kant is sufficiently rigorous and honest to acknowledge the difficulty of linking up this paradigm of reason with the concrete content of the life processes from which it has been abstracted and for which it is supposed to provide the preconditions.

In this Kantian cultural climate, both Marx and Lukács follow in the footsteps of Hegel in attempting to resolve the antinomies of form and content that arise from the formalistic paradigm of rationality. To Hegel they owe dialectics as the method through which the opposites can be reconciled in a higher unity, a totality. The application of the concept of totality to the study of the historically given forms of rationality provides the basis for a social theory of theory which is not reductive, for an ideology-critique in the most interesting sense of the term. In their application of dialectics, the juxtaposition of the abstract theoretical concepts of philosophy with a specific social background both explains the impasses and antinomies of theory on a social basis, and shows a path to resolution through social action. Thus philosophy is not seen as a mere rationalization of covert interests, nor as a merely passive reflection of production relations. Rather, it is shown to be the form in which the actual contradictions of social life are raised to consciousness most generally and most rigorously, *under the horizon* of the given society.

Susan Buck-Morss has argued recently that Adorno's cultural criticism was deeply influenced by this method, as he discovered it in Lukács. She summarizes Lukács' approach lucidly as follows:

Instead of reducing bourgeois thought to the economic conditions of its production, Lukács argued that the nature of those conditions could be found within the intellectual phenomena themselves. . . . Once these thinkers accepted given social reality as *the* reality, they had to come upon a barrier of irrationality which could not be overcome (and which had led Kant to posit the thing-in-itself), because that barrier could not be removed from theory without being removed from society. Conversely, if theorists could see through the reified appearances, they would recognize that the antinomies of philosophy were due not to the inadequacies of reason, but to those of the reality in which reason tried to find itself.[26]

Much the same analysis could be made, in a general way, of Marx's early discussions of political philosophy, or his critique of Hegel's *Phenomenology* in the *Manuscripts*. It is noteworthy too that Marx's most illuminating later comment on the theory of ideology points in the same direction. Speaking of the "relationship between the *political* and *literary representatives* of a class and the class they represent," Marx says:

What makes them representatives . . . is the fact that in their minds they do not get beyond the limits which the latter do not get beyond in life, that they are consequently driven, theoretically, to the same problems and solutions to which material interest and social position drive the latter practically.[27]

The uniqueness of the approach taken by Marx and Lukács, which distinguishes it not only from Kant but also from Hegel, is their common belief that the primary antinomy to be overcome is that of traditional philosophy and social reality. Here the term "meta-theory" applies in a double sense. Not only do Marx and Lukács attempt to relate philosophical abstractions to the social lifeworld, but they claim to identify the intrinsic limitation of the method of formulating abstractions in traditional philosophy. This limitation, they argue, is due to the tradition's systematic refusal to consider the philosophical implications of really fundamental social change. Because traditional philosophy assumes that the alienated foundations of the social order are rooted in the very nature of reality, it concludes that the antinomies can only be resolved speculatively, in thought, and formulates them in view of this sort of resolution. The criterion of philosophical adequacy that guides concept formation in the tradition thus reflects an implicit sense of the limits of social change which Marx and Lukács explicitly challenge. For them, the resolution of the antinomies requires a form of radical social transformation unimagined or rejected as impossible by the tradition. Marx and Lukács defend their point of view by arguing that this transformation is really possible, and on this basis they claim to offer an entirely new interpretation of the antinomies, freed from the limitations of the tradition.

Nevertheless, neither Marx nor Lukács simply dismiss philosophy. Rather, they proceed from the assumption that the split between the concept of reason, as elaborated in philosophy, and its concrete social substratum reflects contradictions in social reality and points the way toward the practical resolution of the latter. Traditional philosophy, in spite of its limits, was able to identify social potentialities, even if only in a speculative form antagonistic to practice. The problem now consists in reconstructing the insights of this philosophy in a new context, oriented toward practical social change. Marcuse summarizes this conclusion as follows: "The philosophical construction of reason is replaced by the creation of a rational society. The philosophical ideals of a better world and of true Being are incorporated into the practical aim of struggling mankind, where they take on a human form."[28]

In sum, the meta-theoretical approach in the sense the term will be used here consists in dialectically relativizing philosophical form and social content, and correspondingly, theory and practice. A standpoint immanent to both theory and the philosophical tradition is equally rejected. Marx and Lukács do not philosophize within the historically given tradition, presupposing the continuing validity of philosophy as such, and *eo ipso* of its forms of evidence and its problematics. Rather, they consider the tradition as essentially completed, and then proceed to study it from "outside," as a relative moment in a larger social process in which practice can intervene. It is in this light, and not in some merely pragmatic sense of urgency, that we are to understand Marx's thesis: "Philosophers have only *interpreted* the world in various ways; the point is, to *change* it."[29]

A NOTE ON THEORY AND PRACTICE[30]

Within the tradition of Western Marxism, these rather opaque formulations of the theory-practice relation have a quite definite meaning. One of the aims of this book is to clarify that meaning as it is understood within that tradition. Since I am writing within that tradition myself, I will continue to use terms like "philosophy," "theory," "practice," and phrases like "the unity of theory and practice," "the realization of philosophy," in much the sense that Marx and Lukács use them. Before proceeding on this basis, I would like to step briefly outside that framework to anticipate certain objections that are frequently made to the Marxist treatment of the theory-practice relation. These objections might be put in the form of questions that implicitly challenge the very idea of a unity of theory and practice or a realization of philosophy in Marx's and Lukács' sense. Here are some examples:

1. Marx and Lukács claim that they are "realizing" philosophy, putting theory into practice. How does this differ from "applying" theory to the solution of a practical problem?

2. Marx and Lukács claim that the philosophical tradition is finished, which would seem to mean that they themselves are not philosophers contributing to that tradition. Yet surely works like Marx's *Manuscripts* and Lukács' *History and Class Consciousness* are philosophical works. Are they then philosophers, and if so how can they elaborate a philosophy on the basis of the proposition that philosophy is dead?

3. Marx and Lukács seem to say that only the revolution can "solve" philosophical problems, and yet they propose their solutions to these problems in philosophical works written before the revolution. Does this not imply that the revolution is after all irrelevant to the solution of philosophical problems?

These questions arise largely from problems in understanding Western Marxism's special terminology. When this terminology is understood it becomes clear that Marx and Lukács are not making quite such wild and radical claims as they at first appear to be making. The chief difficulties stem from ambiguities in the terms "philosophy" and "theory." I will therefore treat these first.

Marx and Lukács do not use the term "philosophy" to refer primarily to the activity of reflecting on the basic assumptions and ideas of a culture. In this sense they are obviously still doing philosophy, and they would not deny it. For them, "philosophy" refers to a specific historical tradition of reflection that develops common themes from the Greeks to Hegel. They do regard this tradition as "completed," and they would deny that they are merely continuing it in their own work. The unity of the tradition consists in certain paradigmatic concepts and methods which run through it from the beginning to the end, in spite of major variations and innovations. It is this paradigm which has been exhausted, not the activity of reflection *per se*.

However unfamiliar this approach to understanding philosophy may be in the Anglo-American context, it is a well identified tendency in Continental philosophy since Feuerbach. The early Marx and Lukács, Nietzsche, Heidegger, and Derrida have all proposed general theories of the unity of the philosophical tradition, and on that basis have announced its end. This amounts to treating philosophy a bit like the monuments of a dying civilization. Reflection continues, and indeed it has no original concepts to substitute for the old ones. But the philosopher's relation to these concepts is no longer immediate, naive; the "death" of philosophy means no more than that thinkers become conscious of the historical limits of the cultural system on the basis of which these concepts arise.

For Marxists, this consciousness is specifically social. They trace the origin of philosophy's eternal truths, its constants and paradigms, back to social causes that, they believe, are in the process of disappearing. There is a particularly clear statement of this position in the *Communist Manifesto*.

The history of all past society has consisted in the development of class antagonisms, antagonisms that assumed different forms at different epochs. But whatever form they may have taken, one fact is common to all past ages, viz., the exploitation of one part of society by the other. No wonder, then, that the social consciousness of past ages, despite all the multiplicity and variety it displays, moves within certain forms, or general ideas, which cannot completely vanish except with the total disappearance of class antagonisms. The Communist revolution is the most radical rupture with traditional property relations; no wonder that its development involves the most radical rupture with traditional ideas.[31]

If we accept the limitation of "philosophy" to a specific tradition bound up with the history of class society, then we need a wider term with which to refer to the general process of reflection on basic assumptions of which this "philosophy" would be an instance. This more general term is "theory." Now we need to distinguish between two types of theory, a type which is identified with traditional philosophy and a new type which is identified with the sort of reflection in which Marxism engages. This is precisely the distinction between "traditional" and "critical" theory that Horkheimer made in a famous essay. Like the Frankfurt School, Marx and Lukács argue that traditional theory has been superseded by a new critical theory. In the works with which we will be concerned, they do not suggest that philosophy should be abandoned for practical activity or simply "applied" in the usual technical sense of the term. The point, then, is not that reflection should cease, but that a new kind of reflection is needed.

This new kind of reflection differs from the old at two levels. On the one hand, it treats many assumptions which the philosophical tradition took for granted as problems. On the other hand, it treats these assumptions as problems at the specific level of the social causes from which they arise. For example, instead of accepting the eternal necessity of the antinomy of public and private interest, critical theory would show that this antinomy has a specific social cause that can be removed. Critical theory still works with the concepts of public and private interest elaborated in philosophy, but it problematizes the social background against which these two forms of interest arise as antagonistic opposites.

The critique of abstract or "pure" theory is to be understood in this context. It is, once again, not that Marx and Lukács reject conceptual generality for empirical specificity, but rather that for them the process of abstraction in which philosophy detaches its concepts from their social basis gives rise to a bias they reject. This is a bias toward treating philosophical issues as though they rested on eternal facts of nature or ontologically necessary dimensions of the human condition. But once conceived in this way, the social background of these issues is occluded and it becomes impossible to imagine human action contributing to changing this background. Marx and Lukács thus do not return to the empirical so much as show the inseparable connection between the most abstract concepts of philosophy and a concrete social context, which can be changed. This type of reflection resembles what Douglas Hofstadter has called a "strange loop": at the very top of the conceptual hierarchy, at the point at which one reaches the most general and abstract concepts, one finds oneself suddenly plunged down to the lowest rung of the conceptual ladder.

Let me return now to the example of the antinomy of public and private interest cited above to illustrate how practice can contribute to resolving a theoretical problem. Plato sets up the problem as philosophy has treated it ever since. Plato's guardians are qualified to rule by the complete elimination of their private lives; they cannot even know their own children. (For the Greeks the abolition of the family is the abolition of the private sphere itself.) The lower classes of the *Republic* pursue private interests but this disqualifies them from rule. The antinomy is evident here. It does not disappear in as different a philosophical doctrine as Rousseau's. Rousseau distinguishes the general will from the will of all as two opposed types of interest. It is true that he does not conceive of a special class as the bearer of the general will, but instead projects the antinomy into the individual. The measure of the split in the individual this produces is the degree of "virtue" required to participate in citizenship. Even a Mandeville, who claims that "private vices are public benefits," readily admits that the intention of the individuals in pursuing private interests is antagonistic to social welfare and only increases it by a paradoxical reversal in contact with other similarly corrupt private interests.

For a Marxist the limitation of this type of thinking is clear. The unquestioned assumption that lies behind the antinomy is the permanency of privately owned means of production, the administration of which places the individuals in an antagonistic relation to each other. Public interests then arise alongside the private ones insofar as the community has needs which are not identical with the mere summation of these antagonistic private interests. But what if this basic assumption was false? What if historical conditions arose in which private ownership of means of production could be replaced by the rational administration of both the economy and the state in the interests of the whole community? Of course some forms of "private" interest would remain, but these would not stand in an antinomial relation to the public interest of the community. Instead of dedication to public interest requiring renunciation of private interests, the two could support each other harmoniously. The traditional philosophical construction of the issue would no longer apply.

The point I want to make is not that such a Marxist reform of society would work—that is another problem—but rather that once one envisages it as a real possibility, social action appears to play a central role in resolving philosophical problems that have traditionally been treated as purely theoretical in character. It is this new role for social action which is intended by the concept of a "unity" of theory and practice. Philosophy is "realized" in this unity in the sense that its old ideal of somehow reconciling public and private interest is finally achieved. The new element is that this realization involves a radical social change, and not a purely conceptual mediation such as Plato's utopia, Rousseau's "virtue," or Mandeville's "invisible hand."

Note that the revolution need not already have succeeded for this new type of theoretical reflection to proceed. Reflection can always go beyond the given achievements of its era toward ideal outcomes. This is true of Marx as much as it is of Plato. But what appears as a real possibility to anticipatory thinking differs drastically with time and place. Even in his wildest speculations, Plato saw no way to abolish slavery. Aristotle once made the fantastic suggestion that slavery could be abolished if tools would activate themselves without human agency. Marx writes in a time when this idle fantasy of the ancients appears as an imminent possibility. On the basis of this changed historical situation, he imagines a wholly different practical context for philosophy than the one prevailing in all class societies. Thus Marxists do not need to wait for the revolution to propose theoretical analyses of the solutions to problems it is supposed to bring about. However, they do generally insist that only by struggling against capitalism has the working class been able to shake up the dominant assumptions of a millenial class culture so that these assumptions can finally be problematized in theory and new solutions to old problems anticipated. Later chapters will explain this connection between theory and practice in more detail.

2

The Meta-Theory of Philosophy: Marx's Formulation

DEONTOLOGICAL GROUNDS FOR REVOLUTION

The ambition of philosophy of praxis is to link the fulfillment of the "demands of reason" to revolutionary political goals. The establishment of this link implies that the practice of a rational life includes revolutionary political action, and that revolution itself can be rationally justified. These are in fact fundamental conclusions of Marx and Lukács in their early Marxist work. In his early works Marx develops a meta-theory of political philosophy and derives original grounds for revolution from it. In *History and Class Consciousness*, Lukács constructs a meta-theory of classical Germany philosophy from which he too derives a rationale for revolution. This chapter will be primarily concerned with Marx's early justification of revolution, while a later one will take up Lukács' related argument.

By way of introduction to the concept of revolution in philosophy of praxis, it will be helpful to consider the traditional idea of the right of revolution. Of course throughout most of its history political philosophy has been more concerned with rational grounds for obedience to government than with the right of revolution. Usually obedience has been justified by reference to functions performed by the state to the benefit of the individuals. However, the expectation of a fair return for obedience may easily be disappointed. Then, when the state fails to fulfill its function, grounds for obedience may become grounds for revolution. Similarly, most justifications of revolution imply a theory of obligation to the post-revolutionary state. This dialectic of obedience and revolt is not a sign of inconsistency in political philosophy, but on the contrary results from its consistent commitment to rationality in a world of contingencies, and its ever enlarging claims for the individual. These observations are confirmed by the early revolutionary theories of Marx and Lukács. In both cases conservative political doctrines, taken as the basis of a meta-theoretical critique, are transformed into their revolutionary opposites precisely in the name of reason.

We can gauge their originality by comparison with earlier revolutionary political theory. The classic ground for revolution, formulated for example by Locke, is teleological or utilitarian in character. Locke believes that "the end of government is the good of mankind."[1] Although Marxists only rarely offer utilitarian arguments for revolution, a vaguely utilitarian concern for human happiness constitutes the moral aura of most Marxist discourse. Marxists implicitly add to Locke's critique of political relations a parallel critique of property relations, both of which, in their view, should be instrumental to human happiness. Locke's main point is conserved: society, as a common creation of human beings, should serve their interests and not the contrary.

Socialism undoubtedly originated in some such sense of revolution as a legitimate collective means to happiness. However, if the early Marx had presented a simply humanitarian justification of revolution, he would have fallen beneath the level of the philosophy of the *Aufklärung* in which he was so deeply schooled. For Marx it is not enough to show that revolution is a means to happiness, since Kant and Hegel question the ethical status of happiness itself. Kant shows that as a rational being man has higher interests than those discovered through a utilitarian calculus, including duties of obedience to the state regardless of "material" consequences. By conceptualizing this "higher" sphere of duty in terms of a dialectical theory of individuation and mutual recognition, Hegel succeeds in basing similar conclusions on a far richer social theory. Thus in Kant and Hegel traditional speculative philosophy takes a conservative turn, denying the pertinence of the utilitarian grounds for revolution put forth in progressive theories such as Locke's.

Marx revives revolutionary theory not by a "regression" to utilitarianism, but rather by developing a new deontological ground of revolution, based on the intrinsic nature of rationality. Deontological grounds for revolution flow from the demand for rational political action, independent of the use to be made of the freedom won by revolution, whether it be the pursuit of happiness, morality, or any other end. The chief representative of this position is Rousseau, who assumes that the citizens of a rational society would use their freedom to achieve happiness, but for him freedom as the actual exercise of self-determining rationality is an end in itself.

The difference between teleological and deontological grounds for revolution is especially clear in Locke and Rousseau's discussions of slavery. Both are against it, of course, but for very different reasons. Locke argues that slavery is illegitimate because "this freedom from absolute arbitrary power is so necessary to, and closely joined with a man's preservation, that he cannot part with it but by which forfeits his preservation and life together."[2] Rousseau, on the contrary, makes no appeal to the right to life, but claims an obligation to moral self-responsibility incompatible with slavery. He argues that "when a man renounces his liberty he renounces his essential manhood, his rights, and even his duty as a human being. . . . It is incompatible with man's nature, and to deprive him of his free will is to deprive his actions of all moral sanction."[3]

Deontological grounds for revolution are usually explained as Rousseau does here, by reference to an absolute value placed on human dignity, the right of each individual to determine himself freely, to secure respectful treatment from others. It is argued that where political conditions prevent this they ought to be overthrown. Here we pass from the mere *right* of revolution, which flows from a concern with human happiness, to an *obligation* to revolution in the name of dignity and freedom. This is very much the sort of problem that preoccupies the young Marx. He writes in one early essay: "To be radical is to grasp things by the root. But for man the root is man himself. . . . The criticism of religion ends with the doctrine that man is the supreme being for man. It ends, therefore, with the categorical imperative to overthrow all those conditions in which man is an abased, enslaved, abandoned, contemptible being . . ."[4] For the young Marx, a revolution *"à la hauteur des principes"* is a revolution for freedom and dignity.[5]

Basic to this theory of revolution is the idea that the rational subject is not fulfilled merely in thought, nor even in private morality, but also requires a sphere of public activity. But where rationality must be deployed, there freedom too is necessary, for "Freedom is the 'formal element' of rationality, the only form in which reason can be."[6] Thus for Marx, as for Rousseau, revolution is a condition for the full exercise of reason. It is comparable with Cartesian doubt or the Enlightenment struggle against superstition as an attack on contingent obstacles to rationality, as a methodological preliminary to the flowering of humankind's highest faculty.

Marx's concern with the problem of revolutionary rationality is formulated explicitly in some of his earliest writings. He tries to show that revolution can satisfy what he calls "the demands of reason," that through it reason, or philosophy, can be "realized" in social reality.[7] This terminology is of course Hegelian. It was Hegel who first proposed to show that "reason" was "realized," that the contradiction between the rational concept of the state and its historical reality had finally been overcome. This philosophical *tour de force* was intended to lay the revolution to rest, to deprive it of the halo of rationality with which the eighteenth century had surrounded it. Starting from such premises, Marx's task is laid out for him: to demonstrate that reason is *not* in fact realized, that it continues to produce "demands" transcendent to the given state of affairs, that revolution is therefore still a rational act.

But after Kant and Hegel, it is not possible for Marx to renew revolutionary theory by returning to the speculative methods of a Rousseau. Kant's conservative political philosophy is based precisely on the implicit grounds for obedience to government contained in the Rousseauian revolutionary theory. This theory itself must therefore be submitted to a radical critique in order to discover how political philosophy had been reconciled—prematurely—with an unjust society, and to find in it elements that can be reformulated to again ground a revolutionary struggle against this society. The core of this effort consists in overcoming the antinomy of need and reason Marx identifies as constitutive of the entire tradition of political philosophy. Marx subjects the concepts of need and reason to a critique and a revision in the course of which he develops his metatheoretical approach. I will show later that the antinomy of need and reason in Marx is only a particular instance of the antinomy of fact and value with which Lukács is centrally concerned in his early work.

Marx's meta-theory of political philosophy is based on a specific construction of the relation between need and reason in political philosophy, one which derives largely from an interpretation of Rousseau as seen through the eyes of Kant. This of course limits the bearing of Marx's analysis, which simply assumes that the essence of the whole tradition is revealed in what is presumably its highest stage. Nevertheless, the analysis is at least an interesting hypothesis about political philosophy in general; furthermore, Marx's approach is sociologically justified because it is the doctrine of Rousseau-Kant that underlies the democratic ideology of the French Revolution and later German liberalism.

Marx assumes with Rousseau and Kant that freedom is not whim but "obedience to self-given law."[8] With them he also assumes that the rules of conduct cannot be *derived* from happiness as an end, but must be derived from the concept of reason: the rational individual owes it to himself to maintain his autonomy from both his own needs and the power of other men. Happiness is not, however, a matter of indifference for Rousseau, nor even for Kant. In Rousseau, for example, freedom is essentially the right and the power to do what is in one's own interests as a member of the community. Freedom is a value in itself, but it is also bound up with the pursuit of collective self-interest in the higher sphere of politics.

It has been argued that in Kant too right conduct establishes general forms of social interaction which maximize the freedom of each individual to follow his merely "natural" end, which is happiness. What Kant does is not so much to reject the pursuit of happiness as to reduce it to an "anthropological" or empirical consideration, thereby clearly delineating the boundaries between deontological and utilitarian grounds for political action.[9] The basis of this philosophical distinction is the praxeological one between ethics and economics. In the ethical form of action, the behavior of all subjects is intrinsically compatible and harmonious, while in the economic form of action, behavior may be conflictual and competitive. Only ethical action, which achieves harmony through conformity to a universal rule, can be granted the dignity of reason. The pursuit of material welfare is mere "content" of experience, determined by nature and therefore contingent, compatible in principle, Kant would argue, with ethical behavior but subordinate to it by right.

For Marx this construction of the relation of reason and need results in a disturbing split between the ideal of freedom and the actual motives which, in real life, freedom serves. This split is particularly significant because it undercuts the protest against poverty in a formally "rational" society, reducing such protest to a marginal concern of merely empirical interest. Life becomes, in fact, a means to rationality in a topsy turvy vision likely to satisfy only those for whom the means of life are assured. What is required is a reformulation of political theory to establish the intrinsic rationality and universality of the pursuit of happiness and the satisfaction of the needs on which happiness depends.

Marx worked out this program in three stages, to which correspond three important early works. In the first part of the essay "On the Jewish Question" he attacks the problem of need, in order to show that the conflictual form of action associated with it is not natural and necessary, but historical and subject to revolutionary change. This essay culminates in a new formulation of the concept of freedom, in line with the revision of the concept of need. The second stage of the analysis is developed in the "Introduction" to the "Contribution to the Critique of Hegel's Philosophy of Right." There Marx arrives by a deduction from principles at the political and social conditions for a realization of his new concept of freedom. This argument leads to the proletariat, which he identifies as the agent of a revolution that will abolish philosophy in realizing it. The last stage is reached in the *Economic and Philosophical Manuscripts* of 1844. There Marx follows the thread to its beginning in the concept of reason itself, which he now sets out to revise.

THE ANTINOMY OF REASON AND NEED

Marx's essay "On the Jewish Question" is an attempt to overcome the antinomy of form and content opposing the ideal of the bourgeois-democratic state to the facts of capitalist social and economic life. Marx conceptualizes this antinomy through the split between moral-political rationality (the basis of the state) and utilitarian-anthropological goals (the basis of the economy) as it appears in Rousseau and the French Revolution, filtered through Kant and Hegel. He argues that this split is reflected in the distinction between "man" and "citizen" in French revolutionary theory, and that this distinction in turn depends on that between civil society, the sphere of private activity, and the state, the sphere of cooperative activity.

Marx shows that the state accumulates all the functions of rationality: consciousness, reflexivity, morality, universality, and "species-life," this last being a term derived from Feuerbach which signifies the consciously social and cooperative nature of man. The merely empirical functions of natural human existence are then consigned to the sphere of civil society, where the individual lives his "real" life, as opposed to his ideal rational life as a citizen in the state. In civil society the egoism of private individuals creates a hell of competition in the pursuit of happiness through economic aggression. There human action does not achieve rational universality, but is rather mere nature. Marx writes:

The perfected political state is, by its nature, the species life of man as opposed to his material life. All the presuppositons of this egoistic life continue to exist in civil society outside the political sphere, as qualities of civil society. Where the political state has attained to its full development, man leads, not only in thought, in consciousness, but in reality, in life, a double existence—celestial and terrestrial. He lives in the political community, where he acts simply as a private individual, treats other men as means, degrades himself to the role of a mere means and becomes the plaything of alien powers.[10]

In presenting the problem in this manner, Marx is not simply criticizing the egoism of bourgeois society. There is that, but more important is the fact that "species life" is decisively linked to reason in the concept of the state. In the political domain, rationality is exemplified by the cooperative, communal aspect of human nature, which takes refuge in the state once it has been driven from the intensely competitive civil society. As Marx put it in his letter to Ruge: "Reason has always existed, but not always in a rational form. . . . As far as actual life is concerned, the political state especially contains in all its modern forms the demands of reason, even where the political state is not yet conscious of socialistic demands."[11] The problem now is to criticize the "irrational" and contradictory form in which reason exists in the modern state in order to understand why reason has been confined to this limited domain, why actual life continues to persist as an empirical and natural residue antagonistic to reason in a civil society alongside the state.

Marx seeks a solution through a critique of the limits of the concept of political revolution, which at this point is equivalent for him with the French Revolution.[12] Political revolution aims to change the principles governing social interaction in order to maximize individual freedom in private life. In practice, the revolution accepts the given basis of private life as received from the *ancien régime*, namely private property, and attempts to lift the burden of feudal restrictions weighing on this basis. "This revolution," Marx says, "regards civil society, the sphere of human needs, labour, private interests and civil law, as the basis of its own existence, as a self-subsistent pre-condition, and thus as its natural basis."[13]

Civil society appears essentially as a sphere of "nature" because it lacks the two most important determinations of rationality, which are *reflexivity* and *universality*. On the one hand, the political revolution does not conceive of civil society as a historical result, as the outcome of a process of mediation, hence as a self-reflected and self-developed sphere of reason. Instead, it is seen as the product of the egoistic individuals whose natural inclinations govern it once all feudal restrictions have been eliminated. These egoistic individuals are simply received by the revolution as "the passive, given result of the dissolution of society [of the *ancien régime*], an object of direct apprehension and consequently a natural object."[14]

On the other hand, as a "natural" man, the merely given product of instinct and need, the egoistic individual of bourgeois society is plunged into a *bellum omnium contra omnes*. The activity of this egoistic individual can consist only in degraded competitive strife. Its form is not rational or universal and no process of mediation can raise it to rational universality. The contradiction between reason and need, the one necessary and universal, the other contingent and particular, cannot, Marx claims, be resolved on the ground of capitalist society.

Marx goes on to show that the bourgeois split in the individual between need and reason, man and citizen is a dialectical one in which each polar opposite requires the other for its existence. The polarity of man and citizen reflects a split in human nature inevitable in capitalist society, a split between its empirical content and its rational essence. The empirical man of civil society is the really existing human being, an egoistic residue standing in perpetual contradiction with its own rational instantiation as citizen. But only through the citizen can the man exist, that is, can the individual freely pursue private interests in private life under the protection of the state. Meanwhile, the ideal citizen, member of the state, is the essence of what it is to be human, a rational political animal. Yet the citizen is there only to protect and defend the rights of man. Existence and essence require each other and also stand in contradiction. Marx says, "Man as he really is, is seen only in the form of egoistic man, and man in his true nature only in the form of abstract citizen."[15]

Political revolution founders on this antinomy. It confines itself to liberating a pregiven "nature" that bears within it the irrationality of private competition. In the face of this nature, reason has a bare "artificial" existence as an "allegorical, moral person" in the citizen.[16] Most abstractly formulated, the dilemma is an example of the fundamental antinomy of form and content with which philosophy of praxis is concerned: *rational form here presides over empirical content not by mediating it and raising it to rational universality, but by leaving it to be in its given condition.*

At this very abstract level, Marx's critique of formal democracy is structurally similar to Lukács' critique of Kantian ethics. In Lukács' terms, the antinomy of reason and need that Marx identifies would be an example of the more general antinomy of value and fact, of "ought" and "is," that arises from the formalistic concept of reason. This concept of reason is based on the acceptance of "immediacy," that is to say, on the failure to discover in the given facts those potentialities and tendencies embodying rationality and driving them toward a rational end. Instead, the given is *defined* as indifferent to reason and value, as the merely empirical, factical residue of the process of formal abstraction in which the concept of reason is constructed. As Lukács put it, "Precisely in the pure, classical expression it received in the philosophy of Kant it remains true that the 'ought' presupposes an existing reality to which the category of 'ought' remains *inapplicable* in principle."[17] This is the dilemma of bourgeois democracy as Marx explains it: political rationality presupposes as its material substratum an irrational social existence which cannot be made to conform to rational principles.

Marx and Lukács, then, arrive at similar solutions to the problem they have identified. In the more abstract terms of Lukács, this solution "consists in annulling [*aufzuheben*] that indifference of form towards content . . ." which is the basis of reified rationality.[18] More concretely, for Marx, it is necessary to transform civil society into a sphere of rational interaction. Mere political revolution is not adequate to the task. Marx writes, "The political revolution dissolves civil society into its elements [egoistic individuals] without revolutionizing these elements themselves or subjecting them to criticism."[19] What is required is precisely the "revolutionizing" of private and individual existence so that it too conforms with the demands of reason. The content of free activity must no longer stand in contradiction with freedom itself.

At this point Marx derives what might be called a new "concept" or *Begriff* of free society from the *Aufhebung* of the contradictions he has identified between the concept and the object of traditional democratic political theory. He does not yet know concretely in what rational social activity would consist, but he knows the condition for such activity, namely, the transcendence of the opposition between private egoism and rational common action. For this it is necessary that collective action in the common interest, action based on the reciprocal recognition of the humanity and needs of all individuals, transcend the narrow boundaries of politics and extend to economic life as well. Then economic activity would have a rational form and human needs would partake of rational universality through their reciprocal recognition by all. Marx concludes:

Human emancipation will only be complete when the real individual man has absorbed into himself the abstract citizen; when as an individual man, in his everyday life, in his work, and in his relationships, he has become a species-being; and when he has recognized and organized his own powers *(forces propres)* as social powers so that he no longer separates this social power from himself as political power.[20]

This new condition for the fulfillment of the "demands of reason" is contained already in abstract form in the modern state. It is the new basis for deontological grounds for revolution and for what Marx calls the "realization of philosophy."

In sum, Marx has shown that political philosophy accepts the irrational form of the pursuit of happiness (civil society) as a natural fact, and so applies the demands of reason only to the state. These demands concern, among other things, the establishment of a true community through the reconciliation of antinomial opposites such as individual and society, private interest and common good, and all the similar displacements of the antinomy of content and form in the political domain. But Marx is able to demonstrate that community cannot be realized in a partial domain, such as the state, alongside a civil society based on a conflictual form of action.

To fulfill the demands of reason, then, it will be necessary to extend them to civil society. To accomplish this, in turn, it is necessary to overcome what Lukács calls the "immediacy" of the sphere of need, its philosophically naturalized form, which admits of no possibility of change and progress. This Marx succeeds in doing when he arrives at the concept of a social revolution which would not just change the state, but also bring about the "revolutionizing of the elements themselves." Community can be realized at all levels of society, including the material level of the sphere of need, when the system of practice governing the pursuit of happiness in class society has been transformed.

THE AGENT OF REVOLUTION

The next step in Marx's analysis consists in finding a possible agent for the radical transformation of man and citizen he proposes. This proves to be a more delicate matter than would first appear. On the one hand, Marx must base his new concept of freedom on some actual social force to escape the merely abstract ethical relation of philosophy to reality he has already rejected in his letter to Ruge. On the other hand, in attempting to base his philosophy on a real social force, there is the danger that he will reduce historical action to a mere instrument of philosophy, which later would then be the real "subject" of the revolutionary process.

In Marx's "Introduction" to the "Contribution to the Critique of Hegel's Philosophy of Right," when he first approaches this problem in a highly speculative form, he does indeed fail to resolve the dilemma posed above. There he arrives at an undialectical construction of the relation of theory to practice which does not so much overcome the abstract character of ethical demands as impute this very abstractness to the demands of an entire social class. Lucien Goldmann suggests that this failure is not of merely biographical interest in the study of Marx's development, but that the undialectical conclusions of this text anticipate the later undialectical construction of the theory-practice relation in the socialist movement: "In fact, it suffices to replace the word philosophy in the 'Introduction' with the word Party (and at bottom in the two cases we are concerned with an ideology-elaborating group) in order to obtain a position very close to that expressed by Lenin in his work *What is To Be Done?*"[21] The discussion of class consciousness in a later chapter of this book will explore Lukács' solution to precisely this problem.

Marx's failure in this essay is due in part to his method, which differs radically from that of his later sociological and economic work. He does not start from an analysis of society but from philosophy. He takes his new philosophical concept of freedom and tests it against the various classes of society to find one which can serve as its representative in practice. As he puts it, "Revolutions need a passive element, a material basis . . ."[22] Or again, "Theory itself becomes a material force when it has seized the masses."[23] Marx's essay has the appearance of a class analysis and indeed some features of it anticipate his later theory of class. Marx tries to prove that previous, merely political revolution have failed to achieve human emancipation because they have liberated not man but particular classes from oppression. The bourgeoisie, for example, was oppressed by the nobility in France *as a class*, in terms of its particular interests in the society. The wrongs done to the bourgeoisie *appeared* to all other classes to exemplify the general injustice of the society and so they supported the bourgeoisie in its revolution. But the liberation of the bourgeoisie from these wrongs was not human emancipation but only bourgeois emancipation. It did not free man but the bourgeoisie to pursue its interests, which in turn came into conflict with the interests of society as a whole.

Thus it is the very principle of class which is the source of the limits of political revolution. Marx concludes, and this distinguishes his method from that of the later works, that his philosophy cannot be realized by a social class in the usual sense but only by "a class in civil society which is not a class of civil society, a class which is the dissolution of all classes."[24] What he is seeking, in other words, is a class that is not a class, a "universal" class in something like Hegel's sense of the term, with no particular interest at all, hence none opposed to that of society as a whole. Having arrived at a rather Hegelian formulation of the problem in his earlier essay, it is not surprising that he here reaches a variant of the Hegelian solution.

Marx argues that the proletariat alone of all classes can go beyond a limited, merely political revolution to a general human revolution, a social revolution, for it has no status within the existing system at all. It is, Marx claims, and here he was right for his time if not for ours, the product of the "disintegration" of other social strata, with no traditional status of its own to defend. For this reason its protest can be truly universal in character, and can bring down the system of class which Marx now identifies as the source of egoistic individualism and the basis of civil society.

The proletariat, Marx concludes, can alone "revolutionize the elements themselves," that is, transform what it is to be an individual in society. For it has no interest in conserving a particular status opposed to the whole, hence no interest in perpetuating the split between civil society and the state to ensure itself a domain of free competitive aggression. The proletariat thus appears as the appropriate instrument of Marx's philosophy and the demand for revolution is now addressed to this class. Marx writes, "Philosophy is the head of this emancipation and the proletariat is its heart. Philosophy can only be realized by the abolition of the proletariat, and the proletariat can only be abolished by the realization of philosophy."[25]

In spite of the elegance and symmetry of this solution, it falls far short of resolving the problems Marx has posed for himself. Here theory and practice are seen to arise independently, and if social revolution satisfies essential demands of theory, it is by no means clear that the proletariat intends this result in revolting. Lukács remarks:

The issue turns on the question of theory and practice. And this not merely in the sense given it by Marx when he says in his first critique of Hegel that "theory becomes a material force when it has seized the masses." Even more to the point is the need to discover those features and determinations both of the theory and the ways of seizing the masses which convert the theory, the dialectical method, into a vehicle of revolution. We must extract the practical essense of the theory from the method and its relation to its object. If this is not done that "seizing the masses" could well turn out to be a will o' the wisp. It might turn out that the masses were seized by quite different forces, that they were in pursuit of quite different ends. In that event, there would be no necessary connection between the theory and their activity, it would be a form that enables the masses to become conscious of their socially necessary or fortuitous actions, without ensuring a genuine and necessary bond between consciousness and action.[26]

Lukács goes on to point out that in this same text Marx briefly lays down the basic condition for achieving a real unity of theory and practice. Marx writes, "Will theoretical needs be directly practical needs? It is not enough that thought should seek to realize itself; reality must also strive toward thought."[27] Both Marx and Lukács thus arrive at the conclusion that it is not only the "indifference of form towards content" that must be overcome, but also the indifference of content towards form.

Marx has so far seen the necessity of creating a form of rational interaction in the pursuit of happiness and to this end he has identified an agent capable of implementing the "demands of reason." But still the form-content distinction persists, because the pursuit of happiness itself has not been raised to rational universality, only its form. The proletariat appears as a passive instrument of philosophy because in revolting to achieve happiness, it unconsciously serves the "cunning of reason" by realizing rational form in actual life. An ungenerous observer could still insist that Marx is tossing "the roasted pigeons of absolute science" into the mouth of the proletariat. Marx now seems to realize that there is no solution within the framework of a concept of reason as pure form, and so he proceeds to a radical critique and revision of the concept of reason itself.

REVISION OF THE CONCEPT OF REASON

In the third phase of his early work, in the *Economic and Philosophical Manuscripts* of 1844, Marx sets out to unify theory and practice through revising the concept of reason as it is formulated both in the philosophical tradition and his own previous writings. To accomplish this, Marx must return to the study of need from a new angle. In the early essays, Marx found a *form* of rational interaction in the pursuit of happiness. But the *content* of the concept of need with which he worked remained unthematized and unanalyzed; it remained, in fact, immediate and hence irrational for Marx as it had for earlier political philosophy. This dimension of the problem now becomes the decisive one.

If there was a still dogmatic element in the earlier essays, it lay in Marx's failure to derive rational social interaction, the "revolutionizing of the elements themselves," from the needs it was to help satisfy. Instead, social revolution still appeared as a philosophical exigency from which the needy could incidentally benefit. The antinomy of need and reason is not abolished in the accidental convergence of philosophy and the proletariat, but rather reproduced in a new guise. The antinomies of philosophy and reality, theory and practice which appear in Marx's discussion of historical agency are simply displacements of the original antinomy of political philosophy.

To resolve these antinomies, Marx will now reverse the terms
of the problem and attempt to found the demands of reason in
the very nature of need. But this amounts to demonstrating
that the content of the sphere of need is rational, is, in fact,
the essential sphere of rationality for a meta-theoretically
reconstructed concept of reason.

In developing this meta-theoretical approach to rationality,
Marx is greatly aided by Feuerbach, who treads a similar path
with more maturity and assurance in the same period. Feuerbach's central idea is that philosophy is secularized theology.
He says, "What lies in the other world for religion, lies in this
world for philosophy."[28] This is particularly true of the
philosophical concepts of subject and object. When
philosophy identifies the subject with reason, with thinking, it
brings the theological idea of "spirit" down to earth. Similarly,
the concept of the object as an object-of-thought, constituted
by thought or obeying rational laws, is a homely transcendental equivalent for Biblical Genesis.

This is on the face of it a crass and reductionist interpretation of the essence of philosophy. What makes Feuerbach
interesting and important is his attempt to go beyond this
basic thesis toward a reconstruction of philosophy. There is a
parallel here with Marx's method in the essays discussed
above. Marx took certain general formal principles of political
philosophy—the demands of reason—and detached them
from their accustomed object, in this case the state, to apply
them to another object, society. Feuerbach does something
similar for philosophy in general, detaching its formal structure from its concept of the subject and object. The
"philosophy of the future," as Feuerbach calls it, will conserve
these formal traits but attach them to a new subject-object
concept. This is a meta-theoretical approach to the critique
and revision of fundamental philosophical concepts because in
it these concepts are relativized through contact with the
concrete existential domains from which they were first
abstracted in their initial construction as philosophical. This is
particularly clear in Feuerbach.

Feuerbach calls Hegel's thought, which he sees as the culmination of the philosophical tradition, a "philosophy of identity." The identity referred to is that of thought and being, reason and reality. This identity Feuerbach sees as a theological principle and to it he opposes what he calls "the true and absolute viewpoint": "the viewpoint of the distinction between I and thou, subject and object."[29] Yet although Feuerbach rejects the philosophy of identity, he tries to conserve its formal principles on another plane.

He first redefines the concepts of subject and object, arguing that they are both sensuous, natural things in the world which cannot be brought together merely conceptually. The identity achieved in and through thought is spurious and ideological, but there is another kind of subject-object identity which can be achieved in nature through sense perception and love. Feuerbach writes, "The identity of subject and object, which in self-consciousness [in other words, in Hegel] is only an abstract idea, is truth and reality only in man's sensuous perception of man."[30] Thus the formal principle, subject-object identity, is taken from Hegel and conserved, while its content in Hegel's own thought is rejected.

The upshot is an enlargement of the concept of the subject to include more than thinking, to include the whole man, so to speak. This enlarged subject retains what might be called an "ontological pathos" through its continued submission to the formal principles of idealistic philosophy. Feuerbach expressed his conclusion in ringing phrases which certainly influenced Marx.

The unity of thought and being has meaning and truth only when man is comprehended as the ground and subject of this unity. Only a real being recognizes real objects; only where thought is not the subject of itself but a predicate of a real being is the idea not separated from being. . . .

From this result the following categorical imperatives: Desire not to be a philosopher as distinct from a man; be nothing else than a thinking man. Do not think as a thinker, that is, with a faculty torn from the totality of the real human being and isolated for itself; think as a living and real being, as one exposed to the vivifying and refreshing waves of the world's oceans. Think in existence, in the world as a member of it, not in the vacuum of abstraction as a solitary monad, as an absolute monarch, as an indifferent, super-worldly God; then you can be sure that your ideas are unities of being and thought.[31]

That is precisely Marx's starting point in the *1844 Manuscripts*. There he attempts to obey Feuerbach's injunction by a heroic effort to overcome the gap between thought and life. As Marx puts it, "One basis for life and another for science is *a priori* a falsehood."[32] Elsewhere in the text, Marx expresses himself in the first person in a manner which indicates his personal stake in the matter.

My universal consciousness is only the theoretical form of that whose living form is the real community, the social entity, although at the present day this universal consciousness is an abstraction from real life and is opposed to it as an enemy. That is why the activity of my universal consciousness as such is my theoretical existence as a social being.[33]

However, Marx is a better dialectician and a more rigorous thinker than Feuerbach. He is not content to retain simply the most general form of the philosophy of identity, while giving an anthropological twist to the concepts of subject and object. He takes far more than this from Hegel in order to accomplish far more ambitious goals than Feuerbach's. Marx follows Hegel in requiring that subject-object unity be grasped as the actual constitution or production of the object by the subject. He also agrees with the Hegel of the *Phenomenology of Mind* that this production takes place in the historical process. He accepts, in other words, what Lukács describes as "Hegel's programme: to see the absolute, the goal of his philosophy, as a *result* remains valid for Marxism with its very different objects of knowledge, and is even of greater concern to it, as the dialectical process is seen to be identical with the course of history."[34] The formal principles Marx retains are thus richer and more complex than those that survive Feuerbach's critical blast.

As Marx works out his program in the *Manuscripts*, it becomes clear that he is attempting not just a "reform of philosophy"—Feuerbach's phrase—but a rigorous *Aufhebung*, or transcendence, of Hegelian idealism, and with it of philosophy generally. To accomplish this Marx develops a meta-theoretical critique of Hegel, designed to show that the latter's attempt to found reason as absolute knowledge is a still theological attempt to overcome social alienation in thought. The *"ordre des raisons"* must be reversed: when alienation is overcome in real life, then and only then will it be possible to overcome the alienation of reason. In line with this approach, which subordinates the truth of reason to a philosophical anthropology, Marx praises Feuerbach, who "founded genuine materialism and positive science by making the social relationship of 'man to man' the basic principle of his theory."[35] Simultaneously, in contra-distinction to Feuerbach, Marx believes that it is capitalism which is responsible for the degradation of the relation of "man to man." Thus the *Manuscripts* do not achieve their end in a mere philosophical reformulation of the concept of reason. Revolution becomes the basis for a new identity, overcoming the opposition of thought and life, thinker and society, by founding reason in life and community in practice. The retention of the formal structure of Hegel's thought infused with this new content yields a philosophy of praxis.

How does Marx go about it? I will first sketch the three dialectical "moments" of Marx's meta-theoretical approach and then elaborate each in some detail. Marx begins by showing that philosophical categories are "in reality" displacements of social ones. This demonstration involves the elaboration of new theoretical categories in terms of which to explain the failure of the traditional theory to understand its own relation to reality. For example, Marx is convinced that the problem of alienated labor is the real foundation of Hegel's philosophy, but that Hegel fails for not posing it clearly. Marx argues that "Hegel's standpoint is that of modern political economy. He conceives labour as the essence, the self-confirming essence of man. . . . [But] labour as Hegel understands and recognizes it is abstract mental labour. Thus, that which above all constitutes the essence of philosophy, the alienation of man knowing himself, or alienated science *thinking* itself, Hegel grasps as its essence."[36] The whole artificial, speculative and ultimately theological structure of Hegel's system results from just this inability to thematize real labor as the ontological core of history.

Having relativized the philosophical categories with respect to social ones, Marx proceeds to the second "moment" of the meta-theory. This consists in casting the social categories in the form of the philosophical ones, as does Feuerbach in the passages discussed above. Finally, in a third phase, the meta-theory demonstrates the philosophical pertinence of social action in resolving the contradictions of the philosophically recast social categories. In this phase Marx is able to show that the problem of the alienation of labor is a fundamental problem *within* philosophy, and not just a contingent problem of practice. This is impossible within Hegel's own thought, which encounters the alienation of labor in history as no more than a passing concern.

In sum, Marx redefines the *terms* of Hegel's philosophy, while retaining in part the *relations* Hegel establishes between these terms. Marx can then set the entire system in motion in history itself because of the social redefinition to which he has submitted it. It is clear that these new definitions do not correspond with Hegel's. It is also clear that Marx shifts back and forth in the *Manuscripts* between his own concepts and Hegel's, using the same terms in different senses. But this is not just an ambiguous use of terms. Marx's substantive thesis is that Hegel's concepts are a misconstruction of a reality better described by Marx's own, that Hegel attempts in a mystified way to solve the very problems that concern Marx.

The first phase of Marx's meta-theory is developed in the conclusion of the *Manuscripts*, in his "Critique of Hegel's Dialectic." There Marx argues that Hegel's term "alienation" stands for the uncomprehended object of thought. To found reason, that is, to demonstrate the unity of subject and object, "It is necessary, therefore, to surmount the object of consciousness. Objectivity as such is regarded as an alienated human relationship which does not correspond with the essence of man, self-consciousness."[37] The return of the alienated, the demonstration of its unity with the conscious subject, consists for Hegel only in surpassing the cognitive immediacy of the object. The appropriation of alienated reality is in fact its comprehension by which this immediacy is overcome. But, Marx argues, in its social application this method leaves the world exactly as it was before, tacking a certificate of rationality onto every form of oppression. Since alienation is, at least for Hegel, really overcome in philosophy, the need to change the world has vanished. Thought can congratulate itself on having *produced* the reality and thereby justified it.

This is once again what Lukács means by philosophy remaining in the standpoint of immediacy. In *The Holy Family*, Marx describes it as "the mystery of speculative construction." He says, "Speculation on the one hand apparently freely creates its object *a priori* out of itself and, on the other hand, precisely because it wishes to get rid by sophistry of the rational and natural dependence on the *object*, falls into the most irrational and unnatural *bondage* to the object, whose most accidental and most individual attributes it is obliged to construe as absolutely necessary and general."[38]

Hegel's conservatism, Marx believes, results from describing real alienation as the phenomenal appearance of the alienation of reason. For Hegel the alienation of the individual in the *ancien régime* did not consist in the fact that he was reduced to an "abased, enslaved, abandoned, contemptible being," but in the fact that the state did not correspond with its concept, that, in practice, it could not command the rational obedience of its subjects. Once the state has been reformed, then it *can* command rational obedience even from an "abased, enslaved, abandoned, contemptible being." There is thus a merely contingent relation between philosophy and Marx's "real" alienation, which consists in human misery and dependence. The philosopher becomes the "enemy" of the human community in demonstrating to it that it should accept its fate without protest. He withdraws the moral credit of the oppressed by rationalizing the established order.

Marx argues that Hegel falls into "uncritical positivism and uncritical idealism" because he begins by narrowing the subject to a mere function of thought. Marx writes,

For Hegel, human life, man is equivalent to self-consciousness. All alienation of human life is, therefore, nothing but alienation of self-consciousness. The alienation of self-consciousness is not regarded as the expression, reflected in knowledge and thought, of the real alienation of human life. Instead, actual alienation, that which appears real, is in its innermost hidden nature (which philosophy first discloses) only the phenomenal being of the alienation of real human life, self-consciousness.[39]

Hence for Hegel, "It is not the fact that the human being objectifies himself inhumanly, in opposition to himself, but that he objectifies himself by distinction from and in opposition to abstract thought, which constitutes alienation as it exists and as it has to be transcended."[40]

In opposition to the formula he ascribes to Hegel, "man= self-consciousness," Marx argues that man is sensuous natural existence, that, therefore, the subject is a natural being.[41] Its essential mode of activity is also natural: labor, not thinking. Similarly, Marx proposes to redefine the concept of the object as an essential correlate of this subject, as a sense object, existing proximally for the human senses as an object of need.

Note that Marx does not return to Locke. He does not found knowledge on the senses in the empiricist manner, but applies the general formal principle of subject-object identity to a redefined subject and object. Thus Marx's "sense object" is not a Lockean "idea" but the actual object itself, as it exists for the senses and especially as it exists as an object of need. With the establishment of these new definitions of the philosophical subject and object, the first phase of Marx's meta-theory is completed.

The second phase of the meta-theory then proceeds to reconstitute the formal structure of philosophy of identity with the help of these redefined terms. It is in this phase that Marx revises the concepts of need and reason to overcome their antinomial formulations in political philosophy. This revision consists, essentially, in transferring the formal attributes of reason to need. In Hegel, reason is self-reflexive, it mediates itself in the course of its own self-development in history; again, for Hegel reason is also universal, both in the narrow sense that its ethical postulates apply equally to all, but also in the broader sense that its unconditioned categories apply to the whole of reality. The formal principles of the philosophy of identity, such as the exigency of a unity of subject and object, are the foundation of this concept of rationality, their fulfillment the essential demand of reason which establishes reason's *imperium.* For Marx all these determinations of rationality are simply transferred wholesale onto "man." And since "man" in Marx's sense is a being of need, this remarkable substitution results in the attribution of the characteristic traits of rationality to the sphere of need. Need therefore no longer appears as the irrational content of a formalistic rationality, but is itself charged with the functions of rationality.

For Marx the philosophical subject is now a natural being, man. As such, this subject encounters its object, nature, in a natural way. The proximate relation of subject to object will be need, which motivates labor for the satisfaction of need.

"As a natural, embodied, sentient, objective being he is a suffering, conditioned and limited being, like animals and plants. The objects of his drives exist outside himself as objects independent of him, yet they are objects of his needs, essential objects which are indispensable to the exercise and confirmation of his faculties."[42] Were this simply a statement about human physiology it would of course be completely banal. It is no news that hunger requires food. However, Marx is attempting to make a statement about being in general, about ontology, and not just about the empirical being of the animal man. He writes, "Man's feelings, passions, etc., are not merely anthropological characteristics in the narrower sense, but are true *ontological* affirmations of being (nature) . . ."[43]

Bertell Ollman has suggested that we use the concept of "internal relations" to describe Marx's theory of need. Indeed, Marx rejects empiricism's nonteleological, external and accidental concept of relatedness. The ontologically primoridal sphere is not that of mechanistic natural science, in which such external relations prevail, but the sphere of need, in which "the need of a thing is the evident irrefutable proof that the thing belongs to my being, that the existence of this thing for me and its property are the property . . . of my being."[44] Hence Marx says that "Nature is the inorganic body of man," to express the idea that man and nature, subject and object, are joined in essential interdependence.[45]

Now too the labor through which need is satisfied will also appear as an ontological category in the forms of philosophy of identity. Labor is in fact the actual process of unifying subject and object, man and nature in the self-development of a humanized rationality. Here Marx passes from the abstract and immediate positing of the unity of subject and object in need, to a reflexive, mediated unity through the production of the object by the subject in labor.

Such philosophically reconceptualized labor Marx calls "objectification," the natural activity of the naturalized subject, man. When human beings transform their environment through labor, they "objectify" their needs and faculties. This they must do, for as a natural being man must "express and authenticate himself in being as well as in thought."[46] The result is a "humanized" nature within which human beings can fulfill themselves and unfold their potentialities in a continuous process of self-creation. There too they can recognize their own existence confirmed and universalized in the transformed objects of labor and, by extension, in all of being. Marx writes, "It is only when objective reality everywhere becomes for man in society the reality of human faculties, human reality, and the reality of his own faculties, that all objects become for him the objectification of himself. The objects then confirm and realize his individuality. They are his own objects, which is to say that man himself becomes the object."[47]

Finally, the third phase of the meta-theory derives philosophical and political consequences from these formulations, consequences that appear once the terms of philosophy have been reconstituted within the domain of history where they can be set into motion through social practice. At stake here is the meaning of the concept of "alienation" which, Marx argues, stands in contradiction to the "human essence." Hegel's concept of alienation is now revised to mean a specific, degraded type of objectification in which the transformed world turns around and dominates its creators instead of serving them. Here the individuals cannot recognize or develop themselves through their objects, but are crushed and oppressed by them. Because alienation, as "loss of the object," is not just a social category but also a determination of being generally, this condition can be reformulated as the antinomy of subject and object. In alienation, subject and object stand in conflict, as opposed principles requiring mediation.

The fundamental exigency of philosophy of identity is that the object appear as a product of the subject, but for Marx the process of this production is now a real one, occurring in history and not in the head of a philosopher. Alienation is a problem for philosophy, splitting subject from object, but not a problem that could be solved in pure thought through a speculative construction. Marx notes that "the medium through which alienation occurs is itself a practical one."[48] Its transcendence will also have to be practical, requiring a reversal in the relations between human beings and the products of their labor. This then is the "real" alienation which must be overcome and which Hegel confounds with objectivity itself.

Philosophy now appears for Marx not as a means through which a subject-object unity is achieved, but rather as the reflection in thought of their unity in history through labor. And where this unity is obstructed by alienation, the consequences will be felt by philosophy too as failure of its project. Thus where Hegel saw actual alienation, alienation in Marx's sense of the term, as the phenomenal form of the alienation of self-consciousness, Marx reverses the terms and defines the alienation of self-consciousness as the phenomenal form of actual alienation.

This alienation of self-consciousness consists for Marx in religion and idealistic philosophy. The human species creates a world through labor which dominates and dispossesses it; in thought too the products of the mind become powers over it. The species' spiritual and intellectual struggle to understand and reconcile itself with its own alienation gives rise to myths and speculative constructions. In them the individuals rationalize their powerlessness and learn to accept its inevitability as a positive good, as "the rose in the cross of the present."[49] In Hegel this form of artificial reconciliation with alienation nevertheless points toward the solution by mythologizing the unity of subject and object in labor.

Such alienated thought, Marx believes, cannot resolve its own antinomies. The concept of reason cannot be founded so long as alienation is accepted immediately in reality. It is the fact that philosophy remains in immediacy, that its transcendence of alienation takes place merely in thought and not in real life, that is responsible for idealism's theological turn toward a supra-sensible reality. But if the overcoming of alienation in practice is essential to the liberation of reason from theological myths, then revolution itself is a *methodological* necessity for philosophy.

A characteristic theory-practice relation now emerges, quite similar to that which Lukács establishes in his early work. If theory attempts to overcome alienation in pure thought, it will fall into various secularized forms of religion. Yet alienation is the obstacle which must be overcome in order to found reason, for to accept it as it is means to fail to unite subject and object, to demonstrate the production of the latter by the former, and this Marx continues to believe is necessary. Thus theory can found itself only by passing into practice to destroy alienation in reality. This can be done through socialist revolution. Marx writes:

It is only in a social context that subjectivism and objectivism, spiritualism and materialism, activity and passivity, cease to be antinomies and thus cease to exist as such antinomies. The resolution of the theoretical contradictions is possible only through practical means, only through the practical energy of man. Their resolution is not by any means, therefore, only a problem of knowledge, but is a real problem of life which philosophy was unable to solve precisely because it saw there a purely philosophical problem.[50]

The purpose of theory on these terms is to provide the proletariat with the "intellectual arms" it needs to solve not only its own problems but those of philosophy as well. No longer does theory appear as the real subject of this process, representing rational form to the proletariat, which latter, as mere need or factical content, can only be a "passive," "material" base for reason. Rather, the domain of need and labor in which the proletariat moves is also the element of reason itself. The contradictions the proletariat experiences in its existence are not accidentally related to the contradictions of philosophy, but are one and the same. Theory and practice have been united.

In reaching this conclusion Marx finally derives a wholly new type of ground for revolution: the ultimate demand of reason is rationality; revolution alone can satisfy this demand by resolving the antinomies of philosophy. If this is true then reason itself requires revolution, and every rational individual is committed by the very nature of reason to lend a hand.

FROM MARX TO LUKÁCS

The preceding discussion has shown that Marx's early meta-theory of philosophy is in fact a critique of formalism, both in politics and more generally in the theory of rationality. In the next chapter, I will show how this critique of formalism is further elaborated in Lukács' early Marxist philosophy. Lukács' theory is deeply dependent on Marx's, even though the most important early philosophical writings of Marx were still unpublished at the time. Insofar as the theory presented in the *Manuscripts* is concerned, this dependency is therefore indirect, mediated by Marx's *Capital*. It is precisely because Lukács studied *Capital* to find in it the basis of a meta-theory of formal rationality that he was able to reconstruct and extend its philosophical dimension in a manner paralleling Marx's own early philosophical work.

Marx arrived at the study of the economy not merely through a change in interests, but through a rigorous philosophical argumentation in the course of which he demonstrates that economics is the science of alienation, the discipline in which is charted the original and basic alienation from which the more complex philosophical forms of it are derived. Although Marx later abandoned the philosophy of praxis of his early works, the trace of this original discovery of the economy is preserved in his later ones. This trace appears most clearly in the continuing use of a meta-theoretical approach.

Marx's *Capital* continues to criticize formalistic abstractions by bringing them into relation to the social substratum from which they were originally abstracted. It is true that these are no longer philosophical abstractions but economic ones; however, Marx treats these latter in much the same way he had treated the former in the *Manuscripts*. The social contradictions he discovers are, in effect, philosophical antinomies reconstructed in a domain where they can be resolved through social action. The "secret" of *Capital*, its frequent obscurities, the "coquetting" with Hegel, the significance Marx attached to it as the basis of a theory of socialist revolution, all this is to be explained in terms of his fidelity to the original meta-theoretical project. Thus *Capital* is more than a scientific work on economics; it is also a chapter in the history of philosophy.

However, given its exclusively economic focus, *Capital* cannot adequately formulate and resolve the philosophical problems to which it is implicitly addressed. This is damaging to the coherence of Marxism; most importantly, it leaves a gap between the critique of capitalism and the socialist solution, a gap often filled by making pseudo-scientific and determinist claims for the theory of the economy. Whatever Marx himself may have said along these lines on occasion, Marxist economics establishes no causal connection between capitalism and socialism. As I will explain in more detail below, socialist revolution and the transition to a socialist society involve a type of cultural change that cannot be theorized on the model of those processes of "natural history" to which the mature Marx once compared them. On the contrary, the meta-theory of philosophy comes much closer to anticipating in philosophical terms the kind of cultural approach that can alone connect the critique of capitalism with socialism.

This was Lukács' great insight: the understanding that the critique of formal rationality implicit in Marx's economic works is the key to developing an adequate Marxist theory of revolution. Lukács thus began with a work, *Capital*, that responded only implicitly, methodologically to his own preoccupations. He made this implicit dimension of Marxist economic theory explicit by reconstructing its meta-theoretical premises. Then, generalizing Marx's concepts, Lukács reformulated the philosophical implications of the economic theory as the basis of a theory of revolution. To accomplish this, Lukács had to supply the missing moment in the meta-theory at the basis of Marxist economics, the moment in which philosophy itself operates with the historicized philosophical concepts to resolve simultaneously both historical and philosophical problems. In taking this step beyond Marx, Lukács developed an original philosophy of praxis.

3

Reification and the Paradigms of Rationality

THE CRISIS OF RATIONALITY

Marx's early work is critical of bourgeois society, but it arises less from the crisis of this society than from an abstract ethical attitude seeking a historical ground which is only just beginning to appear. By the time Lukács approaches the task of reformulating the Marxian theory, bourgeois society is in crisis, a general crisis embracing not only the ethical and political domain, but the very form and substance of rationality and culture. As Lukács put it in one early article: "The culture of the capitalist epoch had collapsed in itself and prior to the occurrence of economic and political breakdown. Therefore . . . it is a pressing necessity, precisely in the interests of culture, in the interest of opening the way to the new culture, to bring the long death process of capitalist society to its completion."[1]

This sense of generalized culture crisis is not unique to Lukács, but he is one of the first to articulate it with deep urgency and anguish. Later, in the period between the wars, a Spenglerian mood of doom comes to dominate much philosophical thinking in continental Europe, especially in the phenomenological and existentialist movement. In his "Vienna Lecture," Husserl expresses this mood while offering phenomenology as a last hope for mankind: "There are only two escapes from the crisis of European existence: the downfall of Europe in its estrangement from its own rational sense of life, its fall into hostility toward the spirit and into barbarity; or the rebirth of Europe from the spirit of philosophy through a heroism of reason that overcomes naturalism once and for all."[2]

What is unusual about Lukács' response to the crisis is his return to Marx for a solution in the *philosophical* domain, basing a "heroic" rationalism on the resolve of the revolutionary socialist movement. Of course in this period the whole socialist movement is imbued with a sense of the crisis of bourgeois society, but nowhere is the philosophical significance of socialist activism raised to consciousness. In the 1920s there are attempts such as Heidegger's to formulate a "decisionist" philosophical alternative to what is perceived as a disintegrating rationalism, but these remain disconnected from socialism, which alone offers some hope of transforming philosophy into destiny, and come to grief in a temporary union with fascism. (Malraux does represent a progressive alternative in this period, but it is an alternative within literature and not philosophy.) Lukács, practically alone, attempts to resolve the crisis through renewing Marx's philosophy of praxis.[3]

Like the young Marx demanding the realization of philosophy through revolution, Lukács insists that what is at stake in the struggle for socialism is not only a change in society, but also the fate of rationality. The revolution is an affair of reason. For, once philosophical ideas are reformulated meta-theoretically as social projects, then historical action has unique philosophical pertinence.

For Lukács the crisis of reason encompasses the dominant paradigm of rationality in all its manifestations, from science and technology to history and sociology, from the market and the bureaucracy to the socialist opposition itself. The concept of "reification," which Lukács applies in all these domains is based on three principal sources: Marx's concept of economic fetishism, Weber's concept of rationalization, and Hegel's concept of appearance. Lukács' theory can best be understood as a generalization of Marxian fetishism in two dimensions, in sociological breadth through Weber, and in ontological depth through Hegel. So generalized, the concept of reification becomes the basis for a critique of capitalist rationality as a system of social thought and organization threatened by its inability to grasp the material substratum of its own formalistic categories and institutional structures.

In *Capital*, fetishism means the substitution of exchange value for use value, relations between social objects for relations between the human beings who produce them, both in everyday life and in the scientific representation of the economy. This condition Marx attributes to the generalization of commodity exchange on the market. Fetishism characterizes a society in which the economic relations between the individuals are governed by the forces they unleash through their unplanned interactions on the market. In such a society, the "law" of the market takes on an independence and power, a "material character," the individuals themselves increasingly lose. Marx derives this condition ultimately from the fact that production itself is splintered and fragmented.

In the form of society now under consideration, the behaviour of men in the social process of production is purely atomic. Hence their relations to each other in production assume a material character independent of their control and conscious individual action. These facts manifest themselves at first by products as a general rule taking the form of commodities.[4]

Marx calls the result "fetishism" because in the market the human relations of producers and consumers appear not as such, but as relations between economic goods and categories, which latter seem to have an effective reality independent of the individuals. The outcome of the myriad interactions of individuals on the market, which none can chart although all participate in determining it, appears as specifically economic "properties" attached to the goods in circulation. Thus goods "have" a price which seems to belong to them much as do their physical and chemical properties. Indeed, so real is this price that it effectively governs the movement of the goods to which it is attached. Similarly, some goods "are" capital, while others take the form of profit or wages or savings, and so on. Yet it is clear that while these categories are in no sense imaginary, neither are they "real" attributes of the things to which they are applied. They are, says Marx, social relations become things, or "reified."

A commodity is therefore a mysterious thing, simply because in it the social character of men's labour appears to them as an objective character stamped upon the product of that labour; because the relation of the producers to the sum total of their labour is presented to them as a social relation, existing not between themselves, but between the products of their labour.[5]

Lukács' treatment of fetishism as reification involves the assumption that Marx's concept refers not only to the economy, but to the general form of capitalist social life. As a generalized fetishism, reification is applied to all the characteristic alienations of the human community in capitalist society, including such noneconomic institutions as bureaucracy and law. Marx himself fails to so generalize his concept of fetishism, or does so on occasion only hesitantly. Lukács does not hesitate; following in the footsteps of Weber, he develops a general cultural analysis of capitalist forms of life in which certain traits Marx identified with fetishism are considered to be exemplary for society as a whole. Weber's importance, in this regard, lies in his emphasis on the role of "rationalization" in the development of capitalism, the submission of social reality to forms of calculability and control. Although this contribution of Weber's may not owe much to Marx, Lukács tries to establish a connection.

Weber's theory of rationalization has to do with the extension of formalistic, quantifying reason to the phenomena of social life. He links this process of rationalization in society to the rise of modern science, with its quantification of nature, and to the emergence of modern capitalism, with its orientation toward economic gain. The two tendencies are joined in the idea of society as an object of technical rationality and control. Lukács incorporates Weber's theory wholesale into his own: wherever in capitalist society quality appears as quantity, or human interactions as the interaction of social things, and wherever the course of social events appears to be determined by quasi-natural laws, Lukács will interpret the phenomena through his concept of reification.

Lukács' originality with respect to Weber lies in his emphasis on the tension between the formal structures of rationalization and the actual human "content" of social life on which they are imposed. Lukács thus borrows many themes from Weber, but treats them in the general framework of Marx's critique of fetishism, as a formal-rational "appearance" in dialectical conflict with a real content it expresses. One might almost say that Weber's theory is recast by Lukács in the mold of Marx's, so that its general tendency is reversed: no longer an account of the inexorable progress of rationalization's "iron cage," Lukács' refurbished Weberianism sets off this trend against a dialectical counter-trend that promises eventual release from subservience to alienated social law. In Lukács, social reality escapes from the net of reified rationality: the increasing rationality of the parts is tied, he claims, to the invincible "irrationality of the total process," to economic crisis and violent resistance from below.[6] With this approach, Lukács has the basis of a specifically Marxist theory of the culture of capitalism, developed later in many dimensions by other Marxists, and particularly by the Frankfurt School. This cultural approach to capitalism will be explained in more detail below.

The tension Lukács identifies in social reality, between its reified form and its living human substratum, is philosophically significant because it represents meta-theoretically a larger conflict in the paradigms of rationality. In this tension, capitalist rationality comes up against a limitation that can only be overcome in an alternative paradigm, one which is theoretically expressed by Marxist dialectics, practically realized in socialism. In his philosophical discussion of these alternatives, Lukács uses the concept of "reification" and its dialectical correlate, "totality," to recapture for Marxism the Hegelian distinction between formal-analytic understanding (*Verstand*) and synthetic reason (*Vernünft.*) Lukács thematizes these two paradigms of rationality as opposed methodologies in social research and opposed cultural formations, with the latter emerging in each case as the *Aufhebung* of the former.

Lukács relates Marxism to the problem of rationality through a revolutionary philosophical interpretation of *Capital*. It was Lukács who first understood that *Capital* is more than a scientific work on economics, but an attempt to redefine that very science in terms of the philosophical background sketched above. He discovered, long before the publication of the *Manuscripts*, that Marx's critique of fetishistic formalism in political economy implies a far more general reconstuction of the concept of reason. The preceding chapter has shown how Marx moved from an early critique of formalism in political philosophy to a broader concern with the formalistic concept of reason, very much as Lukács supposed. Unfortunately Marx did not explicitly follow up this line of thought in his later work; nevertheless, it is clear that his early meta-theory did prepare his choice of a dialectical methodology in social research, and his critical attitude toward the dominant formalistic methods of the day. Marx's ea: ly work stops just short of providing a philosophical justification for a dialectical paradigm of rationality, inspiring the choice of the latter more by its general tendency than by a developed argument. Lukács' theory of reification is an original critique of formal rationality, based on Marx's *Capital*, and pursued to the point where it can actually found a dialectical concept of reason. There is a sense then in which Lukács' early Marxist work anticipates the discovery of the *Manuscripts*, and also goes beyond them theoretically in an important domain.

THE CONFLICT OF PARADIGMS

It is a commonplace that Marx's social theory fails to justify his confidence in the inevitable advent of a socialist future. *Capital* does not succeed in rigorously predicting the social transformation it announces. The resulting gap between the critique of capitalism and the socialist solution is sometimes filled by making pseudo-scientific determinist claims for the economic theory. Marx promises to explain the transition to socialism on the basis of "iron laws," but in fact he gets from capitalism to socialism not by a lawful, causally determined progression but by a philosophical dialectic. It is not surprising that unsympathetic critics speak of a "religious" or ethical exigency of socialism in Marx's work which is unfounded in the objective social theory.[7]

I have shown in the previous chapter that Marx arrives at the concept of socialism not through an ethical argument but through a theory of rationality and its "demands." In fact, Marx's early theory points toward a hierarchy of forms of rationality in economic and social life, corresponding to capitalist and socialist society and connected less by a political than a philosophical mediation. It is true that the later Marx sometimes took this philosophical mediation for a causal link. This was due to his self-misunderstanding in terms of a scientific paradigm of explanation unsuited to the tasks he sets it. Yet Marx could hardly have rested content with a theory so abstract and disconnected from concrete social life as the philosophical one presented in the *Manuscripts*. His dilemma was his inability to elaborate a new model of social change, based neither on a pure philosophical exigency nor on a causal prediction, in short a model of cultural change. Such a theory of culture would be the missing term between the *Manuscripts* and *Capital*, on the one hand, and between the critique of capitalism and the prediction of socialism on the other hand.

When Marx turned to economic research and abandoned philosophy, he left behind a number of vital conceptual tools needed to develop a theory of cultural change. The *Manuscripts* adumbrate such a theory in its discussion of paradigms of rationality, which might have been treated as cultural formations in a more concrete social theory. But Marx fell just short of making explicit the full implications of the meta-theory of philosophy for the study of culture. It is precisely this which Lukács finally achieved in his theory of reification.

Lukács reconstructs Marx's critique of formal rationality as a meta-theory of capitalist culture. On this basis he reconceptualizes class struggle as the dialectical mediation in which formal-analytic rationality, as a cultural paradigm, is transcended historically by an alternative dialectical paradigm. The transition to socialism now appears in a different light; it is not a causal sequence, nor a philosophical or ethical exigency only, but a process of mediation historicized meta-theoretically in the revolution. This mediation arises from the immanent cultural contradictions of the capitalist paradigm of rationality, contradictions between reified social practice and living human beings who resist the imposition of these reified forms. Such a theory of culture can finally link the philosophical concerns of Marxism with its specific analysis of political economy and social reality, and the latter with the projection of a socialist future.

Lukács reinterprets Marx's critique of political economy in

terms of this new approach. He treats the capitalist economy as the source of a cultural system, a paradigm of rationality prevailing throughout the social order: "What is customarily called the economy," he writes, "is nothing but the system of forms of objectivity of real life."[8] But then the discovery of contradictions in the economic sphere takes on a larger, cultural significance. What Marx describes as the economic crisis and breakdown of capitalism, Lukács reconstructs as the system's cultural crisis and breakdown. He thereby avoids a mechanistic social theory which would derive revolution from simple dissatisfaction with the level of welfare that capitalism can (in theory) deliver to its working class. Instead, Lukács develops a broader crisis theory, once again adumbrating the later efforts of the Frankfurt School.

This Lukácsian crisis theory is concerned with the generalization and breakdown of formal rationality as the governing principle of capitalist social life. The crisis appears "in the conflict between existence in its immediacy together with its expression in thought in the categories of reflection, and living social reality."[9] Here we have once again the contradiction between "true actuality" and "existing actuality" identified by the early Marx. Lukács' formulation implies a contradiction between form and content at two related levels, epistemologically and socio-politically.

On the one hand, Lukács does not dismiss bourgeois political economy as a mere epistemological error. Rather, it is the immediate theoretical expression of the social structure (that is to say, of "existence in its immediacy"). It is this structure itself which, because of its formal-rational character, stands in contradiction with "living social reality." Thus Lukács explains the emergence of political economy in terms of the relative success of the bourgeoisie in imposing its reified categories on actual social life.

Nor is it an accident that economics became an independent discipline under capitalism. Thanks to its commodity and trade arrangements capitalist society has given the whole of economic life an identity notable for its autonomy, its cohesion and its reliance on immanent laws. This was something quite unknown in earlier forms of society.[10]

On the other hand, even this relative success of capitalist economic theory and practice will meet its limit in inevitable resistance from below. Thus for Lukács formal rationality enters into crisis at both of the two connected levels under discussion here, epistemologically, in the ultimate failure of capitalist economic and social categories adequately to grasp the content of social life; and socio-politically, in the failure of the objects of these categories, the real institutions and relations they reflect, adequately to shape the lives of human beings in the society. At both levels, the formal limitation of the bourgeois standpoint testifies to what might be called its "eccentricity with respect to the real."

Nevertheless, Lukács does insist that political economy can advance science and formulate more or less exact calculations and predictions in every sphere by abandoning qualitative explanations for formal, quantitative ones. Partial abstract systems of laws can be constructed, each one embracing a specific segment of the economy in a form that allows it to be successfully manipulated for individual advantage. But the strength of this method is also its limit. A concept of knowledge which proceeds in terms of universal and atemporal laws such as those of political economy cannot grasp the deeper processes in which social practice constitutes social reality in its very lawful regularity. Thus it cannot comprehend those shifts and transformations at the level of the "totality" in which the foundations of the social system are laid and changed. It can only take the results of such changes as its presupposition and attempt to reduce them to their most abstract, reified form, without ever grasping the process of change itself.

As change accelerates and becomes more far-reaching with

the progress of capitalism, the control of events that the bourgeoisie seeks never ceases to become more problematical. In appearance the society continues to be composed of partial subsystems, internally rational and contingently related. The theory and organization of these reified sectors becomes ever more developed. But in reality, in the totality, these various subsystems and sectors interact in ways that no reified theory can grasp. Thus the management of society as a whole becomes more and more difficult even as the rationalization of its partial sectors is perfected. "The whole structure of capitalist production rests on the interaction between a necessity subject to strict laws in all isolated phenomena and the relative irrationality of the total process."[11]

This "irrationality of the total process" is reflected in the economic crises of capitalism, in which Lukács sees an unconscious rebellion of use value against the exchange value which is its phenomenal form. The reified form here fails to mediate successfully the production and distribution of the required quantity of real contents—use values—needed to maintain the system and the individuals who live under it.

This same "irrationality" appears consciously in the class struggle. In class struggle, "Force . . . appears as the concrete embodiment of the irrationality limiting capitalist rationalism, of the intermittance of its laws."[12] In class struggle economic, political and social acts react profoundly on each other, in direct opposition to the rigorous separation between them that bourgeois theory and practice attempt to establish; this constitutes an immediate refutation of the reified point of view. To the bourgeoisie the result appears as imminent barbarism and social disintegration. But, Lukás argues, in fact it is only the uncomprehended content of that abstract labor power which the capitalist pays at the factory gate, shattering its own reified form of objectivity and manifesting itself directly in historical action. Here the totality, as the actual moving force of history, the reality behind the reified appearances, emerges independently of the social laws and confronts them with forces they cannot control.

In this reformulation of the Marxian breakdown theory, reification is a process of partial autonomization which produces relatively independent spheres of social life that interact externally. The autonomization of the partial subsystems is the condition of their restructuration under a formal technologic of control and rationalization. The ultimate dialectical "mediation" of reified social reality consists in the real practical subversion of the social order through the breakdown of the boundaries of its partial subsystems. Making connections between the artificially isolated subsystems is the most threatening oppositional strategy for this reified social order, the strategy through which a new paradigm of rationality imposes itself on the inherited material of the old society. The very fact that the connections can be made and that the various partial subsystems can be related to each other in original ways proves their dependency on the human substratum of the society. It is through such subversive mediation that the human community, conscious of itself, assumes control of its own history.

CULTURE AND RATIONALITY

Lukács' theory of reification has fascinating methodological implications for both social science and philosophy, yet these have been largely overlooked. In this section and the next, I will begin to draw out these implications and try to account for the difficulty with which they are understood. There is a significant precedent for this problem of interpretation in the treatment of Marx's concept of alienation. Several researchers have discussed the transformation of Marx's critical concept of alienated social reality into the affirmative concept of alienated "consciousness" that now prevails in the social sciences, and according to which alienation is a subjective state of the individual and not an objective fact of social life.[13] The gutting of Marx's concept as it is incorporated into social psychology is paralleled by a similar misconstruction of Lukács' concept of reification. One of the main purposes of this chapter is to explain why reification cannot be understood as a category of social psychology, an "ideology" or mode of "consciousness." Yet this is the standard use of the concept in social theory today. Berger and Luckman, for example, write that "reification is a modality of consciousness, more precisely, a modality of man's objectification of the human world."[14] While it is true that such a definition would apply to the concept of "reified thought," the subject of my next chapter, the recovery of the critical content of Lukács' concept requires its reconstruction as an objective dimension of social reality. To this end I treat reification as a *cultural* category, an approach which offers a valuable alternative to both subjectivist and mechanistic misconstructions of Marxist social categories.

Although Lukács uses the term "culture" relatively infrequently, his interpretation of Marxism is in fact quite close to a modern cultural approach. The concept of culture is of course notoriously vague, but it has served anthropologists well to the extent that it orients them toward the historical specificity and system-wide unity of the societies they study.[15] "Culture" is a *monistic* concept which presupposes a unity of pattern and purpose characterizing the entire social system beneath the surface distinctions of social subjectivity and objectivity. The concept of culture points toward the common structures of social life at all levels, in artefacts, behavior and belief systems, in character and institutions. It assigns the researcher the problem of discovering the overarching paradigms of meaning and value that inhabit all the various spheres of society. It is some such orientation which Lukács attempts to capture for Marxism with his theory of "forms of objectivity."

According to this theory, social being and social thought cannot be separately conceptualized and then related by a theory of reciprocal causal interaction, as in most Marxist theory. This view, Lukács argues, leads to an insoluble antinomy of thought and things which can be overcome "only by conceiving of thought as a form of reality, as a moment in the total process . . ."[16] From this standpoint the focus is shifted from the mechanistic "influence" of social conditions on ideology and consciousness to the generalized patterning of all dimensions of society by a single form. Form in this sense is culture as an emergent property of social behavior, a property which is irreducible to the traditional categories of subjectivity and objectivity because they are in fact constituted by culture.

It is on these terms that I interpret Lukács' generalization of Marx's critique of formal economic rationality as a wide-ranging critique of formalism in all areas of capitalist social life. Lukács treats formal rationality in its social dimension as a specific cultural pattern, that of capitalism, and reconceptualizes the Marxist critique of capitalism as a cultural critique of this paradigm of rationality. To the extent that social science, like political economy, is based on a formal paradigm of explanation, this approach to social rationality has puzzling methodological implications. I would like to consider now the implications for social science of Lukács' critique of formal rationality.

For phenomena to be taken as possible objects of social scientific explanation, they must first be stripped of the natural immediacy in which they appear to everyday consciousness. For example, social theory cannot interrogate the fact of inequality until such time as that fact no longer seems natural, but appears as a historical accident. More recently, histories of childhood, death and other similar institutions have revealed just how much of what we take for natural in the human condition is in reality social. But what of the moment of immediacy in social theory itself? Social theory is also a social activity which would lend itself to social explanation if only we could be freed, as theorists, from an unreflective practice of reflection on society. Alvin Gouldner, among others, has called of late for a "reflexive" sociology that would overcome the traditional blindness of social theory to itself. In this regard, Lukács has a unique contribution to make, for he first proposed a sociological reflection on the very paradigm of rationality employed in social scientific explanation.

Undialectical social thought presupposes formal rationality as the *a priori* of scientific explanation, both of nature and society, to which is correlated the *a priori* ontological structure of the world. For any thought which starts out from the assumption that formal rationality is the highest type of rationality and the one in which the truth and being of things is revealed, the existence of formal rational laws of society poses no problem of principle. One simply takes it for granted that society, like nature, in which formal rational laws are first discovered, exhibits a rationality of this type. From the point of view of laws of this rationality, the individual human beings of which society is composed appear as mere vanishing points, mere instances of the generalities under which their being and their action can be shown to fall. Here is the origin of the extravagant deterministic claims of much social thought, including various schools of Marxism.

In opposition to this deterministic approach, there are romantic and humanistic counter-theories which derive society from an ontological base outside it, from individual human beings. In its extreme formulations, this approach leads to various forms of reductionism, for example, in terms of individual psychology or the actions of great men. Such an approach may save some degree of freedom for the social individual, but at the price of dissolving society as an object. This is no more satisfactory than sociological determinism, because we have ample evidence that society is an object *sui generis* with its own structure, and not simply a sum of individual actions.

Lukács theory of reification attempts to transcend this antinomy by treating the formal rational laws of the social world not as its ontological basis, but as a cultural system in interaction with the human beings who comprise that society. This position is designed to account for the irreducibility of the social object and also for its contingency on human actions which may transcend any given set of laws.[17] This approach undercuts the assumption that formal rationality is a universal ontological feature of nature and society, hence also any attempt to treat formal rational laws as the foundation of the social system. On Lukács' terms, formal rationality and its laws is a specific cultural product of capitalism, which itself requires explanation and therefore cannot serve as the paradigm of explanation. Lukács has recourse to the dialectical concept of totality to describe the structure of a social object in which formal rationality is a moment rather than an ontological presupposition.

Considered methodologically, Lukács' approach bears a certain resemblance to the contemporary theories of rationality of Weber and Husserl. It will be useful to draw out the comparison briefly, especially since Lukács was certainly influenced by Weber, and very probably by Husserl as well.

In his methodological writings, Weber suggests that systems of rationality can be reconstituted as ideal-types for the study of social objects by abstracting from their internal logic and forms of validity so as to treat them simply as behavioral models. The multiplication table, for example, exists not only as mathematical truth, but may be used as a more or less adequate ideal type of actual mathematical behavior.[18] Weber argues that sociology can suspend belief, in some sense, in systems of rationality in order to study them in their sociocultural dimension.

When one considers the enormous importance of the concept of "rationalization" in Weber's sociology, one might almost say that such suspension of belief is a constitutive, *a priori* foundation of sociology as a science, through which it establishes its field of objects in contradistinction from the other sciences. Yet this sociological "bracketing" of rationality is in Weber still incomplete because it does not include sociology itself in its scope. Thus Weber finds no contradiction in suspending belief in the type of rationality involved in "rationalization" while continuing to employ precisely this type of rationality to explain "rationalization." As Merleau-Ponty remarks, "Weber is well aware that history as science is itself a product of history, a moment of 'rationalization,' or of the history of capitalism."[19] Science would thus begin at the point at which reflection ceases, at the point at which formal rationality is taken for granted in its self-evidence and no longer interrogated as a social phenomenon.

Weber's ideal-typical reconceptualization of rationality resembles to some extent Husserl's much more radical interrogation of rationality in his transcendental phenomenology. Like Weber, Husserl begins by suspending belief in rationality through a procedure he calls the phenomenological reduction or bracketing of the natural attitude. After suspending all "positings of being" and corresponding truth claims in this manner, Husserl then attempts to analyze in "pure consciousness" the production of the effect of being and truth. Without going into a detailed description of Husserl's philosophy, I want to point out that this suspension is not merely methodological, as is Weber's, but goes to the ultimate epistemological credentials of the bracketed attitudes. Thus for Husserl, there is no easy regression to an unreflective faith in rationality. The reduction is not just a scientific technique, which presupposes science itself as the domain which is never truly reduced, but rather it is designed to open up the methodological space within which an integrally reflective form of phenomenological rationality can be deployed.

Husserl's example is suggestive for understanding Lukács' position. Lukács transforms Weber's purely methodological bracketing of formal rationality into a radical cultural critique of reification, affecting the epistemological claims of any formal rational study of society. He not only treats formal rationality as a cultural dimension of capitalist society, he includes the formal rationality of the social sciences themselves in this bracketing. Thus, like Husserl's phenomenology, the Lukácsian cultural approach involves a reflective reduction of truth claims which Weber still continues to take for granted. And like Husserl, Lukács attempts to arrive at an integrally reflective paradigm of rationality, capable of explaining the suspended formal one as well as itself.

However, at another level, Lukács remains closer to Weber than to Husserl. For like Weber, Lukács studies the bracketed form of rationality as a cultural pattern, comparable with others in its relative power to shape society, but also comparable, Lukács would add, in its limits as a basis for explaining the system it governs. Lukács' radicalized Weberianism thus remains at the social level, achieving the more highly self-reflective position of Husserl not by a retreat to the transcendental, but by relativizing the truth claims of social science.

It is important to note that this approach does not require the rejection of the epistemological validity of formal rationality in the specific domains to which its application is uniquely appropriate, such as mathematics and logic. Lukács also grants natural science a certain independence of social practice, in its validity if not in its genesis. These domains, Lukács argues, lack a dialectic of subject and object and so come under the horizon of formal rational explanation. Society, on the other hand, is constituted in the dialectic of subject and object, and so can never be fully grasped by a formal rational logic.[20]

Thus Lukács' point is not that formal rationality is "arbitrary" in the same way and to the same degree as such things as table manners—a truly irrationalist position, and one which would make the dependency of dialectical rationality on the *Aufhebung* of formal rationality completely incomprehensible. Rather, it is as a *cultural* system, governing for an entire social world that formal rationality requires a properly cultural explanation. Lukács argues, in effect, that as a cultural pattern formal rationality is as culturally relative as any other, that is to say, that society is no more essentially "rational" in this sense than it is totemistic, to mention another cultural logic to which reification might be compared.[21]

This interpretation of Marxism is an extremely controversial one in spite of these qualifications, which are often overlooked. Commentators of the so-called "scientific" school of Marxism, such as Lucio Colletti and Althusser, protest that Lukács' theory of reification leads back to the romantic culture criticism from which Marx is supposed to have liberated radical social thought. For them the Lukácsian approach signifies the revival of philosophy, that is to say, of ideology inside the *cordon sanitaire* surrounding the "science" of Marxism.

Thus Gareth Stedman Jones writes that *History and Class Consciousness* "represents the first major irruption of the romantic anti-scientific tradition of bourgeois thought into Marxist theory."[22] Colletti has a similar opinion, complaining that Lukács "entered the factory not with *Capital* but with the *Essai sur les données immédiates de la conscience* . . ."[23] In sum, Lukács would have transformed the Marxian critique of capitalism into a romantic critique of reason *per se* by conceptualizing formal rationality through the concept of reification as a cultural dimension of capitalist society, rather than considering such rationality in the approved "scientific" manner as a universal ontological property of being itself in both the natural and the social world.

I will return to this controversy in a later chapter. Here the most important point to be made is that Lukács had no need to study Bergson to arrive at his intellectual destination: Marx and Hegel would have sufficed. To give an example, there is ample material in the first volume of *Capital* to support Lukács' critique of the alienating affects of the division and mechanization of labor; it is simply not true that Lukács is hostile to machinery *per se,* as is sometimes charged. Lukács' argument leads not to an opposition to reason in general, but like Hegel's philosophy on which it is based, it rejects the universal pretensions of formal rationality in order to validate the claims of dialectical rationality. All this is clear enough from the texts and need not be belabored.

What really is questionable in Lukács' procedure is also what is most original and fruitful, namely, the discovery that linking all the phenomena of capitalist society Marx criticizes, from fetishism to mechanization and crises, there is a common structure, a pattern constituted by the imposition of formal rationality on the social world. It is this discovery which is the basis for Lukács' generalization of Marx's approach in the theory of reification.

It is true that Marx himself did not thematize this patterning process; his analysis therefore falls short of a specifically cultural approach. Lukács' leap from the critique of political economy to a theory of capitalist culture is thus a step beyond Marx, and it is fair to say that his reading of Marx involves a certain distortion of the latter's position insofar as Lukács fails to make clear the originality of his own views, but attributes everything to Marx. This step beyond Marx was inspired, however, not only by Lukács' reading of philosophy and sociology, but still more by real social changes in capitalism with which many of his critics today have still not come to terms after fully fifty years.

Like Weber, Simmel and a number of other thinkers of the period, Lukács believed that in advanced capitalism fetishism extends into every domain of social life. This made it necessary to develop concepts unifying the diverse phenomena Marx criticized more or less separately in his work. This, rather than any retreat into irrationalism, inspired by *mauvaises lectures*, is what lies behind the introduction of the concept of reification and its application in a cultural critique of capitalism.

REIFICATION AND REASON

I would now like to show that the place of Lukács' theory of reification within his construction of Marxist theory can only be understood by examining the second dimension in which he generalizes the concept of fetishism, the ontological dimension. It is for failing to explore this aspect of the theory that many commentators have gone astray. It is here that Lukács reformulates Marxist theory in terms of Hegelian categories. The basis of this reformulation is Hegel's distinction of paradigms of rationality, between "understanding" *(Verstand)* and "reason" *(Vernünft)*. As Hegel employed this distinction, it referred to different ontological levels in reality, as well as to different faculties and methods. Hegel does not pretend to "refute" understanding as in error, so much as to cut down its claim to being the ultimate paradigm of rationality. Reason, for Hegel, arises not in opposition to understanding, but dialectically from it, through a process of mediation.

Lukács' turn to Hegel in the interpretation of Marx is justified by Marx's frequent use of the Hegelian category of "appearance" in the discussion of economic fetishism, and by his reference to the Hegelian distinction of abstract and concrete in his most important methodological essay, the "Introduction to the Critique of Political Economy." These categories are all derived from Hegel's distinction of understanding and reason. There is no doubt that this aspect of Hegel's theory influenced Marx. These Hegelian usages in Marx are easily identified because Hegel substitutes his own very characteristic definitions of these terms for the conventional ones.

Hegel's distinction of appearance and reality does not correspond with the usual one between what is merely for consciousness and what is in itself. Instead, appearance and reality are related as real moments in the dialectic of being. Appearance is not in the mind, but is the "immediate" reality of being, the form in which it reveals itself proximally. Through the discovery of the implicit "mediations" uniting these appearances, being passes into "reality." Similarly, in place of the usual distinction of abstract and concrete in terms of the degree of conceptual generality, Hegel substituted a distinction between the unilateral and the holistic. The abstract is the partial "moment" in a concrete "totality." Lukács' concept of reification covers approximately the territory of Hegel's concepts of appearance and abstraction.

For the most part Marx himself follows the Hegelian usage of these terms. However, there is a significant ambiguity in his theory of fetishism. There Marx seems to rely on the conventional distinction between the abstract and the concrete to describe the process in which money "appears" as the general equivalent for all economic goods. This "identity" of all commodities is ultimately rooted in the equivalence of the labor they contain. The comparability of all the forms of labor, their "abstract" identity (in the conventional sense of the term) is rooted in turn in the capitalist transformation of the labor process. In the course of capitalist development, the concrete, qualitative specificity of the various types of craft labor is eliminated and all are reduced to the mere quantitative expenditure of time and energy. They thus become comparable, or equivalent in becoming more "abstract" through the loss of their qualitative specificity.

However, in spite of Marx's apparent reliance on the conventional distinction of abstract and concrete in these discussions, his constant reference to the former as the "appearance" of the latter indicates that something more complex is involved. In fact, the "Introduction to the Critique of Political Economy" shows that Marx's use of the conventional distinction is embedded in a Hegelian dialectic of appearance and reality.

There Marx explicitly employs the Hegelian distinction of abstract and concrete to describe his own method, and relates it to the distinction of appearance and reality. Marx writes, in a famous passage, "The concrete is concrete, because it is a combination of many objects with different destinations, i.e. a unity of diverse elements. In our thought, it therefore appears as a process of synthesis, as a result, and not as a starting point, although it is the real starting point and, therefore, also the starting point of observation and conception."[24] Marx applies this distinction to the theory of fetishism, and shows that the abstract generality of the categories of the capitalist economy is the result of a process of development which, to be fully comprehended, must be reinserted into the social totality from which it arises.

The "synthesis" through which thought brings together all the various determinations and categories of the capitalist economy in a concrete totality, concrete in the Hegelian sense, thus overcomes their unilateral character precisely in the course of explaining their historical and origins and social functions. This synthesis is simultaneously, however, the demonstration that abstractness in the sense of conceptual generality, is the necessary form of appearance of the social reality which underlies the economy. So Marx writes that "the categories are therefore but forms of expression, mani-festations of existence of this subject, this definite soci-ety . . ."[25] Marx's method, as he himself describes it in this text, condenses the two concepts of the abstract and the concrete into one through inserting them into a dialectic of appearance and reality.

The unity of these two concepts of the abstract and the concrete is in fact adumbrated already in Hegel's own discus-sion of the appearance/reality dialectic. Of course the entire *Logic*, indeed all of Hegel's work, is based on a method of exposition that passes from the abstract, in his own sense of the term, toward the concrete. However, the category of "appearance" thematizes precisely this distinction as a general ontological attribute of being. Appearance in this Hegelian sense is the "whole" insofar as it is "manifested" in "parts" which themselves have the apparent form of independence and autonomy. It is this form which is dialectically trans-cended in the synthesis of the parts in a "totality," a "reality."

The pivotal moment in this transition from appearance to reality is the transcendence of what Hegel calls the "law of appearance." This category refers to the type of connection between objects established by analytical "understanding," for example in natural scientific explanation as the latter is interpreted by Kant. Scientific laws in this sense presuppose the independent existence of the objects they draw into external relation, and fail to found these objects in their existence through the relations that are defining for them. Law thus establishes, Hegel argues, only "immediate because abstract unity" and must be transcended by reason *(Vernünft)* in the concrete and mediated unity of a totality of essential relations.[26]

These considerations on Hegel should help to explain why Lukács conjoins social ontology and methodology in this theory of reification. His starting point is the *appearance* of autonomy of the economic system and, modelled on it, the reified culture of capitalism generally. The autonomy of system is that aspect of reification by which it constitutes a logically coherent, law-governed world of social objects. For Lukács this appearance of autonomy can neither be treated as an illusion, ideology or "worldview," nor as a reality in the full sense of the term. Rather it is *Erscheinung*, "appearance," that is to say, it is the real *in* that aspect which reveals a systematic order, a lawful form.

It is important for understanding Lukács' relation to romanticism to note that he does not contrast this lawful order with an immediate and concrete experience. His philosophy is not one of romantic protest against reification; he is too much of a Hegelian for that. Rather, he seeks to transcend the category of appearance through mediating it at a higher level, a level richer in form as well as in content. In Hegel's *Logic*, this is the level of "totality," as a complex of essential relations between form and content, appearance and reality, law and its determined objects. Hegel's treatment is extraordinarily difficult, in part because of the high level of generality of his presentation. Lukács' own presentation of this dialectic of appearance in a specific social context does succeed in making clear in what such a mediation would consist.

Lukács argues that Marx's method in *Capital* corresponds closely with Hegel's. The autonomized partial moments of the whole appear as "facts" of social life, raised to consciousness in the categories of political economy and comprehended through its formal rational laws. These latter are not, for Marx, illusions or errors, but pivotal moments in the transcendence of the immediate appearances. This is why Marx's own theory is presented as a "critique" rather than as a canonically formulated alternative to political economy. As Lukács understands Marx, bourgeois economics thus represents the moment of appearance, formulated as a law through the understanding, while Marx's critique represents reason's discovery of the reality which appears.

There is however a significant difference between this Marxian and the original Hegelian approach: where Hegel assumes the contrast of understanding and reason to be an atemporal distinction in ontological levels, Marx offers a historical explanation for it. The sphere of appearance, which consists for Marx in the reified facts and laws of capitalism, is bounded historically by a possible transcendence in action. Reification is thus not merely subjective, but neither is it a permanent reality that can never be changed. It is the failure to grasp reification as social appearance in this sense that leads to its philosophical representation as an eternal foundation of knowledge and experience, rather than as a historically specific cultural form. It is on this aspect of the theory of reification that Lukács' own analysis focusses.

Lukács argues that the Kantian analytic understanding represents in philosophy, at the highest level of generality, the same reified formalism found in bourgeois political economy. Just as Hegelian reason transcends the understanding through a synthetic process of mediation, so Marx accomplishes the same sort of radical critique of political economy. For Lukács, however, Marx is not simply applying Hegelian dialectics to a particular domain, the economy, nor are the formalistic categories of political economy merely categories of a specific social science. Bourgeois economics and the forms of existence of which it is the expression are the archetypical domain from which formalistic rationality arises as a cultural pattern. Lukács observes that "the structure of commodity relations [can] be made to yield a model of all the forms of objectivity of bourgeois society together with all the forms of subjectivity corresponding to them."[27] The general predominance of formalistic rationality in philosophy, science, law and the other areas of the superstructures can now be explained on this basis.

From Lukács' meta-theoretical standpoint, the economy is the concrete substratum and the real basis of the philosophically abstracted categories which define formal rationality and its antinomies. The meta-theoretical reconstruction of these categories *in* the economy alters the problematic of rationality and points toward a very different kind of solution to its antinomies than those offered by philosophy in the past, namely, a historical solution. On these terms, Marx's critique of political economy becomes the basis for a more general critique of formalistic rationality. In linking political economy, as form of appearance, to its base in the totality, Marx indicates the lines along which the concept of rationality would have to be revised to lose its formalistic limitation. Lukács thus rediscovers the whole Marxian problematic of rationality from these indications in the economic works.

Lukács claims that his own approach unites philosophy and science, theory and history in a historical dialectic. The split between these domains he regards as due to an illusion of history into which every era falls, the illusion that its own most general formal structures, its "form of appearance" is suprahistorical. Philosophy then proceeds to elaborate abstract and atemporal systems based on the implications and contradictions of this apparently suprahistorical form, while the material life of society, history, is viewed as mere factual content of this form.

Bourgeois society itself makes possible a transcendence of

this split between philosophy and history through the development of an integrally historical method that leaves no domain of form beyond its reach. This society is unique in that in it the domain of universal form appears as analytic understanding, corresponding to the actual categorial structure of the economy which is its archetype and source. Thus here the science of the economy can transcend its own boundaries as a specialized discipline and contribute to the resolution of properly philosophical problems. This is accomplished by showing the historical and social roots of the specific, dominant paradigm of rationality of the bourgeois era. In so relating economy to rationality, the immediacy of form can finally be overcome, and it can be historicized in contact with its substratum and content. This historicization can be extended to all the more abstract philosophical theories that arise on the basis of the formal structure of the economy when that structure is posited as suprahistorical in essence. Thus philosophy can be swept into the movement of history, and history itself can become the study of reason, no longer a mere contingent collection of facts. It can be shown "that history consists precisely in the constant transformation of those forms which earlier modes of thinking, undialectical and stuck fast in the immediacy of their present as they always were, regarded as suprahistorical."[28]

In sum, Lukács identifies formal rationality with capitalism and dialectical reason with socialism as successive stages in the history of rationality, and not as atemporal and alternative paradigms, each potentially valid throughout all of history. This historical identification of the forms of rationality Lukács regards as the specific contribution of Marxism to the resolution of the problems raised by Hegel's theory of rationality.

The great advance over Hegel made by the scientific standpoint of the proletariat as embodied in Marxism lay in its formulation of the categories of reflection [*Reflexionsbestimmungen*] not as an "eternal" stage in the comprehension of reality in general, but rather as the necessary forms of existence and of thought of bourgeois society. Marxism thus grasped these categories as reifications of being and thought, and therewith discovered the dialectic in history itself.[29]

It is to Lukács' application of this approach in an original meta-theory of philosophy that I will now turn.

4

The Meta-Theory of Philosophy: Lukács' Formulation

THE HERITAGE OF CLASSICAL GERMAN PHILOSOPHY

For Lukács traditional philosophy is in essence theory of culture that does not know itself as such. Philosophy is reflection on cultural structures misinterpreted as eternal principles disconnected from the accidents of history and social life. Yet in spite of this systematic misconstruction of culture, philosophy is important insofar as it thematizes cultural presuppositions and exposes them to discussion and criticism. Philosophy has a unique contribution to make to a social theory which wants to understand its own place in a process of cultural transformation of which it is a part. This explains why the heart of Lukács' most important work is devoted to an extended analysis of the history of philosophy.

Lukács had, of course, an important predecessor in the Marxist study of the history of philosophy. In the foreword to *History and Class Consciousness*, he says that "it is of *practi-*

cal importance to return in this respect to the traditions of Marx-interpretation founded by Engels (who regarded 'the German workers' movement' as the 'heir to classical German philosophy.')"[1] However, this statement is misleading to the extent that it would incline the reader to seek in Lukács a treatment of classical German philosophy similar to that which it receives from Engels and his orthodox Marxist followers. In fact there are few important similarities, for Lukács returns less to Engels' specific interpretation of the heritage than to the general question posed by Engels of Marxism's relation to its philosophical forebears.

Engels was the first to describe the broad sweep of the history of ideas from the French Enlightenment through Hegel and Feuerbach as a vast intellectual prologomena to Marxism. For Engels the German working class movement was the heir of this great intellectual tradition, continuing it within a new framework. However, this new framework, as Engels understood it, bore little resemblance to the heritage which it was supposed to assume. Engels presented Marxism as a science, comparable to the other sciences, while Marxist philosophy became for him a new natural philosophy, synthesizing all the sciences into a materialist worldview. The final traces of classical German philosophy that remain were to be found in a revised dialectic, which presumably continued the Hegelian theory of reality as process. But neither this materialist worldview nor this dialectic can carry the weight of the inheritance Engels claims for them.

In fact for Engels the heritage of the bourgeoisie is not so much philosophy as science. The epistemological and ontological concerns of classical German philosophy go by the boards. Bourgeois philosophy served a function in developing dialectics, in stimulating the growth of the natural sciences and of historical and economic theory, and in combatting religion with materialism. But, if Marxism can assume this heritage, it is only by everywhere substituting new scientific modes of thought for the old speculative ones. In the process, reason ceases to be problematical—hence philosophical; it regains the immediate self-certainty of early modern science, distinguishing itself from philosophy as this science distinguished itself from that of Aristotle.

The uncritical, or precritical theory of truth Engels postulated as the basis for the inheritance is particularly evident in those passages where he discusses the legitimacy of the proletariat's claim. For Engels the essence of the heritage is science, the sciences created by the bourgeoisie, because only science is *universal*, not bound by the class conditions on which it nevertheless depends for its birth. The proletariat alone in bourgeois society *needs* the truth, and it alone, therefore, can rise to the universality and honesty required for the continued pursuit of scientific truth in the period of the decadence of bourgeois society. Even in the natural sciences the declining bourgeoisie cannot accept the truth it discovers, because at every turn new ideas undermine the foundations of bourgeois ideology and subvert the static worldview and the *"post festum"* religious conversion of a class menaced by the repercussions of its own rationalistic traditions. Hence the task of reason devolves on the proletariat, which is prepared to accept this task in the proper spirit and carry it forward.

Like Engels and the mainstream of the Marxist tradition, Lukács too sees more at stake in the socialist movement than a change in property relations; the struggle will also decide the fate of reason itself. However, for Lukács, gone is the enlightenment optimism and faith in science of the Marxist mainstream, gone the supreme self-confidence of Engels, who still could say of the petty bourgeoisie, "Let [them] cast in their lot with the anti-Semites until they have convinced themselves that they get no help in that quarter."[2] Both the rationalism and the irrationalism of bourgeois society now appear to Lukács to be infinitely more problematical than ever they appeared to earlier Marxists. For the first time there arises within Marxism an interrogation of enlightenment itself, and not just of its limits or abuse in bourgeois society. In this sense, Lukács' critique of reified rationality foreshadows the later work of Adorno and Horkheimer in their *Dialectic of Enlightenment*. Like them, Lukács sees in modern irrationalism not a mere regression behind the achieved level of rationality, but the dialectical correlate of the later. In his own terminology irrationalism is described as a reaction against reification under the horizon of reification itself.[3] In any case, the heritage of classical German philosophy now appears in a very different light than it did to Engels, not as the salvation of the scientific debris of the Enlightenment from an increasingly obscurantist bourgeoisie, but as a great attempt to validate and found rationality itself, an attempt which had inevitably to fail on the ground of bourgeois society but which may yet succeed on proletarian soil.

For Lukács, bourgeois thought reaches its peak in classical German philosophy, but at the same time its contradictions manifest themselves there with more clarity and rigor than elsewhere. These contradictions Lukács sums up as the "antinomies of bourgeois thought," the split between subject and object, freedom and necessity, value and fact, form and content, which philosophy attempts to overcome in what Lukács calls a "totality." For Lukács as for Hegel, "To transcend such ossified antitheses is the sole concern of reason."[4] The resolution of the antinomies is the fundamental exigency of this philosophy, through which it attempts to found its concept of reason. But, Lukács argues, in spite of the most strenuous intellectual efforts, the antinomies emerge intact from bourgeois philosophical reflection. Kant's philosophy is for Lukács the highest and purest expression of the antinomies of reified thought, and the greatness of Hegel lies principally in having developed the dialectical methodology by which Kantianism could be subjected to a rigorous critique and transcended. Marxism then appears as the completion of the Hegelian critique of Kant, a completion which requires a radical change in orientation, but which in essence prolongs Hegelian dialectics. Lukács' own contribution consists in the appropriation of Hegel's dialectical critique of Kant and of reified thought generally from within Marxism.

From this standpoint classical German philosophy takes on a wholly new importance for Marxism. It does not belong to Marxism's prehistory, but rather poses for the first time, if in a still relatively unconscious form, the fundamental problems that Marxism is called upon to solve. Lukács therefore reexamines the development of this philosophy, from Kant to Hegel, in order to understand the earliest formulations of the problems to which Marxism is addressed, and the general conditions of their solution. The study of classical German philosophy is a study of the outer reaches of bourgeois thought, as it approaches the point at which its transcendence in Marxism will finally show the way to resolve its antinomies. For Lukács, the theory of the antinomies of bourgeois thought is a summum of the fundamental methodological exigencies of a new concept of reason: the dialectical unification of subject and object, freedom and necessity, value and fact, form and content. These were already the goals which classical German philosophy set for itself and Lukács accepts them as valid, rejecting only the method by which this philosophy hoped to attain them.

The failure of classical German philosophy then demonstrates that reason requires, on purely *methodological* grounds, a step beyond bourgeois society, beyond philosophical speculation into revolutionary practice. Classical German philosophy, Lukács says, "is able to think the deepest and most fundamental problems of the development of bourgeois society through to the end—on the plane of philosophy . . . And—in thought—it is able to take all the paradoxes of its position to the point where the methodological necessity of going beyond this historical stage in mankind's development can at least be seen as a problem."[5] Henceforth the founding of a universal concept of reason is impossible without this *historical* progress. This historical progress has therefore become, as such, a demand of reason.

Lukács' Marxism thus refuses either to attempt a speculative resolution of the antinomies of philosophy, or to ignore them in the naive self-certainty of science. For Lukács the only possible reconciliation is the practical transcendence of the opposition between the antinomial terms at the level at which they arise. The procedure of Lukács' meta-theory of classical German philosophy consists in large part in identifying this level as social and demonstrating the continuing traces of their social origin in the most abstract concepts of this philosophy. This is the theoretical basis for what Lukács calls the unity of theory and practice.

THE REIFIED THEORY-PRACTICE RELATION

Lukács' approach to the study of philosophy is deeply disconcerting for it asks us not only to believe that philosophical abstractions are rooted in social life, but, stranger still, to believe that the problems arising from these abstractions can be resolved in social life. This approach implies a question not ordinarily posed about philosophy, namely why it *is* philosophy in the first instance.

This question makes no sense in terms of the usual Marxist theory of ideology. That theory contrasts an apologetic abstractionism, starting out from the problems of social life and rising to philosophy with, on the contrary, a direct practical assault on these same problems in order to resolve them practically. Clearly, such a philistine position leads to the simple dismissal of philosophy in order to turn to the serious business of practical affairs. Yet the point Lukács wants to make is that the kind of social problems that become the basis of philosophical reflection simply cannot be solved by such an unreflected practicality. They arise, rather, at the points where such practice invariably fails, or still more critically, at those points at which its very success raises further questions it knows not how to address practically. For Lukács, therefore, it is not any and every practice which might resolve philosophical problems, but only a very special kind of practice the nature of which will have to be specified further.

This dialectic of theory and practice might be approached from another angle. Most Marxists consider practice as a more or less conscious implementation of theory (of bourgeois or proletarian ideology, for example), but it would conform more to Lukács' intent to reverse the terms of the equation in order to consider theory as a specific type of practice "raised to consciousness" and there conceptualized. One might ask then what it is about the type of practice prevalent in bourgeois society that generates the problems with which philosophy is concerned. This question could also be reformulated more precisely as follows: What is the inner limit on practice in bourgeois society which prevents it from resolving practically the types of problems that then appear in philosophy as antinomies? What is there about this practice that makes of it the source of problems it cannot even begin to resolve, which in fact do not appear to be practical problems at all, but rather to be philosophical problems? Already, the very form of these questions begins to indicate unaccustomed reasons why philosophy should arise through a process of abstraction from practical life, leading it ever further from its own material substratum. In a complementary fashion, one also begins to see just why instead of recommending an immediate return to practice, Lukács proceeds to a meta-theoretical critique of philosophy in the course of which everyday practice too is subjected to critical analysis.

Most abstractly formulated, the limit on everyday practice with which Lukács is concerned is reification. The previous chapter has discussed the ramifications of this concept in detail. Here I will confine myself to an exposition of those aspects of the concept most relevant to Lukács' meta-theoretical critique of philosophy. These are the social origins of the reified theory-practice relation, and its consequences for what Lukács calls "reified thought," that is to say, thought which accepts reification as the horizon, the intrinsic limit of practice generally.

According to Lukács, it is the capitalist transformation of the work process which is the basis of all forms of reification. The reification of labor is therefore the origin and model of all forms of reification throughout the society. "The destiny of the worker becomes the general destiny of the entire society."[6] In practice, capitalism imposes this particular destiny on ever larger segments of the population as it everywhere divorces workers from their means of production and organizes them in factories. Ideologically, the capitalist class itself justifies its right to possess these means of production by claiming that they are the fruit of its own labor or that of its ancestors. Labor thus has new social and ideological functions in capitalist society, different in principle from those it possessed in earlier times. It is no longer a special concern of a particular estate as in slave and feudal society. Labor is not seen as a degraded, subhuman activity, but as the source of all social utility, as an eminently human occupation. This is not merely an ideological change; the key traits of reification workers experience also affect the upper classes. "The problems of consciousness arising from wage-labor are repeated in the ruling class in a refined and spiritualized, but for that very reason, more intensified form."[7]

Lukács seeks the *"Seinsgrund"* of reified thought, even in its highest philosophical manifestations, in the structure of the capitalist labor process.[8] Under capitalism, the productive system faces the worker as a completed and independent object world, which imposes its own rhythm and order on his or her laboring activity. The more advanced is the mechanization, the more the expenditure of this labor power becomes the simple control of the autonomous productive activity of the machines themselves. Here work tends to become "the contemplative stance adopted towards a process mechanically conforming to fixed laws, enacted independently of man's consciousness and impervious to human intervention, i.e. a perfectly closed system."[9]

It is characteristic of reification that this appearance of autonomy and objective lawfulness obscures the fact that the machine itself is a product of human labor, that its essence is not to be found merely in the structure of its operation, but also in the human activity which first created it and gave it that structure. In short, obscured behind the synchronic rationality of the given productive system is the diachronic development of the human species itself, of its knowledge and powers, and of the class relations of the society which created it.

The capitalist too confronts reified reality in his economic activity in a similar manner at another level. His much vaunted entrepreneurial "creativity," says Lukács, consists entirely in calculating as exactly as possible what will happen despite his intervention. The capitalist then attempts to so position himself with respect to this predetermined outcome that he can profit from the objective evolution. Like the worker confronted with the autonomous activity of the machine, the capitalist is confronted by the autonomous activity of the market.

Thus the activity of the individual subject in capitalist society is not the transformation of *reality*, in Lukács' ontological sense of the term, but rather conformity to it, and especially to its laws, in order to realize its potential benefits for the individual. The intervention of the subject is exhausted in the taking up of an orientation with respect to reality. Where this orienting activity reflects unconscious social laws, massive regularities of behavior will appear which may indeed have a significant effect on the real world. But the subjects do not assume this effect as their common goal, but rather relate to it yet again as the presupposition of an individual calculus of losses and gains. Thus, "the attitude of

the subject becomes purely contemplative in the philosophical sense."[10]

Reified thought is thought which arises from just such a
confrontation of individual and reality. It is not confined to the
bourgeoisie, but affects all classes in bourgeois society, including the proletariat. Not surprisingly, however, it is particularly suited to the life conditions of the bourgeoisie, which
are individualistic in essence. Solidarity between members of
the class has a very limited (primarily defensive) function, and
the form of their interaction is generally one of competition
and conflict, not cooperation and common struggle. Therefore, what the class creates in common, as a class, it generally
accomplishes unconsciously, through mechanisms which
work behind the backs of the individuals. Each capitalist is
aware of the activity of the class as a whole "as something
external which is subject to objective laws which it can only
experience passively."[11]

The individual bourgeois perceives himself as an active
agent, a subject of history, while the activity of his class
appears to him in its reified form, as an object. From the
bourgeois point of view, activity can only be predicated of
conscious individuals and only conscious individuals can appear as subjects. However, Lukács argues, individual activity
in capitalist society consists primarily in adjusting to the
necessary course of events, the better to profit from them.
The conscious activity of the individual bourgeois therefore
makes no essential contribution to the course of events but is
exhausted in the more or less successful calculation of what
will happen in any case. In this sense, the activity of the
individual bourgeois is really passivity, is really an objective
aspect of the social process and not a subjective, creative
aspect.

The level at which the true activity of the bourgeoisie is to
be found is precisely that of the class as a whole, of which the
individual is only conscious as pure objective force. This level
of true activity is unconscious because it results from the

mutual interaction of the thousands of decisions of the members of the class, and from the unforeseen consequences of these decisions. It is this which the individual bourgeois experiences as the objective laws of the economy which, like Bacon's nature, must be obeyed to be controlled.

These sociological considerations form the essential background to a discussion of Lukács' meta-theoretical procedure in the critique of philosophy. The antinomy of value and fact can serve here as an exemplary philosophical problem that arises from the reified theory-practice relation, and which can usefully illustrate Lukács' general approach.

From the standpoint of the reified theory-practice relation, the individual is condemned to accept the existing social reality in fact, free only to take up one or another inner attitude toward it. The reified objectivity of social reality takes the form of a pitiless determinism, indifferent to the needs and values of the individual, while these latter now appear to be purely subjective, inward, with no basis in a "reality" of any kind. Value stands opposed to fact, freedom to necessity. This correlation of inner freedom and outward necessity, of subjective value and objective reality is the immediate theoretical consequence of a practice which refuses all solidarity, all conscious *Aufhebung* of the unintended consequences of individual action.

The struggle of the individual with reified reality can play itself out in two complementary forms. "The reified consciousness must also remain hopelessly trapped in the two extremes of crude empiricism and abstract utopianism. In the one case, consciousness becomes a completely passive observer moving in obedience to laws which it can never control. In the other it regards itself as a power which is able of its own—subjective—volition to master the essentially meaningless motion of objects."[12] These two antinomial opposites reappear everywhere in reified theory, in the opposition of a psychology of adaptation to an ethics of duty, in the opposition of a philosophy of history which emphasizes the lawful course of events to one which emphasizes the role of great men and ideas, in the opposition of a legal theory emphasizing environmental causes to one emphasizing personal responsibility, and so on and so forth.

For the individual, the dilemma is a painful and inescapable one. He or she may accept the given reality as is, and attempt to achieve a personally advantageous position within it. Freedom is now restricted to movement within the framework of the necessary laws of existing reality. No attempt can be made to transform or alter this world or what must necessarily come to pass within it. That way lies utopia, and the hopeless struggle against the inevitable. However, the psychic costs of the realistic capitulation before reification have also been calculated from Stendhal to the modern critiques of conformism, and found to be considerable. Society as a market, indeed a racket in selfhood, is ultimately what Lukács' discussion suggests.

The other horn of the dilemma is a utopian struggle to realize higher values in the world, against all the force of resistance of the latter. The individual may refuse the existing reality and oppose to it moral exigencies that would give it a meaning. However, Lukács argues, this attitude splits the subject in half, dividing its substance between empirical needs and desires that can best be satisfied in conformity with existing reality, and the authentic selfhood that derives from conformity with a moral law. This position, which Kant developed into a coherent ethical philosophy, is no more successful than "realism" in resolving the antinomy of value and fact. Indeed, by incorporating the split between these dimensions into the inner life of the subject, it intensifies it to a tragic degree. An unyielding reality, mechanistic in the unfolding of its autonomous course, proves unresponsive to the moral promptings of utopian aspiration which it threatens in the inner citadel of the self. "Freedom," Lukács writes, "is neither able to overcome the material necessity of the system of knowledge and the soullessness of the fatalistic laws of nature, nor is it able to give them any meaning."[13]

Lukács arrives by this route at a theory of alienation quite close to that of the early Marx. He shows how, from the structure of everyday practice in capitalist society, "The activity of man, his own labor becomes something objective and independent of him which is submitted to the alienated autonomy of the natural social laws . . ."[14] This is the core of the Marxian critique of capitalist alienation, the demonstration that in this society, even in his most strenuous self-assertion man remains "object and not subject of events."[15]

REASON AND DOMINATION

So far the discussion of Lukács' meta-theory of philosophy has shown that the antinomies of practical reason can be derived from the immediate lifeworld of practical activity in capitalist society. This is, perhaps, not so surprising since practical reason is inevitably close to actual practice in its concepts and problems. However, more difficult will be the parallel demonstration that the antinomies of pure reason, specifically the antinomy of subject and object, can also be derived from this same practical lifeworld. Lukács' meta-theory of pure reason is based on the demonstration of the intrinsic dependence of the philosophical subject-object concept on the capitalist technical "conquest" of nature. This particular way of dealing with the antinomy of subject and object links Lukács' work once again to the Frankfurt School, which has on various occasions called into question, if not denied, the achievements of technical progress and the universal validity of the natural sciences.[16] At the same time, implied in Lukács' approach is also a remarkable critique *avant la lettre* of another tendency of contemporary social thought, structuralism, with its privileged emphasis on the moment of synchronic system in social life, and its attempt to derive development from pattern. I will return to some of these themes in more detail in later chapters; here I will focus primarily on the epistemological aspects of what I take to be one of Lukács' most suggestive innovations in Marxist philosophy.

How, on Lukács' terms, can one understand the subject-object relation of bourgeois philosophy, which claims to be founding for practice rather than founded by it? In an argument full of hesitations and obscurities, Lukács suggests an answer to this question which I will reformulate as a meta-theoretical critique of this philosophy's subject-object concept. A study of this argument will also show how Lukács derives the antinomies of pure reason from the structure of reified practice. This example will thus continue to clarify the sense in which Lukács' approach to "ideology" is based on a theory of practice rather than on a theory of the reflection of the base in the superstructures.

According to Lukács, the reified paradigm of knowledge is rooted in the practice of technical control which is the central project of the bourgeoisie from its origins as a class. More precisely, it is the universality of this project that distinguishes bourgeois thought from earlier forms of thought. In precapitalist society, human beings carved out of nature only a narrow sphere of activity for themselves, frequently ascribing their power over this small humanized enclave of reality to divine intervention. Technical rationality was thus always bounded at its limits by another type of thinking, a condition which reflected the feebleness of the human species and its limited understanding of the world. Never before the emergence of capitalism did human beings see their destiny as the total and integral domination of nature.

In capitalist society the ancient impotence and restraint gives way for the first time to a Faustian ambition to overcome every residue of uncontrolled nature, to humanize it and submit it to desire, and this new project completely transforms the concept of reason. Corresponding to the gradual fulfillment of this ambition, there is an increasing extension of reification which, projected to the limit, would make it possible to represent every aspect of existence by its quantitative essence and to control it.

Of course this tendency toward total reification exists practically only as a tendency. Theory comes to the aid of the still incompletely realized project of total domination by demonstrating its possibility in principle. This demonstration at first takes the form of the construction of formally rational models of the universe which reveal it to be available for domination. Capitalism was thus accompanied by the development of rationalistic philosophy and mathematical science, as attempts to validate its project. (The similarity of this argument to Heidegger's later discussion of technique is striking.) Bourgeois class consciousness required such a demonstration to found itself as a universal and coherent worldview, capable of organizing the infinite and unending extension of the exploitation of nature.

In the theoretical sphere, the validation of bourgeois society requires the demonstration that the entire universe is rational, reified and controllable in principle. Bourgeois thought believes it has comprehended reality only when the human and qualitative dimensions of the real have been reduced to formal, quantitative relations between things. The subject that is dialectically correlated with this concept of reality is an agent of individual technical practice, hence a contemplative subject in the sense of this term explained in the previous section. From this standpoint, the recognition of the inviolability of the impersonal, autonomous laws of reality is the very condition of the comprehension and domination of reality by the individual. Indeed, for reified thought, "only a reality caught in the net of such concepts can really be mastered by us."[17]

Might there not be another basis for control of objects: not individual manipulation on the basis of laws but conscious collective decision about the laws themselves? This would seem to be a possibility at least with respect to the laws of society. This possibility is foreclosed by reified thought which understands law in every sphere as the precondition, not the outcome of instrumental action. For this thought, in sum, the reified is the rational and therefore also the controllable. The concept of knowledge is accordingly narrowed to include only such a rationality.

To show that the world is rational in this sense is to derive its *form* from the very structure of reified reason; what exists as reality in the outer world also exists as truth in the subject. The point can be made in another way. For reified thought "our" domination of nature, that of the human species in general, is only possible insofar as nature conforms to "our" reason. "The salient characteristic of the whole epoch is the equation, which appears naive and dogmatic, of formal, mathematical, rational knowledge both with knowledge in general and also with 'our' knowledge."[18] What is produced by "us" in thought as rational knowledge must find its validation in reality as universal and objective. Then the deduction of the world from the principles of an autonomous and free reason can be shown to correspond with the nature of things. Thus the ambition of capitalism to dominate and transform the earth leads to the theoretical exigency of the demonstration of the identity of subject and object.

Lukács points out that this rationalistic philosophy involves a curious reversal of perspectives. Practically, the subject stands in a contemplative relation to the world. It is on this condition alone that subjectivity can dominate reality within the horizon of reification. But theoretically, the subject attempts to produce the world actively in thought. It is on this condition alone that reification can appear as the essence of reality. Practical contemplation and theoretical activity compass this basic antinomy of reified thought.

Lukács summarizes the problem as follows.

The contradiction that appears here between subjectivity and objectivity in modern rationalist formal systems, . . . the conflict between their nature as systems "produced" by "us" and their fatalistic necessity as distant from and alien to man, is nothing but the logical and methodological formulation of the state of modern society. For, on the one hand, men are constantly smashing, replacing and leaving behind them "natural," irrational and factical bonds, while, on the other hand, they erect around themselves in the reality they have created and "produced by themselves," a kind of second nature the operation of which opposes itself to them with exactly the same lawful necessity as was the case earlier on with irrational forces of nature (more exactly: the social relations which appear in this form.) "To them, their own social action," says Marx, "takes the form of the action of objects, which rule the producers instead of being ruled by them."[19]

In capitalist society, then, the unmastered alienated form of social life takes shape as the dictate, no longer of irrational religious powers, but of "scientific" laws. In its reified form reason itself becomes an expression of this alienation.

Reified thought believes it has found the essence of reality in the formal rationality of the system of determinants which expose it to reified practice. Like the individual confronted with the machine, the individual confronted with reified social reality discovers the nature of the object in its *structure* and not in the process of its *production*. Thence arises what Lukács describes as the antinomy of logical genesis of the "categories" in terms of which reality is understood, and the actual (collective) production of the social world in the course of history. This is the major methodological contradiction that results from the antinomy of subject and object in reified thought. According to Lukács, the bourgeois social sciences exemplify this methodological contradiction. They all seek to understand their objects through their logical structure, in abstraction from the process of their historical becoming. The illusory priority of "structure" over "process" (and its romantic inversions) arise from a confusion in ontological levels characteristic of reified thought: the individual subject confronts the products of the collective activity in which it unconsciously engages as though they were an objective reality, independent of man. Thus the "categorial" level of cultural forms and the corresponding analytic concepts seems to represent a more basic level of being than historical development, a level of eternal laws and principles that is fundamental for history.

What is really happening belies this approach. In fact, if history appears to be a subordinate domain, this is because the reified individuals do not act on social reality through a conscious collective practice, nor, therefore do they signify "reality" as the object of such a practice. As we have seen in the previous section, reification's technical paradigm of subjectivity and objectivity presupposes an individual subject in principle. The more or less unconscious collective practices in which capitalism really consists appear to reified thought to lie *on the side of the object.* What the individuals cannot consciously and individually accomplish is thus not "accomplished" at all, but rather suffered as a fate by them. Of course, the individual does relate to the products of these unconscious activities, but not as to human products. Rather, all he perceives of the collective practice in which he is willy nilly engaged is its results, and behind these its *form*, imprinted on the objects of his control. This form appears as an impersonal and autonomous law which preexists and predetermines social behavior.

Lukács argues that this form is not a law but a principle of practical synthesis of reality by an unconscious social practice. It is only insofar as the object has been submitted to this form that it enters the circuit of capitalist technical domination. Thus priority would go to history in explaining apparent social laws and not vice versa. Reified thought refuses to see this social practice as a practice, as a creative historical intervention. Instead, it sees the historical process in which its objects are reified and dominated as unveiling the preexisting essence of these objects. For reified thought this essence is precisely that dimension of the object through which control of it can be achieved. Thus in submitting to the formal rationality of reification, the object surrenders its own vital mechanism to human control, revealing its true essence as a potentiality of manipulation which has always slumbered within it. Lukács' point, once again, is that this way of representing the subject-object relation reverses the picture by occluding the unconscious social practice which "prepares" the object for instrumental manipulation, both materially and through the work of social signification in which it takes on its lawful form.

FROM KANT TO HEGEL

Lukács' conception of reified society as a "second nature," the laws of which are created by man but which appear as objective as natural laws, suggests an important philosophical parallel. This is, after all, approximately the form of the Kantian doctrine, which proclaims that experience is governed by laws imposed on it by the subject and which, in turn, necessarily determine the knowledge of the subject. What is the significance of this parallel?

Once again, it is necessary to insist that Lukács understands theory as practice "raised to consciousness," and not as the mere reflection of an objective condition. Thus Lukács does not claim that Kant's theory is an unintended or unconscious metaphor for realities of which Kant was only dimly aware. Rather, Kant's theory is a perfectly rational and conscious way of understanding these realities, *under their horizon*, that is to say, within the framework of reification. More precisely, this means that when Kant founds the identity of "our" knowledge and objectivity in the concept of transcendental synthesis, he is not merely *reflecting*, but rather *explaining* the social realities Lukács also explains, but as those realities emerge from reified practice and appear to reified theory. It was thus Kant, in a sense, who first discovered the reification of reality by social practice discussed in the last section, but only insofar as that process can be constructed speculatively as an imaginary individual practice.

This inability of classical German philosophy to go beyond a speculative theory of reification has complex consequences which Lukács elucidates in the course of his meta-theoretical critique. In short, where practice does not "penetrate" reality, affecting it in its essence, the limits of practice will leave their mark on theory; Kant's idea of the thing in itself is the clearest example of a *theoretical trace* of that domain of objectivity of which reified practice has renounced the transformation. However, in arriving at a concept such as the thing in itself, philosophy does succeed in indicating, at least negatively, the preconditions of unreified practice and the corresponding theory for which the antinomies of reified thought would not arise. This is the kernel of truth to be found in philosophy once the mystical shell of speculative construction has been stripped away by the meta-theoretical revision of its concepts.

From this standpoint, Kant's philosophy is an enormous theoretical advance over earlier rationalism, which simply assumed the rationality of the universe without "noticing" the constitutive functions of the subject. The progression from Kant to Marx can then be understood as the gradual working out of Kant's original intuition in ever more concrete, ever more adequate forms, culminating in the final recognition of the social practice behind the reified appearances. At the center of *History and Class Consciousness* is an extraordinary discussion of the development of classical German philosophy, seen in this light as a step in the intellectual progression leading to Marxism. In the course of this discussion, Lukács shows that Marxism is the veritable *Aufhebung* of this philosophical tradition, arising from its inner dynamic and on the basis of its results. In this section, I will recount the main lines of Lukács' discussion.

Considered as a grand hypothesis concerning the philosophical development from Kant to Hegel and Marx,

Lukács' philosophy of praxis is rich in suggestive ideas but also in problems and difficulties. Lucien Goldmann's study of Kant and the later Lukács' study of the young Hegel have given evidence of the fruitfulness of the general approach sketched below.[20] It is impossible here to evaluate this research into the history of philosophy, interesting as that would be. All that we can do now is to consider how Lukács' hypothetical history functions inside his own conception.

In brief, Lukács argues that classical German philosophy is torn by the conflict of two principles. On the one hand, it understands rationality as the basis for overcoming the contingency, the merely "factical" givenness of objects. This principle can be formulated in terms of the exigency of an identity of subject and object as the condition for founding a universal rationalism, unbounded by supernatural mysteries or unknowable realities. In Kant this unification of subject and object takes the form of the "production" of the object in thought through its derivation from rational form. On the other hand, classical German philosophy assumes a reified, formalistic concept of reason which necessarily secretes contingency and facticity as the residue of the process of abstraction from concrete content in which it is constituted. Such a formalistic concept of reason can never be fully united with its corresponding objects. Thus this philosophy's paradigm of knowledge comes into conflict with its method of validating the claims of knowledge. Lukács regards the principle of identity of subject and object as necessary for any consistent rationalism, including Marxism, but he regards the reified paradigm of knowledge as tied specifically to capitalist society. Marxism succeeds where classical German philosophy failed precisely through meeting the demands of an identical subject-object in terms of a different, dialectical paradigm of rationality.

Lukács' extremely complex argument for this conclusion is presented as a quasi-history, behind which it is possible to identify a static model that in fact organizes his presentation.

This model is the Kantian "system" itself, with its threefold division into critiques of pure and practical reason, and of judgment. The history of classical German philosophy, as Lukács presents it, is in fact the successive thematization of each of these three aspects of Kantian doctrine *qua* solution to the contradiction described above. As one after another attempt fails, the emphasis shifts from one to another of the elements of this structure, culminating finally in the Hegelian dialectic. All along the way, Lukács draws out the implicit conclusions established by this "philosophical experiment," conclusions which will later form the basis of the Marxian solution to the problem of founding a new concept of reason.

Lukács begins his discussion not only with a critique of Kant, but with a critical appreciation of that aspect of Kantian philosophy which already anticipates dialectics. It is most of all the extreme rigor with which Kant confronted the contradictory demands of founding a universal concept of reason and the limits of his own reified conception of theory that leads him to the threshhold of dialectics. As noted above, reified thought encounters an insurmountable contradiction between its ambition to "produce" its objects in thought by deducing them from their forms, and the impossibility of embracing the content of these forms with a formalistic concept of reason. Instead of arbitrarily dismissing this contradiction, as had earlier rationalistic metaphysics, Kant conceptualizes it in the notion of the "thing in itself."

This concept serves many functions in Kant's thought, which Lukács groups into two main types. On the one hand the thing in itself is the material substratum of the rational forms in which the object is comprehended. On the other hand it is the ultimate end of knowledge, as God, the soul, and so on, which "are nothing but mythological expressions to denote the unified subject or, alternately the unified object of the totality of the objects of knowledge, considered as complete (and completely known.)"[21] These different functions of the thing in itself have in common the fact that in each case it represents an absolute limit to (reified) human knowledge, a barrier beyond which thought cannot penetrate. The thing in itself thus blocks the attainment of systematic knowledge of the universe as a whole in both the direction of the deduction of the content of knowledge from its forms, and the unification of the totality of forms in a single universal system.

The problem of the content of the concepts of the understanding arises from the seemingly "impenetrable" character of the empirical facts presented through these formalistic concepts, the impossibility of deriving the material substratum of the concepts from the concepts themselves. Earlier dogmatic metaphysics had not even recognized this problem, although its trace can be discovered there too in unconscious forms. Spinoza, for example, had postulated an infinity of mediations linking substance (form) with its particular modes (content), thereby affirming the possibility in principle, if not in practice, of deducing the entire universe from its logical structure.

Kant rejects this assumption of earlier systematic philosophy and shows that the concepts of the understanding cannot be related abstractly in a metaphysic, but require a material substratum of irreducibly contingent facts to be deployed correctly. With this the very notion of building a philosophical system on the model of mathematics is refuted. Kant argues "that pure reason is unable to make the last leap towards the synthesis and the constitution of an object, and so its principles cannot be deduced 'directly from concepts, but only indirectly by relating these concepts to something wholly contingent, namely *possible* experience.' "[22] Because the concepts of the understanding must always be employed in relation to an entirely contingent "possible experience," which cannot be produced by the subject, irrationality invades the terrain on which the traditional rationalistic systems were constructed. And, Lukács argues, "it is clear that this principle of systematization [of rationalism] is not reconcilable with the recognition of any 'reality,' and 'content' which in principle cannot be deduced from the principle of form and which therefore has simply to be accepted as a facticity."[23]

Kant's critique of metaphysical system building shows the connection between the two aspects of the concept of the thing in itself; for now the deductive presentation of the concepts of the understanding no longer appears, as it did for rationalism, as a legitimate grasp of the totality of knowledge and of the world. The concepts of the understanding have been tied to their content, and this content cannot be deduced from these concepts. The greatness of Kant's philosophy is that it rejects any return to irrationalism or dogmatic metaphysics in the face of this difficulty. Kant's thought is truly "critical" with respect to dogmatic rationalism to the extent that it recognizes the insuperable opposition of form and content for a formalistic concept of reason. But in another way Kant is as uncritical and dogmatic as his predecessors, in assuming that rationality is essentially formalistic. To this extent, Kant too accepts the basic framework of reified thought without question.

It is precisely because Kant both accepts this framework and criticizes the artificial solutions to its problems that he is driven beyond the limits of earlier philosophy. The struggle to maintain a systematic of reason in the fact of this apparently insurmountable difficulty brings him to the limits of reified thought. Now that the unity of reified thought and reality has been fundamentally undermined, the maintenance of a concept of reason capable of "producing" its objects is only possible beyond the horizon of pure theory. The methodological exigency of a unity of subject and object, of a philosophical validation of the power of reason must be fulfilled in another region of human existence.

Thus Kant was led to pose the fundamental demand of reason which was to preoccupy classical German philosophy thereafter, and eventually to lead to Hegel's dialectic: the exigency of a "subject of thought which could be thought of as producing existence without any *hiatus irrationalis* or transcendental thing in itself."[24] In contrast to the dogmatic metaphysics of the seventeenth century, which begins by accepting the reified form of objectivity of its objects and then attempts to unify subject and object by deducing this form of objectivity from reason, the new philosophy will attempt to discover a level of reality at which the duality of subject and object is transcended, and starting out from which the empirical duality of both can be deduced.

But this exigency, in turn, can only be satisfied by transcending the contemplative point of view, by discovering a practical subject which, in generating its own world of objects, transcends the rigid dichotomy of form and content of contemplative thought. This new orientation toward practice is motivated by the desire to find a subject, the object of which is integrally and fully its own product. Lukács explains:

Theory and praxis in fact relate to the same objects, for every object is given as an indissoluble complex of form and content. However, the diversity of the attitudes of the subject orients practice toward what is qualitatively unique, toward the content and the material substratum of the object concerned. As we have tried to show, theoretical contemplation leads to the neglect of this very factor. . . . The very moment when this situation, i.e. when the indissoluble links that bind the contemplative attitude of the subject to the purely formal character of the object of knowledge becomes conscious, it is inevitable either that the attempt to find a solution to the problem of irrationality (the question of content, of the given, etc.) should be abandoned or that it should be sought in practice.[25]

Responding to this dilemma, Kant turned from epistemology to ethics, from the thinking subject to the ethical individual to find the level of subject-object unity. The empirical duality of subject and object seems to be transcended in a deeper unity at the level of being at which this subject operates. No merely given facticity, resistant to subjectivity and independent of it appears to trouble the genesis of reality.

However, in Kant's work this identical subject-object of ethics still confronts the reified reality described in the

Critique of Pure Reason. Its practice encounters a world in which "laws still operate with inexorable necessity."[26] As we have seen in an earlier discussion of the value-fact antinomy, the subject divides into an empirical self, given over to the laws of this world, and a transcendental self, which is free to obey the ethical law. The determinism of outward reality now penetrates into the inner life of the individual. A similar split between the empirical and the transcendental haunts the ethical act, through which the individual strives to realize absolute principles in reality. This act is always an act in the world, where it must take on a phenomenal form determined by the laws of the world just like any other thing. The ethical act is perfectly integrated into the course of this outer determinism, and thus there is a sense in which no value enters reality through it. Rather, in passing from an intention of the will into the positive form of ethical behavior, the higher values seem to be irretrievably lost. It is only the inner form of the act in the mind of the actor which distinguishes it from an unethical act, only the disposition of the will of the actor and not the act itself which is ethical in essence. Lukács sums up this dilemma in a passage already cited in a previous chapter, the significance of which should now be clearer: "For precisely in the pure, classical expression it received in the philosophy of Kant it remains true that the 'ought' presupposes a being to which the category of 'ought' remains *inapplicable* in principle."[27]

Ethical practice does not successfully fulfill its function in the system, but rather reproduces the same contradiction that arises in the sphere of pure reason. All that this ethic can show "is the point where the real interpenetration of form and content *should* begin, where it *would* begin if its formal rationality *could* allow it to do more than predict formal possibilities in terms of formal calculations."[28] But the actual unity of form and content, the actual unity of subject and object in the ethical act remains an unknowable thing in itself, transcending all experience. The ethical solution to the form-content problem which arises in the sphere of knowledge has merely reproduced its terms.

Kant fails to discover what Lukács calls "the principle of practice," the essence of which "consists in annulling *that indifference of form towards content* that we found in the problem of the thing in itself."[29] The principle of practice is not discovered through the mere transcendence of the theoretical orientation toward reality, unless this transcendence is toward a kind of practice which is "tailored to the concrete material substratum of action, in order to impinge upon it to some effect."[30] Nevertheless, Kant's move beyond pure speculative metaphysics and reified contemplation toward practice represents important progress in the direction of a solution he could not work out. It was left to his successors to attempt to find it.

Kant's aesthetics provided the starting point for this attempt, because it includes the concept of the "creation of a concrete totality that springs from a conception of form oriented toward the concrete content of its material substratum."[31] The aesthetic subject is not a formalistic, rationalistic subject, incapable on principle of penetrating the content of the objects toward which it is oriented, but a sort of synthesis of theory and practice. It is an "intuitive understanding," "whose content is not given but 'produced,' and which . . . is spontaneous (i.e. active) and not receptive (i.e. contemplative) both as regards knowledge and perception."[32] Adumbrated in this concept is the principle of a practical synthesis of reality on which Lukács bases his theory. Kant himself did not employ this aesthetic principle for such a general purpose; however, his successors, notably Schiller and Fichte, saw and exploited the possibility of using it to resolve the antinomies of philosophy.

In Schiller the problem of the production of objective reality in thought begins to recede into the background as a new problem of a similar type arises in relation to the subject itself. Both the philosophical and the real social development increasingly fragment the subject into opposed faculties which no longer form a unity. The comprehension of the totality now no longer proceeds through the deduction of reality from the subject, a task the limits of which have been revealed by Kant, but through the deduction of the unity of this subject itself from the subject of aesthetic experience.

The aesthetic subject cannot reconcile the faculties of the mind without being generalized beyond the sphere of artistic production. This Schiller does in his theory of the "instinct of play" and aesthetic education as the means of overcoming the rigid specialization of bourgeois social life. The aesthetic principle then reconciles all the contraries of human nature, both in theory and practice, and shows the way back to a unified and total humanity. But this attempt to generalize the non-formalistic intuitive understanding of aesthetic practice and to make of it a new concept of reason is not successful. Outside the sphere of actual artistic production, it ceases to be a true subject of *practice*. Schiller generalizes it by taking up an aesthetic *attitude* toward the existing world, an attitude which reproduces the world in thought as a finished work of art, in this way apparently overcoming its reified facticity. But here the "action" of the subject is reduced to yet another form of contemplation, if not that of calculating reason, still that of aesthetic appreciation.

Fichte, who also attempted to construct a new concept of reason on the basis of the intuitive understanding, transforms it into a transcendental faculty of the mind from which proceeds the rest of the subject and the entire existing world. Now philosophy turns not toward an attitude, as with Schiller, but toward a renewal of speculative metaphysics. But this position too falls short of practice. The activity which was to unite the faculties of the subject, subject and object, form and content, turns out to be no more than another form of contemplation.

In one important respect, however, Schiller and Fichte do represent an advance over Kant. Although they no more than he discover the true principle of practice, they do finally challenge the dogmatic assumption that formalistic knowledge is the only kind of knowledge. With Hegel this challenge is brought to fruition in the dialectical method. The unique feature of this dialectic is its self-conscious approach to overcoming the irrationality of the contents of knowledge. Hegel was the first to attempt to embrace the material substratum of thought through dialectics, to create a logic of the concrete concept, of the totality.

HEGEL'S DIALECTIC

In Kant's thought, the subject "synthesizes" the real, thereby producing an objective world of experience. This means that the objects of our knowledge are not immediately given but are always worked up by thought before we become aware of them. The synthesis of experience consists in its submission to forms of objectivity, such as space, time and causality, without which it would not take shape as a coherent world of objects at all. Where earlier philosophy had, for the most part, taken for granted the objectivity of objects and the immediacy of experience, Kant showed that objectivity is the product of a synthesis performed by the subject on the raw materials of experience through the imposition of these abstract forms. This was Kant's famous "Copernican Revolution," which placed the subject at the center of the epistemological universe where formerly the object held sway.

As Lukács explains it, German philosophy after Kant attempted to use the concept of an intuitive understanding, drawn from Kantian aesthetics, to radicalize still further this revolution in epistemology. The subject was not only to play the chief role in epistemology, but in ontology as well by constituting not only the forms of knowledge but also the content, the thing in itself which for Kant lay irrevocably beyond knowledge. The Kantian concept of synthesis is thus transformed into a metaphysical principle of world constitution. This is the starting point for the elaboration of the Hegelian dialectic. However, Hegel is able to arrive at his dialectical conception only by taking an important step beyond earlier philosophy. He realizes that the demand of the principle of practice cannot be fulfilled starting out from the individual subject, however much this subject may be sublimated in the transcendental. The dialectical unification of subject and object cannot take place at this individual level, but requires a subject which is also an object, a subject commensurate with the reality which it knows. This is the demand that the "subject be substance." Lukács explains:

Only if the subject (consciousness, thought) were both producer and product of the dialectical process, only if, as a result the subject moved in a self-created world of which it is the conscious form and only if the world imposed itself upon it in full objectivity, only then can the problem of dialectics, and with it the abolition of the antitheses of subject and object, thought and existence, freedom and necessity, be held to be solved.[33]

In sum, not a mythologized transcendental subject modelled on the individual, but some larger, collective principle alone can be adequately imagined as the basis of the resolution of the antinomies.

From this starting point, Hegel was led to make a new type of radical generalization of Kant's Copernican Revolution. Hegel's innovation was to take the Kantian construction of the subject-object relation and to shatter its ontological basis in the traditional concepts of subject and object, which Kant and his followers still presupposed.[34] If thought and things are no longer defined as ontologically independent and primary domains of being, in what form then can they be grasped? Hegel employed what I have called a meta-theoretical procedure to answer this question. He "released" the correlated attributes of subjectivity and objectivity from their reification in the hypostasized subject and object in order to reconstruct their relations in a different context and at a different level. Once released from the grip of their traditional ontological base, these attributes could then be thematized in new combinations in a dialectical ontology.

In this ontology functions of the subject, such as reflection and appearance, are treated as functions of the real itself. Thus the concepts of synthesis and abstract form, which in Kant belonged to the subject as its essential content, are transferred to the real where they organize its dialectical movement. The traditional "things" identified with the subject and object no longer appear in antinomial opposition, but are now derived as secondary spheres from a more basic unity established in this dialectic.[35] On this basis, Lukács argues, Hegel was finally able to discover a way of uniting form and content, the rational categories of philosophy and their material substratum, in real experience.

The ontological region Hegel found to be uniquely suited to the elaboration of this approach was history, a region which embodies a type of objectivity that lends itself to explanation in terms of a non-formalistic concept of reason, and which requires as its subject a collective principle that can truly be found *in* reality. This historical subject must be shown to produce the actual content of the object, not simply speculatively in thought but in reality itself. As Lukács interprets his thought, Hegel was concerned to show that in history the process of "synthesis" of the real, its "logical genesis" at the level of the categories of philosophy, is identical with the practical production of social reality by its subject. Then form and content, philosophy and reality can be united, and the antinomies which emerge in the Kantian system finally overcome. As Lukács explains it:

To go beyond . . . immediacy can only mean the genesis, the "production" of the object. But this assumes that the forms of mediation in and through which it becomes possible to go beyond the immediate existence of objects as they are given, can be shown to be the *structural principles of construction and the real tendencies of the movement of the objects themselves*, that therefore intellectual genesis must be identical in principle with historical genesis.[36]

Thus Hegel chooses to treat history as *reality*, as the ontological region in which the antinomies are resolved, because here the rational genesis of the object by the subject and the self-moving, self-producing activity of practice are one.

Hegel's turning toward history marks a sharp break with rationalism. Rationalism finds in history its least suitable object because history involves newness and qualitative change. Formal reason can only grasp history in terms of a system of foreseeable possibilities, derived from abstract, atemporal laws. But history as a process of concrete becoming escapes this approach. On the other hand, history appears as an ideal object to which to apply dialectics. Here a logic of contents finds an object which is in constant qualitative transformation through the interaction of subject and object, form and content in a totality.

But, Lukács argues, history only points in the direction of a solution to the problems of classical German philosophy; the mere pointing is not yet the solution. For that it would be necessary to discover the subject of history not only speculatively but *in fact*, to find the real "we" whose action is history. The historical subject Hegel proposes is the "Spirit of Peoples." But the Spirit of Peoples does not understand the significance of its own action in the course of history. It is not in principle conscious of the truth of its deeds, but only comprehends them once they are completed, once history has passed on to a new stage and the past is delivered over to philosophical reflection.

This limit Hegel conceptualizes by creating a second collective subject, the World Spirit, which uses the Spirit of Peoples to attain ends which this latter does not understand. (Hence the phrase "cunning of reason.") Between the activity of the historical subject and its own self-consciousness stands a mediation which itself transcends history. Lukács concludes that Hegel's subject of history can never claim its acts as its own. It is not the self-consciousness of its own process, the "subject as substance" which, in achieving self-consciousness, transcends the antinomies of reified thought in the theoretical and practical transformation of reality.

History itself never really achieves self-consciousness. Only the World Spirit can accomplish this as it comes to self-awareness in the head of the individual philosopher at the "end" of history. Reason thus fulfills itself in history only by transcending history. As a result,

History is not able to form the living body of the total system: it becomes a part, an aspect of the totality that culminates in the 'absolute spirit,' in art, religion and philosophy. But history is much too much the natural, and indeed the uniquely possible life-element of the dialectical method for such an enterprise to succeed.[37]

This, according to Lukács, explains why Hegel is obliged to confront the original problems of classical German philosophy outside of history in the realm of absolute spirit. The dialectical method can only establish the identity of subject and object where historical and dialectical genesis coincide. As soon as dialectics deploys itself outside of history the problems of form and content arise once again. In the theory of absolute spirit, in pure logic, the dialectical categories continue to "develop," but now as pure and eternal forms abstracted from any specific content and from the real becoming of the world. The time of this dialectical process is a purely ideal time, no longer corresponding to a real practice of objectification.

Hegel's philosophy ends up in the supra-historical realm of pure thought not because his construction of the problems is essentially reified or false, but rather because he has not discovered the true subject of historical practice. Hegel's work is the culmination of classical German philosophy, drawing the logical conclusions from its various experiments and discoveries. These conclusions can be summed up in

three "demands of reason" which must be fulfilled to overcome the horizon of reified thought. They are: 1) the principle
of practice; 2) dialectical method; 3) history as reality. In spite
of his limitations, Hegel did discover the dialectic and the
special affinity of dialectics for history, and these discoveries
suffice to develop the basic outlines of the principle of practice.

However, not until the actual subject of this practice is also
discovered can reason be founded rationally. This, Lukács
believes, required the historical developments which finally
culminate in the Marxist theory of history. Marxism arises
directly on the soil of the Hegelian system, but informed by a
far deeper insight into the empirical stuff of history. In
Marxism the speculative character of the Hegelian approach
to history is finally overcome in a correct appreciation of the
role of social practice in the real production of history. "In this
sense Marx's critique of Hegel is the direct continuation and
extension of the criticism that Hegel himself levelled at Kant
and Fichte."[38]

THE FAILURE OF CLASSICAL GERMAN PHILOSOPHY

Lukács' meta-theory of classical German philosophy
identifies a common failure to overcome the limits of reified
thought. This philosophy attempts to go beyond reification,
Lukács argues, only theoretically, through resolving its contradictions in thought. But at every stage in the progress of
this philosophy one dimension of reified thought is sur-
mounted from the point of view of another, theoretical contemplation by ethical practice, ethics by aesthetics, formalistic knowledge by a dialectic cut off, in the last analysis, from
history. And precisely because the higher level from which
the lower is deduced as a special case is itself reified, the
original problems of the lower level simply reappear at the
higher one in a new form.

The ontological foundation of classical German philosophy

is reified capitalist society. Lukács tries to show that the antinomies of this philosophy are vast generalizations of the practical "antinomies" of life in this society. Where the individual confronts the opposition of value and fact in day to day practical activity as the undecidable alternative of principled and realistic behavior, the opposition of subject and object as the impossibility of fully controlling and understanding the alienated rationality of the capitalist world, philosophy confronts these same contradictions theoretically and raises them to their concept. But philosophy cannot overcome them where it accepts reification as the only possible framework for thought and action.

The contradictions arising objectively from capitalist reification, between individual and social law, between this law itself and the content which it determines, between, in short, the historical subject and object, cannot be transcended from within reification. Instead, reified thought produces more and more complex speculative mediations uniting the antinomial opposites, mediations which are pure mental constructions. This, Lukács calls "conceptual mythology," which is "nothing more than the expression in thought of some fundamental fact of life that men can neither grasp nor reject."[39]

Even where this philosophy strives hardest to base itself on a practical principle, it remains in the reified attitude of contemplation because it can offer no real challenge to the fixed and finished character of the capitalist world from which its problems arise. The very concepts of subject and object, of thought and being, which it employs immediately express the rigid oppositions of this world. Objectivity can only be united with subjectivity in a speculative, mythological manner because no real practical unity can be conceived in the untranscended framework of capitalist society. As Lukács writes, "But how to prove this identity in thought and being of the ultimate substance?—above all when it has been shown that they are completely heterogeneous in the way in which they present themselves to the intuitive, contemplative attitude?"[40] Even Hegel cannot escape this dilemma once the dialectic develops itself outside history, in the medium of pure thought.

Nevertheless, Lukács concludes, within these limits classical German philosophy does succeed in indicating the direction in which a solution to its problems can be found. "To go beyond this immediacy can only mean the 'production' of the object."[41] In this exigency is contained the condition for a transcendence of conceptual mythology toward a solution to the riddle of philosophy. Lukács believes he has discovered this solution in the meta-theoretical revision of the concept of subject-object identity.

It will be recalled that Marx too developed a meta-theoretical critique and revision of the identity of subject and object in his early work. This critique consisted in redefining the subject and object of philosophy in terms of their concrete social substratum, relating the redefined subject and object according to the forms of philosophy of identity, and then "setting in motion" historically the redefined concepts in order to resolve the contradictions of this philosophy. Now Lukács reaches much the same sort of conclusion, starting out from a similar evaluation of the demand for identity as the decisive philosophical result of traditional speculation.

REVISION OF THE CONCEPT OF SUBJECT-OBJECT IDENTITY

Lukács' concept of subject-object identity is a particular target of attack for critics ranging from the Althusserian to the Frankfurt School. The former explain Lukács' identity philosophy as a consequence of his supposed "romantic" rejection of natural science; the latter reject identity philosophy as rooted in the project of domination of nature of the bourgeoisie, and assert the insuperable separation of subject and object in opposition to any and all theories of identity. In his 1967 "Preface" to *History and Class Con-*

sciousness, Lukács himself dismissed his own earlier theory of identity as an "attempt to out-Hegel Hegel," as a philosophical flourish designed to cap off an overly abstract argument without regard for the realities of social life.[42] In contrast to all these critics, I will argue that the Lukács of 1923 revised the concept of subject-object identity to explain the basis of the possibility of a socialist social practice and to elucidate its philosophical implications.

Puzzling as his concern with this abstract conception may seem, Lukács has good reasons for not simply abandoning it as a historical curiosity. There is more to this demand for identity than the capitalist project of the domination of nature. (The error of the Frankfurt School's critique of identity philosophy is to accept this narrow restriction of the concept at the outset.) More generally, the identity aimed at includes the larger project of establishing the rationality of reason, the universality of its claims and the freedom of the human species from mystical powers, including those of outer and inner nature and of society as well. More concretely formulated, the identity of subject and object means that humankind is or can be at home in the universe, that it can hope to understand the world and itself, and to subsume both nature and society under the exigencies of its own expanding life process. Once again, the form of this subsumption is not necessarily to be identified with capitalist technical domination.

I would like now to turn to Lukács' meta-theory of identity philosophy. My discussion will be limited to those aspects of the theory most relevant to the concerns of this book.[43] The discussion will have to be divided into two complementary parts. Lukács' arguments works from two sides at once, closing the gap between philosophical speculation and history. On the side of philosophy, abstract conditions are posited, while on the side of history a reality is identified satisfying these conditions. The argument as a whole proceeds, as does Marx's similar one, to bring philosophy down to earth by discovering realities which possess the dignity of the Concept. In the remainder of this chapter and the following ones I will reconstruct the argument in its two phases, philosophical and sociological, beginning here with the former.

The philosophical argument contains an ambiguity to which I will return in the concluding chapters of this book. As we have seen, bourgeois identity philosophy establishes only a commonality of form of subject and object. Lukács' meta-theoretical revision of the concept of subject-object identity aims to go beyond this toward a deeper unity based on the production of the object by the subject. But what is the meaning of the concept of "production" with which Lukács works? Two answers are possible, and I will review them both here. On the one hand, Lukács' discussion of the principle of practice leans toward an idealistic concept of production as creation of the object. On these terms, the identity of subject and object implies the radical preeminence of the subject in the theoretical system. Yet even in the passages that argue most consistently for this conclusion, Lukács is careful occasionally to qualify the argument, to note that as an object in the world the subject of practice operates under given historical conditions that determine the limits of its creativity. These qualifications are elaborated into an alternative interpretation of the concept of production in other parts of Lukács' book. In these passages the concept of production is taken to mean *not the creation but the mediation of the object.* Here the subject in no way resembles a collective *cogito*, a transcendental consciousness outside a world it constitutes. As an agent of social practice, the subject is also and necessarily an object. It does not *posit* society but is a moment *of* society, determined as well as determining. Such a subject "penetrates" its objects by altering their form of objectivity in accordance with their real potentialities. The significance of this distinction for social theory is discussed in the remainder of this chapter; its relevance to the philosophy of nature is taken up in the conclusion of this book.

The core of Lukács' argument is common to both these conceptions of the identity of subject and object. In briefest compass, Lukács' argument might be paraphrased as follows. Reified practice is the basis of the antinomy of subject and object and the other antinomies of philosophy. These antinomies arise because the reified subject of practice treats the product of its combined action with other similar subjects as a law-governed, objective reality. It is the unconsciousness of the collective social practice of these subjects which condemns them to actively reproduce a world foreign to them and to their aims. Lukács' point might be reformulated to say that reification arises from the unintended consequences of individual activities feeding back into the latter and giving them the form of a law-governed process. Reified theory also arises on this basis as the conceptualization of the reified form of objectivity that the objects of this practice acquire as such. This form of theory is adequate to understanding the world only in the framework of this practice. But it cannot recognize its own limits because it treats the most general consequences of a historical situation in which decision-making processes are separated as though they were metaphysical realities. In grasping the unintended consequences of these processes as a law, it hypostasizes ontologically what is in reality only a dimension of a specific type of practice.

What Lukács suggests, following Marx, is that the individuals might come together, under certain objective conditions, to make conscious collective decisions about their social activities, thereby interrupting the feedback mechanism which chains them to the perpetual reproduction of their alienated condition. This is Lukács' explanation of the Marxian idea of socialism as "human control of history."

This conception of socialism suggests an intriguing possibility: if philosophy arises from reification and reification itself arises from the unconsciousness of social practice, then could one not imagine a unique kind of "action" which would consist in bringing this social practice to consciousness and thereby changing it? Might it not be possible to de-reify the world, dissolving the social basis of the philosophical antinomies, simply by becoming aware of the unintended consequences of one's actions and, in common with other social actors, bringing these consequences within the domain of conscious social choice and control? Here theory, as consciousness of social reality, would become a practical act with real social consequences and would no longer be comprehensible on reified terms as value-free contemplation of reality from a mythic epistemological "outside." As Horkheimer puts a similar point, "in genuinely critical thought explanation signifies not only a logical process but a concrete historical one as well. In the course of it both the social structure as a whole and the relation of the theoretician to society are altered, that is both the subject and the role of thought are changed."[44]

Practice as Production. The central question left unanswered by this brief description of the theory concerns the nature of the "action" in which thought would consist. As noted above, Lukács offers two different answers to this question. The first of these proceeds from the analysis of the failure of classical German philosophy to elaborate an adequate principle of practice. The problem, as Lukács poses it, consists in finding a type of practice which does not presuppose reification as its horizon but which transcends this horizon and changes reality itself. This problem first emerged as such (although in a different formulation) with classical German philosophy. Hegel, for example, argued that the subject of such a practice would also have to be substance, that is to say, that its subjective activity would also have to be its own self-production as a real object in the world. Classical German philosophy reached this conclusion by the negative demonstration that any practice operating on a world of alien objects must accept the law of those objects as its horizon, as an autonomous order of reality which it cannot alter. The only practice capable of "penetrating" its objects thus proves to be one in which the subject is the object of its own practice, in which therefore its subjectivity is already an objective reality. Then changes in its subjective orientation would be immediately reflected in real changes, fulfilling the exigency of the principle of practice.

Classical German philosophy has already explored the limitations of many types of practice in its search for this identical subject-object. Technical practice and, Lukács would add, natural scientific knowledge proceed from a reified subjectivity for which the problem of the thing in itself inevitably arises. Ethics, aesthetics and the wisdom of the philosopher at the end of history all suffer from an inner resignation, even reconciliation with reified reality, toward which they take an attitude rather than effecting a change. Historical action remains as the only domain in which to find a practice that can affect by its action not only its own orientation toward reality or partial segments and superficial traits of reality, but the very essence of the phenomena. Since, unlike nature, history is the product of human action, it is conceivable that here self-change would be an objective change in (historical) reality, as the principle of practice requires.

Equally important, the type of practice in question must affect "reality" as a whole and not just marginal aspects of it. Artistic practice, to give a counter-illustration, cannot satisfy the exigency of an identity of subject and object because there always exists a social world on its margins which is founding for it and which it cannot touch. What is needed is a practice that is "total" in the sense that it is unbounded by dimensions of reality it cannot alter and which, therefore, persist as a reified residuum, a thing in itself. In Lukács' view, the dialectical identity of subject and object can only be established through history because history is not a mere sector among others, but can be grasped as the primary and basic reality. Only where history is *the* reality can the demonstration of the identity of subject and object in history have the general significance required to resolve the antinomies of reason. This means, however, that all other subject-object relations must be derived from that of the historical subject and object, that they must all be interpreted through their historical dimension. Lukács takes Hegel himself as the demonstration *in contrario* of this position, for the residue of unhistorical reality remaining in Hegel's system becomes the point at which the reified subject-object relation is reintroduced.

Lukács argues that the antinomies of value and fact, knowledge and reality would finally be overcome for the identical subject-object of history. The knowledge of a self-conscious collective subject of history would also be a practice affecting the substratum of reality. For it theory and practice would be united: the immediate repercussions on its behavior of its own self-understanding would transcend the gap between mind and matter, creating a new type of practice unlike the technical one of reification. The "contemplative" limits of the traditional philosophical subject would be transcended, as would the rigid opposition of subject and object, value and fact. In *knowing*, this subject would be *producing* the object of its knowledge or, more precisely, changing the form of its objectivity by overcoming its own immediacy. This would be a Kantian "intuitive understanding" based not on a mythic principle, a transcendental ego or a hypothetical god, but on actual finite subjects in the world.

Practice as Mediation. Interpreted along these lines, the Lukácsian concept of subject-object identity leaves more questions open than it answers. The argument is so formal and abstract that it is difficult to relate it to any really imaginable historical practice. It would even be possible, if one stopped short at this point in interpreting Lukács' text, to conclude that for him the proletariat freely creates a world after its own designs. Yet Lukács did not intend us to stop short here, and he explicitly denies this interpretation of his thought. He writes,

> It is true that the proletariat is the conscious subject of total social reality. But the conscious subject is not defined here as in Kant, where "subject" is defined as that which can never be an object. The "subject" here is not a detached spectator of the process. The proletariat is more than just the active and passive part of this process: the rise and evolution of its knowledge and its actual rise and evolution in the course of history are just the two different sides of the same real process.[45]

Can one specify more precisely the exact sense in which the proletariat functions in the medium of objectivity even in its role as subject? This is the decisive question of whether Lukács' theory leads to an essentially romantic assertion of the proletariat as free creative power, breaking the chains of capitalist convention in a unique act of untrammeled self-expression. In fact it is essential to Lukács' conception that the proletariat *not* be conceived as such a generalized romantic subjectivity, which would still move within the framework of a reified worldview as the incarnated freedom antinomially opposed to the "pitiless necessity of the laws" of the system. Rather, if the proletariat as subject is also an object, this is because its freedom is a specific mediation, a "determinate negation" of the given, hence actualization of real potentialities in the Hegelian sense of the terms, rather than a utopian will.

On this basis, Lukács redefines the proletariat as a knowing subject to explain its "true" consciousness as a function of its social insertion rather than in terms of the usual concept of scientificity. For this class knowing cannot be understood as liberation from existence but rather as a concrete mediation within existence. Thus the transcendence of the premises of capitalist culture in proletarian class consciousness implies no epistemological withdrawal to a free *cogito*, to a pregiven,

undetermined ground of truth. The precondition of this transcendence is capitalist society itself, its culture, its forms of
thought, which can only be transcended through a reflection
in which they are criticized, mediated and comprehended
historically. Capitalist culture is the foundation of true knowledge of society precisely insofar as it is relativized dialectically.

Proletarian thought does not require a *tabula rasa*, a new start to
the task of comprehending reality and one without any preconcep-
tions . . . [but] conceives of bourgeois society together with its
intellectual and artistic productions as the *point of departure* for its
own method. . . . It implies that the "falseness" and the "one-
sidedness" of the bourgeois view of history must be seen as a
necessary factor in the systematic acquisition of knowledge about
society.[46]

Thus for Lukács truth is a mediation, and the transcendence
of the capitalist standpoint rests on a specific socially determined and rule-governed operation performed on it to which
it is intrinsically and uniquely susceptible.

Lukács meta-theoretical revision of the subject-object concept makes possible a true dialectical unity of category and
history, and avoids the dissolution of the former into the
latter. This unity is achieved by emphasizing the objective
side of the subjectivity which constitutes the social world, and
through which it is bound by a determinate order in which it
exercises its socially specific freedom. Lukács argues that
history must be explained through human action, but human
action itself is as much product as producer of history. "Man
has become the measure of all (societal) things," he writes,
and the understanding of history consists in the "derivation of
the indissoluble fetishistic forms from the primary forms of
human relations."[47] In this sense, "man is the measure"
specifically in opposition to all attempts to "measure" history
from an "above" or an "outside" of history itself, such as a god,
nature or transhistorical laws conceived as founding for his-

torical objectivity. Yet this is no humanism in the sense of a doctrine which would derive history from a prior concept of man, or from a quasi-theological creative power attributed to the human species.

For if man is made the measure of all things, and if with the aid of that assumption all transcendence is to be eliminated without applying the same "standard" to himself or—more exactly—without making man himself dialectical, then man himself is made into an absolute and he simply puts himself in the place of those transcendental forces he was supposed to explain, dissolve and systematically replace.[48]

To argue for the possibility of a mediated subject-object identity is to argue that history would become increasingly "rational" once grasped by a self-conscious humanity. It would cease to appear as a law-governed domain of alienated objectivity and become instead the objective preconditions of a process of subsumption and transcendence of a wholly different order. Like a tree adapting to its environment in the very assertion of its unique identity, so humanity would rework the stuff of circumstance by bringing it under the law of its own self-development. This is the very opposite of a reified technical practice, not in the sense of being absolutely free from all objective conditions and limits—that is the utopia of technique—but in the sense of representing a higher, unreified relation to these objective conditions and limits. The dialectic is the paradigm of rationality corresponding to such a practice because it posits no eternal laws, but explains the transcendence of objective conditions through their incorporation into the project of a life process.

With this, the philosophical "deduction" of the identical subject-object of history is completed, and the sociological work of fleshing out that concept must begin. This second phase of the argument is discussed in detail in the next two chapters. For it Lukács relies primarily on traditional Marxist contributions to understanding how the experience and life conditions of the working class prepare it to engage in a new type of conscious collective social practice that might ultimately replace the market as the organizing principle of an industrial society. Lukács tries to show that such practice is de-reifying by its very nature, overcoming the gap between private decision-making processes and therefore capable of transcending the horizon of reification.

What is lacking in Marx's own discussion is a theory of the possibility of the proletariat becoming conscious of these objective potentialities of its class situation, the "revolutionizing of the elements themselves" Marx identifies as the precondition of social revolution. Lukács focusses precisely on this dimension of the problem. Thus the sociological counterpart of his concept of subject-object identity is presented as an analysis of proletarian class consciousness. This argument reaches the same conclusion as the preceding one, but from the "below" of history instead of from the "above" of abstract conceptualization.

5

Culture and Consciousness

MARXISM AND SUBJECTIVITY

Like the early Marx, Lukács formulates a concept of revolution as a methodological necessity, a demand of reason within philosophy. Their philosophies of praxis differ, however, in a number of important respects. After several false starts, Marx focusses on the question of the rationality of the needs that drive workers to revolt, content to show the rationality of revolution by procuration so to speak, as a logical consequence of this initial revision of the relation of need to reason. At first Marx simply assumed capitalism's incapacity to satisfy workers' needs and workers' capacity to establish a new disalienated society. The rest of Marx's life was occupied with the confirmation of these premises by further research into economics and history.

Lukács' discussion scarcely touches on the question of need, although he presupposes the results of Marx's later research. As a good reader of *Capital*, Lukács takes it for granted that adequate motivations for proletarian revolution exist under capitalism. Lukács is not, however, particularly interested in the question of the rationality of these motivations, of need *per se*. Rather, Lukács is primarily concerned with the cultural significance of the paradigms of rationality corresponding to the different social practices of capitalist and socialist society. As a result the meta-theoretical revision of philosophical concepts is oriented not toward the relation of need to reason, but toward the relation of practice to theory. The critique of contemplative, reified thought and of the antinomies of philosophy flows from this initial choice.

As we have seen, on the horizon of Marx's philosophical work there arose a number of important empirical problems that could not be decided in philosophy. Lukács too encounters the same difficulty; philosophy of praxis simply refuses to remain within the boundaries of the meta-theoretical revision of philosophical concepts. In Lukács' case the new problems that arise on the margins of philosophy concern the class consciousness of the proletariat. These are cultural questions in the most general sense of the term.

Lukács needs the concept of class consciousness to measure the epistemological credentials of different class standpoints. He concludes that for all classes but the proletariat, class consciousness is "false," remains "an *unconsciousness* determined in conformity with the class, with its own economic, historical and social situation."[1] In these cases, class consciousness not only defines what the class at its most lucid could be expected to know (its "possible consciousness"), but also the boundary of its understanding, beyond which it cannot penetrate.

This boundary is, ultimately, the boundary of culture, more specifically of the culture of capitalism. The most basic question to which Lukács' theory of class consciousness is addressed concerns whether any standpoint exists *inside* the given culture from which that culture appears not as a transhistorical limit on consciousness but as a merely historical stage in the development of consciousness. Is there any vantage point within capitalist society from which that society appears as a passing historical stage, not merely in its economic and political dimensions but in its most basic cultural presuppositions? Lukács answers, that the proletariat can in principle achieve such a perception, overleaping its own age from within, in defiance of Hegel's pessimistic restriction of wisdom to knowledge of the past.[2]

To demonstrate this, Lukács needs to show two things: that philosophy could be realized by the proletariat if that class became conscious of itself, and also that self-consciousness is compatible with the life conditions of the class. These are not claims that can be made *a priori;* in the Marxist tradition, the theory of class consciousness is supposed to supply an empirically informed demonstration.

Unfortunately, the classics of Marxism offer only a rudimentary program for understanding consciousness and ideology. Yet the focal importance of subjectivity for Marxism is evident from the role it is assigned in the revolutionary process. Traditional Marxism lacks a sufficiently developed account of the passage from objective economic existence to social subjectivity, and through the latter to revolutionary changes in the economy. This has been especially troubling since the Russian Revolution revealed the possibility of wide gaps between the level of development of the economy and of class consciousness. To explain this, or indeed any revolution, more "mediations" are required linking objectivity to subjectivity than Marx and Engels explicitly provide.

As the title of Lukács' most important work indicates, this was the major problem in Marxism he hoped to solve. The historical context of Lukács' project is important for understanding it. The Russian and European revolutions of the period in which he wrote *History and Class Consciousness* brought the question of the role of subjectivity to the center of the theoretical stage. These revolutions were, in fact, incomprehensible from the standpoint of the then-current Marxist orthodoxy, with its scientism and determinism. For the latter consciousness was a thoroughly "secondary factor" in the objective unfolding of the iron laws of history. The political consequences of this representation were disastrous.[3]

Yet this orthodoxy could appeal to Marx as its founder. The official Marxist program for the explanation of the relation between social objectivity and social subjectivity derived directly from Marx's own formulations in such basic texts as the "Preface" to the *Critique of Political Economy*. The terms of this program are familiar: the "mode of production" is supposed to be "reflected" in ideology and the superstructures, these latter influencing the economy in turn through a "reciprocal action" of thought on things. This program, which Marx and Engels constantly propose in general terms but never seriously elaborate in detail, is an attempt to accommodate an earlier meta-theoretical theory of ideology to the traditional causal paradigms of explanation and materialist ontology of their later work. Unfortunately, this accommodation introduces a whole series of antinomies into Marxism which can only be "resolved" through methodological dogmatism or speculative constructions.

Lukács' great innovation is to detect in the background of this official Marxist program, the meta-theoretical reconstruction of the functions of subjectivity in the domain of the material life process. On this basis Lukács rejects the causal paradigm of subject-object relations, with its external interactions between separate spheres of reality—being and thinking—and instead shows the dialectical interdependency of the antinomial opposites. In Lukács' meta-theory, much as in Marx's *Manuscripts*, the abstract concepts of subject and object of traditional philosophy are redefined in order to attach consciousness to its substratum in the actual life process of society. This provides the basis for a cultural interpretation of the old Marxist problematic of the relations of social being and social thought, base and superstructure. In terms of Lukács' new cultural approach, society no longer divides into separate spheres of material objectivity and spiritual subjectivity, body and mind metaphorically reconstituted as dimensions of the social world. Historical subjectivity and objectivity are no longer seen as externally related independent domains, but rather as functional elements in systems of social practice.

In Marx's meta-theory, the philosophical construction of the ideal, as subject or consciousness, was revised and attached to its concrete substratum in the living individual. This relativization of thought with respect to social being still shapes the earliest formulations of the distinction between base and superstructure, for example, in *The German Ideology*. There passages such as the following abound: "Consciousness can never be anything else than conscious existence, and the existence of men is their actual life-process."[4] While open to a mechanistic interpretation, such passages take on their full significance only in the context of the meta-theoretical revision of the antinomial opposites, consciousness and life, which Marx first developed in the *Manuscripts*.

There Marx's critique of the idealistic construction of the concept of consciousness is far more radical than his later programmatic position on the question of the superstructure. In the *Manuscripts* the meta-theoretical reconstruction of philosophical concepts involves an immanent critique of both the abstract ideal and its antinomial correlate, the equally abstract "real" to which it stands opposed. Thus Marx not only revises the concept of reason but also its opposed correlate, the concept of need. In fact, the revision of the one is inherently the revision of the other, the demonstration that the sphere of need has the function of rationality. This double movement of the meta-theory is purged from the later theory of ideology and the superstructures, which treats the opposed correlates as independent real objects and then relates them according to a hierarchy of causal efficacy.

This hierarchy is the exact inversion of the dominant idealistic ontologies of the day, according to which matter finds its source in mind. Marxism's program for explaining the role of the subject in history is based on a general ontology which affirms the primacy of matter *per se*. The general ontological primacy of matter over thought is analogically identified with the specific preeminence of the "material" life process of society over its "ideal" expressions. That this is an analogy is clear: no evident boundary between social "matter" and "spirit" can be drawn since ideology is, admittedly, "a material force when it seizes the masses," and since production incorporates the knowledge of the producers. However, the analogy draws its force less from the concrete content of Marxist historiography and social theory than from its polemic opposition to their idealistic counterparts, which first attempt to distinguish social "matter" and "spirit" and to order them in a hierarchy of significance. Marxism has recourse to a general ontology, a materialist ontology, in opposition to such idealism, and emphasizes economic motivations (metaphoric "matter") as against ideal ones. Engels says as much in a famous letter to Bloch:

Marx and I are ourselves partly to blame for the fact that the younger people sometimes lay more stress on the economic side than is due to it. We had to emphasize the main principle *vis-a-vis* our adversaries, who denied it, and we had not always the time, the place or the opportunity to give their due to the other elements involved in the interaction. But when it came to presenting a section of history, that is, to making a practical application, it was a different matter and there no error was permissible.[5]

Engels here admits that Marxism's theoretical practice in the explanation of the superstructure differs from its materialist program. This difference is due to a greater continuity with the original meta-theoretical approach in the case of Marxist historiography.

As it is generally formulated, the materialistic program leads to insoluble dilemmas. Once social matter and spirit are conceived as independent domains, how can they be brought into communication? The mind-body problem returns to haunt Marxism, which must seek in the theory of ideology a social pineal gland to join what it has conceptually sundered. Like all other solutions of the mind-body problem, that of Marxism is a failure. Once social thought is explained as a "reflection" of social being, it is impossible to understand the "reciprocal action" of the former on the latter, of the image on its original. Yet without this "reciprocal action," Marxism collapses into an economic determinism of which Engels does not hesitate to say that it is "a meaningless, abstract, senseless phrase."[6]

These dilemmas show that a given problematic is not transcended by reversing the value signs attached to its terms. Rather, the same antinomies appear within the inverted problematic which arose from its original formulation, but in inverted form. Thus where idealistic historiography ends up in the hazy indetermination of a theory of "values" and "free will," the materialistic correlate results in a determinism so rigid as to be incompatible with any concept of historical agency at all. The trace of the original idealistic problematic bends Marxism toward such conclusions, in spite of the actual tendencies of the application of the theory.

Lukács formulates a similar conclusion in relation to a parallel problem in epistemology as follows:

But how to prove this identity in thought and existence of the ultimate substance?—above all when it has been shown that they are heterogeneous in principle in the way in which they present themselves to the intuitive, contemplative mind? It becomes necessary to invoke metaphysics and with the aid of its overt or concealed mythical mediations thought and existence can once again be reunited. . . . The situation is not improved in the slightest when the mythology is turned on its head and thought is deduced from empirical material reality. . . . As long as thought and existence persist in their old, rigid opposition, as long as their own structure and the structure of their interconnections remain unchanged, then . . . [materialism] is incapable of explaining the *specific* problems that arise here by reference to *this principle*. It is forced to leave them unsolved, to solve them with the "old" methods and to reinstate the mythology as a key to the whole unanalysed complex.[7]

In sum, adequately relating infrastructure to superstructure requires not only more mediations between the terms than materialism provides, but a definition of the terms themselves that will admit of a mediation in principle.

This is precisely what is lacking in the materialist program because it is a prisoner of the traditional ontological distinction of subject and object. As such it conceives the domain of the objective as self-subsistent and unreflected, as existence in the mode of thinghood. The domain of the subjective appears now as the correlated opposite of existence, as insubstantial thinking, pure reflection, which enters the world of existence only accidentally, through a problematic incarnation. The mark of this "rigid opposition" of thought and things appears clearly in the familiar methodological dilemmas of the materialist program.

Lukács could not rest content with this theoretically stillborn conception. His entire philosophical effort requires a type of analysis of the consciousness of classes and of the function of consciousness in history to which this program is incapable of contributing. The implicit starting point of Lukács' own social theory is a recognition of this failure and a recovery of Marx's original meta-theoretical insight as a basis for a new approach to understanding social consciousness. In this chapter and the next, I will explore his contribution to a Marxist theory of subjectivity.

THE CONCEPT OF "SPECIFIC RATIONALITY"

Lukács' theory of consciousness is best understood as an investigation into what I will call the "specific rationality" of historical practice. Historical development is not utterly unpredictable and irrational, but through a "cunning of reason" achieves results which correspond very generally to a *telos* that can be constructed after the event by the historian.[8] In a famous letter, Engels suggests that this specific rationality of history reflects the statistical regularities generated by the unintended consequences of the myriad interactions of the individual wills in conflict.[9] While it is no doubt true that certain historical "laws" arise from the totalization of the unintended consequences of individual acts, this construction of the rationality of history seems greatly to underestimate the role of consciousness, which does frequently bear a significant, if ideologically distorted relation to the actual outcomes.

The dilemma is thus as follows: history exhibits overwhelming evidence of rationality, but the individuals and classes which act in history do not often intend the result achieved. Human beings make their own history, but with illusions, and the outcome of their actions rarely corresponds with their expectations. And yet, Marxists would add, the outcome does tend to correspond with their interests, to the extent that they can defend these, and to a progressive development in which ever higher levels of human potentiality are actualized over the long run.

The fact that classes frequently pursue their interests more consistently and rationally than they are able to conceive them is puzzling viewed from the traditional voluntaristic standpoint according to which rationality inheres in the first instance in thought. The rationality of historical behavior is apparently not entirely a function of the rationality of its conscious motives. The locus of rationality can no longer be identified with the thoughts of individuals, as it has been by modern philosophy since Descartes. Rationality inheres not so much in these thoughts as in acts. And these acts belong to a *system* of behavior, relating practices at different social levels and in different social spheres, a system which includes the beliefs of the individuals as a merely *subordinate* element. Reason can no longer be identified with the sphere of belief, for even where beliefs are false they may motivate an action which corresponds to a far deeper understanding of society than that of thought itself.

Lucien Sebag draws the following conclusion from these implications of the Marxist approach:

A critical theory of knowledge is possible; revealing a gap between what is said and what is done, it brings to light the non-fulfillment of that which is implied by a given ideology. This presupposes that the domain of Doing [*le Faire*] can be autonomized, becomes its own point of reference. Ideologies then simply are added to it to veil it, deform it, or on the contrary, unveil it; but this deformation, when it exists, can always be objectively demonstrated.[10]

In this view action does not simply execute the goal contained in thought; it has a *telos* of its own which may contradict and transcend that of thought. In the case of false consciousness, action aims at a result which lies hidden to the actor himself. Here the conscious goal of the actor is an illusion which serves to motivate a historically necessary deed without comprehending it. In such cases, the historical necessity which accounts for the emergence of the false consciousness must also account for its ability to motivate practices that exhibit a greater specific rationality than their own apparent motives. The same reasons that make it a false consciousness also make it the source of actions which achieve the objective "goal," the immanent tendency of the historical process. The determinate error of false consciousness and its functionality in the class strategies of the class are but two sides of the same coin. It is in this sense that the error of false consciousness is not merely arbitrary, but can be said to be "adjusted" to its historical function.

Deterministic theories modelled on the natural sciences usually account for this remarkable coincidence of cognitive deficiency and practical functionality by arguing that the individual subject is a mere link in a causal sequence that leads beyond him or her while leaving its trace in a false consciousness of the real process. Thus the "real" subject of the action of the individuals is not their own consciousness, but a larger historical process which is impersonal and non-teleological in character. Or rather, it would be more accurate to drop the language of subjectivity altogether and to describe history as a "process without a subject or a goal," as does Althusser.[11] Consciousness now appears as a residual product of historical analysis, a precipitate which, if not simply thrown out, might be recaptured for scientific study by a suitable psychological approach. In any case, the illusory teleology of consciousness is only that of a mystified and mystifying observer.

The defect in this mode of explanation is to consider the determinants of class practice, such as class situation and interest, as causal factors on the same plane with and able to affect actual individuals and their behavior. This is a paralogism: the class situation and interests of the individuals are not factors external to them, but are the social stuff of individual life. The "interest" of the bourgeois in the maintenance of the conditions of his existence is not a "factor" interacting with his individuality, but is a dimension of that individuality itself. It is only by a methodological sleight of hand that this dimension is reconceptualized as something in the environment which determines the individual causally.

On the other hand, it also needs to be emphasized that a social conception of individuality excludes the correlated opposite of pseudo-scientific determinism, namely a philosophy of freedom. To say that interest and situation are constitutive of individuality is at the very least to break with quasi-theological concepts of individuality and to situate the subject, at the outset, in its specific (social) finitude. The individual is neither a thought nor a thing, and can be explained neither in the language of causality nor that of freedom. This is because the individual exists as such through his or her social relations. We need in short a radically different model for explaining historical causality than that of the natural sciences, and a radically different model for understanding historical freedom than that of traditional philosophy.[12]

The alternative suggested by Lukács consists in regarding the subject as essentially a being of social practice and not of thought. In this respect, Lukács anticipates a number of recent theories of practice, which it may be interesting to mention briefly in concluding this section. Pierre Bourdieu calls the view according to which practice is merely the execution of a project formulated in conscious thought or unconscious mental structures "objectivist voluntarism."[13] Lukács refuses such an identification of meaning and mind. Meaning and its formal structures are now detached from this, their usual locus, and settled in a dialectic of practice and theory. In a discussion of Marxism much influenced by Lukács, Lucien Sebag traces this position back to Marx: "Marx breaks with every limitation of signifying activity to the understanding alone, the true subject no longer being the subject of knowledge alone . . . but the real human being inserted into the concrete life of the society of which he is a member."[14]

Lucien Goldmann has insisted on the similarity of this approach to that of Heidegger, whose *Being and Time* resembles Lukacs' early Marxist work in attempting to explain the social world on the basis of an ontologically primordial practice. For Heidegger, practice is not simply the execution of theory, but it is an original mode of "concern" with "its own kind of sight."[15] It is interesting to note that a similar point is made by Alfred Schutz, also from a phenomenological perspective, who writes, "that theory is completely wrong which maintains that one's behavior is distinct from one's conscious experience of that behavior and that meaning belongs only to the latter."[16]

These phenomenological formulations contribute to clarifying Lukács' position. For him as for the phenomenologists, practice must be understood as the bearer of meanings which theory can raise to consciousness by thematizing the operative significance of its activity. The field of intentionality is broader than the field of thought and the subject's acts may therefore possess a meaning hidden to its consciousness. The consciousness of the subject must now be related to practice not as its source, but as a functional element within it, necessary for its performance but not for that matter the producer or truth of that performance. Practice must be considered as in itself teleological, meaning-bearing, and not simply as the execution of a teleology and a meaning-content first disclosed to the subject in thought.

At the same time, for Lukács if not for the phenomenologists, practice contains moments of objectivity insofar as it is real activity in the world, and not simply an activity of and in the subject, a thought activity. Goldmann summarizes this conception by saying that "the subject belongs to the world and introduces meaning into it practically, but this world belongs to the subject and constitutes it."[17] Methodologically, this constituting of the subject by the world implies the rejection of the traditional individualistic assumption according to which the subject of practice is the single biological organism, the person. Instead, practice is always a function of a wider context of social relations in which it is inserted. In capitalist society the significant context of practice is the class, starting out from which an analysis can be made of individual practices, and not vice versa. It is on this basis that Lukács proposes his theory of class consciousness.

CLASS CONSCIOUSNESS AS IDEAL-TYPE

Lukács' theory of class consciousness involves a two-sided interpretation of the specific rationality of class behavior. On the one hand, this rationality itself can be represented theoretically in a model which would correspond with the rational content of class action, quite apart from the actual thoughts or motives of the individuals. This model Merleau-Ponty defines in his discussion of Lukács as "the inner principle of activity, the global project which supports and animates the productions and actions of a class, which designates for it an image of the world and of its tasks in this world and which, external conditions taken into account, assigns it a history."[18]

On the other hand, the functional relations between thought and action need to be explained in particular cases to show how the conscious motives of the individuals interact with their behavior in a system which, as a whole, exhibits the level and type of specific rationality derived by the first approach. Since Lukács is dealing with the social behavior of classes, this functional approach must include a discussion of the social mechanisms working to adjust thought to action and action to its own rational ends, for example, the specific methods of reality testing, class organization and inculcation of beliefs appropriate to the class in question and the type of activity in which it is engaged. This two-fold method of analysis underlies Lukács' theory of class consciousness, although some of the most important articulations of it are implicit rather than explicit in the text.

Lukács' first approach is based on a synthesis of ideas from Marx and Weber. Weber introduced the concept of the "ideal-type" as a methodological device enabling the sociologist to define a pure abstract model of a more complex and ambiguous reality. Never identical with the reality it described, the ideal-type could be useful in isolating the probable causes and motives of behavior which more or less conformed to it.

For purposes of causal *imputation* of empirical events, we need the rational, empirical-technical and logical constructions, which help us to answer the question as to what a behavior pattern or thought pattern . . . would be like if it possessed completely rational, empirical and logical "correctness" and "consistency."[19]

Lukács constructs the concept of class consciousness as an ideal-type in this sense from an examination of the relations of the form of objectivity of the society and the class situation and interests of the class. The specific rationality of class practice may be defined on this basis because these are the very factors which determine it in reality, at least in the case of the "historically decisive acts" of the class.[20] On the other hand, the actual beliefs of the individuals are not necessarily similar to the model of class consciousness, so derived. In fact, Lukács writes that class consciousness is not "the sum nor the average of what is thought or felt by the single individuals who make up the class."[21] Thus class consciousness comes to refer not the actual beliefs of the individuals but to the implicit and more or less rational core of their practice; it signifies the understanding of reality manifested in the total behavior of the class, independently of the degree to which this understanding also informs its thought.

On these terms, class consciousness must be distinguished from what Lukács calls "real consciousness," the actual thoughts and beliefs of the members of the class. Class consciousness may not be the truth of the historical process as a whole, but it is the adequate rationale of the practice of a group with a definite perspective on society. Real consciousness, on the contrary, may even fall below this level of rationality, exhibiting not only the historically necessary "error" of the class revealed in the model of its class consciousness, but a still less rational response to social reality that is merely functional in the system of behavior of the class.

Lukács writes as follows:

By relating consciousness to the whole of society it becomes possible to infer the thoughts and feelings which men *would* have in a particular life situation if they were *able perfectly* to assess both it and the interests arising from it in their impact on immediate action and on the whole structure of society. That is to say, it would be possible to infer the thoughts and feelings appropriate to their objective situation. . . . Now class consciousness consists in fact in the appropriate and rational reactions "imputed" [zugerechnet] to a particular typical position available in the process of production.[22]

To the extent that the concept of class consciousness is properly constructed in each case, "plausibly motivated" in Weber's words, it would describe the teleology of class behavior.[23] The concept of class consciousness is thus tailored to the basic tendencies of class action from the outset, while the real consciousness of the individuals frequently mystifies them as well as the observer, or trails behind the activity of the class, rationalizing it *post festum*. With respect to this real consciousness, class consciousness would only be the horizon of rationality, the "objectively possible" beliefs that the individuals could hold at their most lucid and rational moments.[24]

Lukács seems to have found Weber's method of ideal-typical description useful in explaining class consciousness because with it he can express the priority of social being over social thought without falling into either mechanism or metaphysics. Lukács could continue to define class consciousness in a perfectly Marxian way, by reference to its social determinants, without having to deny the relative autonomy of thought and the complexity of the processes in which it is formed. Class consciousness would not be a mere statistical sum, nor would it be some sort of collective unconscious, which would mysteriously disclose itself to the individuals in a peculiar self-relation, apart from social interaction. Class consciousness is a model of a reality, not just a statistical average. It does not, however, represent a mysterious psychological process in the individuals but, much more simply, the *telos* of their action.

Lukács' theory of class consciousness distinguishes the models constructed according to the determinants described above from the real thoughts and beliefs of the individuals of which it is the consciousness. As noted above, class consciousness is based on the determinants of class action, not those of class belief. This distinction makes it possible to avoid vulgar determinism by granting social thought a relative independence. But it is essentially negative to say that thought has a relative autonomy, that class consciousness is merely the horizon of the "objectively possible" rationality of real consciousness. This formulation eliminates the threat of mechanistic determinism, but is not yet a theory in the proper sense of the term. Many critics of Lukács note this limitation and comment unfavorably on the difficulties it introduces into his theory of proletarian revolution. A whole school of American commentators has focussed on this problem, which is treated as the weak link between Lukács' philosophy of praxis and social reality.

These interpreters rely heavily on the similarities between Lukács' method and that of Weber, while ignoring Lukács' own concept of practice. The effect of these emphases is to eliminate some of the complexities from Lukács' work, but at the same time to make him appear to be a Stalinist *avant la lettre*, so naive as to announce the repressive colors of Soviet practice admiringly and in a theoretically consistent form. This interpretation is neither textually nor historically plausible, as I have argued elsewhere.[25]

How do the critics justify such extraordinary charges? Since they overlook Lukács' original approach to linking class consciousness and class action, the ideal-typical construct of the former appears to them to have no basis at all in the life of the class. Lukács is supposed to have no way of "getting" from his construct of class consciousness to real consciousness, but can only juxtapose the one to the other as "ought" to "is." Lukács is thus confronted with the very question he himself had posed in relation to Marx's early critique of Hegel, i.e. whether he is not foisting his own revolutionary goals on a proletariat with quite other aims. But in the era of the Russian Revolution, this question has tragic implications; Marxism has become imperious and demands of classes that they conform to an essence it imputes to them, rather than deriving its understanding of the classes from their own thought and action. Such an approach, as Lukács elaborates it, constitutes an anticipatory justification of Stalinist voluntarism.

Thus Morris Watnick writes that Lukácsian class consciousness is not discovered by a study of the actual existing proletariat, but ascribed to the class "by a process of bilateral imputation" proceeding in abstraction from "proletarian class interests and . . . the subjectively infected outlook that goes with them."[26] And James Miller argues that Lukács' approach "doubles" the proletariat into a real class, not necessarily revolutionary at any given moment, and an ideal one possessed by definition of revolutionary class consciousness. Theoretically, the consciousness of the ideal proletariat is represented by Marxism, while practically it is represented by the vanguard party. Thus in Lukács' theory the revolutionary subjectivity of the class would be surreptitiously attributed to the party, while the real proletariat is dismissed as stuck in "reified facticity." The tension between proletariat and party, real and ideal class is left unresolved in fact, while conceptual equivocations prevent its recognition in theory. "The subject's objective subjectivity is 'held safe' in the party, but the subject himself becomes a mere abstract object for the party. The equivocation of Lukács was the equivocation of Lenin—and this equivocation was 'transcended' not in utopia, but in concentration camps."[27]

Is there really such a yawning abyss between class consciousness and real consciousness in Lukács' presentation? At least programmatically, Lukács does suggest a solution. This solution would consist in the development of the second approach to class consciousness mentioned above, the one in which the Weberian model would be applied to the study of the functional relation of thought and action in the system of behavior of the class. Schooled in Weberian methods as he was, Lukács could hardly fail to acknowledge that the definition of an ideal-type requires some such empirically oriented approach to complete it and cannot stand alone. He does note that the difference between class consciousness and real consciousness is not just a heuristic gap, but a socially significant one. Thus, immediately after the lengthy definition of the ideal-typical approach quoted above, he writes,

This analysis establishes right from the start the distance that separates class consciousness from the empirically given, and from the psychologically describable and explicable ideas which men form about their situation in life. But it is not enough just to state that this distance exists or even to define its implications in a formal and general way. . . . We must discover . . . the *practical* significance of these different possible relations between the objective economic totality, the imputed class consciousness and the real, psychological thoughts of men about their life situation. We must discover, in short, the *practical, historical function* of class consciousness.[28]

Unfortunately, Lukács does relatively little with this general program; he fails to develop it with the degree of explicitness and analytic rigor of the first approach. He does attempt to explain the theory of the vanguard party on the basis of a dialectic of real and class consciousness, but in formulations so obscure and ambiguous as to have given rise to systematic misinterpretations of all kinds. Long before it occurred to anyone to charge Lukács with Stalinism, his politics earned him the accusation of anarcho-syndicalism. Lukács' contribution is, I believe, defensible from both these imputations. I have written at length on these questions elsewhere, and repeating that discussion would not advance the argument of this book.[29] Instead, I would like now to turn to the more general problem of whether Marxist theory has the resources to articulate the mediations implied in the working out of a complex conception of class consciousness such as Lukács'. In the next section and the conclusion to this chapter, I will draw on several Marxist theoreticians to indicate various ways in which this might be done.

THE MEDIATIONS

The suggestion that Lukács' theory of class consciousness leads to Stalinism because it is based on the theoretical construction of a specific rationality is so fundamental an objection that I would like to begin by dealing directly with it. For this purpose I want to consider Gramsci's theory of the party briefly. It is widely agreed that this theory is a properly Leninist one in some sense that distinguishes it from Stalinism. I would argue that the same is true of Lukács' theory of class consciousness, and that Gramsci's *Prison Notebooks* offer a striking complement to Lukács' theory in which precisely the least developed sides of Lukács' presentation are brilliantly elaborated within a generally similar theoretical framework.

Gramsci starts out from the same view of practice as Lukács. As he puts it, worldviews are "implicit" in the action of classes and become "explicit" in the elaboration and propagandizing of the appropriate ideologies. Gramsci has little to say about the origin and nature of these worldviews. What interests him is the process in which what Lukács calls "class consciousness" is realized in the "real consciousness" of the individuals; in other words, the process in which the difference between the specific rationality of action and thought is reduced so far as possible, and the individuals provided with views that "raise to consciousness," or make explicit what is already latent in their practice.

Gramsci treats the problem historically. In the beginning a new class will act in function of its real situation in society, even if it still has to conceptualize its acts through the already established ideologies of the old classes of the society. There results an opposition between the meaning embedded in the acts of the class and its beliefs. But in the long run, the level and type of class consciousness embodied in action must prevail and real consciousness must be brought into harmony with it. The determinism of class consciousness is therefore felt not through the literally unthinkable relation between real consciousness and a theoretical construct, as Lukács' critics have charged, but through the relation of social thought to social practice, through, in short, the urgent need of the class for beliefs which articulate its historically necessary behavior.

To bring belief into harmony with behavior requires, in Gramsci's words, the "cultural deployment" of the worldview implicit in action (Lukács' "class consciousness"), and this process consists in "adjusting culture to the practical function."[30] Class consciousness is not immediately realized in class thought, but must be spread through real, historically effective mediations. First, a theory must be elaborated which corresponds with the class consciousness of the class by falling under the horizon of the specific rationality implicit in its class behavior. Second, intellectuals and organizers must emerge as specialized strata of the class, capable of communicating to it the ideas which correspond with its own implicit worldview. In the modern world, Gramsci argues, it is political parties which are primarily responsible for these function.

The role of the party is to socialize the class consciousness of the class, a process which is "objectively possible," in Lukács' terms, because the class is predisposed to believe ideas that rationalize its ongoing behavior. But parties are relatively autonomous groups of individuals, with their own real consciousness. Who is to say that the views they "impute" to the class in their theory and propaganda actually correspond to the needs of the class? Gramsci argues that the class itself will always be the judge of the adequacy of the ideology offered it by the party. The excessive deviation of the party from the class consciousness of the class will result in the class abandoning the party. It is through the determinate contingency of the relation between party and class that class consciousness influences real consciousness. Where assent is given the party, its propaganda serves the function of progressively bringing real consciousness into line with class consciousness.

Class consciousness, the worldview implicit in action, is the invariant and tendential goal of real consciousness to the extent that the class unifies itself behind representatives who have a real consciousness which is much nearer to class consciousness than that of the mass of individuals. The adjustment of real consciousness to class consciousness is thus a social process which takes place in a relation between different real consciousnesses, some of which have the leading, others the following role. The problem raised by the critics of the gap between "objective possibility" and actuality is solved in Gramsci by showing that the real consciousness of the members of the class approximates to their class consciousness through the development of specific kinds of social relations.

In Gramsci as in Lukács the party does not have the proletariat at its disposal, but rather vice versa. When Lukács writes that the party is "the *visible* embodiment of proletarian class consciousness," he means not that the party is the true subject of the revolution, but on the contrary, that it is the privileged *object* of the working class as subject, the object through which the class "sees" its own situation and potentialities most clearly.[31] Even in its acts, the party "appears" to the class, which can accept it or reject it, follow it or oppose it, as the explicit formulation of a class project inarticulately present in the life of the class itself. The party is thus not a mechanism of social control in the service of the revolution—an impossible contradiction: it is there to be "seen," and the sight of it is a moment in the constitution of a subject of history.

DETERMINANTS OF CLASS CONSCIOUSNESS

Despite all this controversy about its political implications, the main purpose of Lukács' concept of class consciousness is to serve as a heuristic device for the study of the epistemological limits of the specific rationality of each class standpoint. This application of the concept depends on one of the critical, and one of the least adequately explained, articulations in Lukács' early Marxism, that which links his theory of the *culture of capitalism* to his discussion of *class situation and interest*. The first concerns socially general determinants affecting all awareness under capitalism; the second explains how these general determinants function in the worldviews and strategies of survival of particular social classes. This articulation is implicit in every essay of *History and Class Consciousness*, explicit in none of them. Even ·the chapter entitled "Class Consciousness" assumes a certain solution to the problem of the relation of culturally general and class specific determinants of consciousness, without actually presenting that solution as such.

This lack of clarity and explicitness has given rise to considerable disagreement about the meaning of Lukács' theory. In an interesting critique, Andrew Arato suggests that Lukács has not one but two theories of consciousness. The first theory, presented in the essay on "Class Consciousness," "distinguished between the social existence of bourgeois and proletariat in terms of class interest," while the second, presented in the essay on "Reification and The Consciousness of the Proletariat," is based on the different relation of these two classes to the reified form of appearance of the society which defines immediate objectivity for both.[32] Arato thus suggests that Lukács began with a traditional theory of ideology, and only later, in his essay on "Reification," offered a cultural approach based on the form of objectivity shared by all members of society.

While there is clearly a difference in the treatment of proletarian class consciousness in the two essays, the one emphasizing interest, as Arato argues, the other emphasizing the capacity of the proletariat to transcend reification, I believe that Lukács presents the same basic theory in both. The essay on "Class Consciousness" also mentions the importance of the transcendence of reification, arguing that the interests of the proletariat drive it beyond immediacy to a true comprehension of society. The essay on "Reification" not only recapitulates this argument, but also adds to it a discussion of the epistemological implications of the class situation of the proletariat.³³ These are complementary approaches, not alternative theories, in Lukács as already in Marx who mentions "material interest and social position" side by side as determinants of class consciousness.³⁴

In fact, Lukács' theory of class consciousness relates three basic determinants, the culturally general "form of objectivity" or "form of appearance" of society, the social situation of the various classes of society, and their class interests. Lukács dispersed his discussions of these various determinants throughout his text; this makes the reconstruction of his theory difficult, and accounts for Arato's suggestion that there are actually two theories offered instead of one.

The most fundamental determinant of social awareness is the form of objectivity of the society, the level of the culturally general schemata of perception and experience discussed in the previous chapters. Under capitalism this form of objectivity is reification, the appearance of social relations as relations between things or, more precisely, in the form of thinghood. Lukács argues that the economy in capitalist society has a double character, as instrumental to survival and as the source of these basic schemata of experience. The individuals constitute the *Lebenswelt* of their daily activity through a practice, the form of which they then perceive as the essence of their objects. In the course of their activity, which plunges them into the immediate appearance of the economy, the form of this appearance, reification, is released from its specifically economic content to become the basis of thought and perception in general. The economic categories thereby become models of a specific type of objectivity, shaping consciousness in all domains.

Through this cultural generalization of its categorial structure, the economy contributes to the process of its own social reproduction. Lukács shows how consciousness both is shaped by its relation to immediate appearances and contributes in its turn to orienting practice toward the activities required to reproduce the system. The forms of appearance and the mode of consciousness based on them are thus essential mediations in the process of social reproduction. In the next chapter I will discuss in detail Lukács' view that the economy itself is the most basic reproductive mechanism of capitalist society. With this the circle is closed, practice producing a world of objects which, by their form, shape a consciousness that orients practice toward the reproduction of these same objects.

This dialectical circularity of the system of practice is the basis of its systematic misperception as a solid reality constituting for practice. Lukács writes that "history is the history of the unceasing overthrow of the forms of objectivity that shape the life of man."[35] And yet each form of objectivity presents itself immediately to consciousness as an atemporal system, without roots or history. In fact the very efficacy of forms of objectivity, their appearance as such forms, rests on the misperception of them as unhistorical, natural and necessary. Reification too has precisely this character.

Can this circularity of culture be broken? This is the question of the possibility of a "true" or revolutionary consciousness in capitalist society. Lukács' whole theory of class consciousness is constructed to identify the conditions for a transcendence of immediacy, for a demystification of the reified form of objectivity of society. Among these conditions is the class situation of the various classes in society. Lukács writes that "in capitalist society reality is—immediately—the same for both the bourgeoisie and the proletariat . . ."[36] And again: "The proletariat shares with the bourgeoisie the reification of every aspect of its life."[37] However, Lukács argues, reification is differently experienced from different class situations. It is interesting that Lukács cites as evidence for this theory one of the few Marxian passages on alienation to which he had access:

The property-owning class and the class of the proletariat represent the same human self-alienation. But the former feels at home in this self-alienation and feels itself confirmed by it; it recognises alienation as its own instrument and in it it possesses the semblance of a human existence. The latter feels itself destroyed by this alienation and sees in it its own impotence and the reality of an inhuman existence.[38]

Thus the "same" alienation is experienced by bourgeois and proletarians, Marx claims, but experienced from a radically different vantage point. Class situation refers precisely to this socially determined vantage point of the classes of society, the point of view from which they "look out" at the world that surrounds them.

Lukács suggests two ways in which class situation affects class consciousness. In the first place, situation determines the relation of the class to the immediate form of objectivity of society, as in the passage from Marx. In the texts cited by Arato to support the idea of a "second" theory of class consciousness, Lukács is in fact working out the implications of the different class situations of the proletariat and the bourgeoisie for their ability to understand the reification that confronts them both. In the second place, class situation determines what Lukács calls the "immediate objects" of the class, that is to say, the objects which most preoccupy it in its daily activity and which become paradigmatic for it in interpreting more "distant" social spheres. For terminological reasons, I prefer to call these initial objects of class consciousness its "proximate objects," to distinguish them clearly from the immediate form of objectivity of the society as a whole.

Lukács argues that the proximate objects of class consciousness form a sort of inner circle of awareness, starting out from which the class strives to reach a universal comprehension of all sectors of society. Whether it succeeds or not in transcending the limits of its own proximate objects will depend on its place in the productive process. Lukács believes that classes engaged in secondary economic activities will fail to understand society as a whole in any satisfactory form, and so will not be able to construct a coherent worldview. Only a class which has some significant involvement in the central productive activity, from which its proximate objects are therefore drawn, can succeed in encompassing the entire society in thought by generalizing from its particular situation.[39]

An adequate understanding of society cannot be based on the uncritical acceptance of the immediately given form of objectivity, but only on its mediation. For a class to attain a true knowledge of its own social world, it must be able to apprehend the immediate social appearances as dialectical moments in a comprehension that goes beyond them to their basis in social reality itself. This requires, Lukács argues, three conditions, corresponding to three determinants of class consciousness. First, the form of objectivity of the society must admit of such a mediation from a possible class situation in society. Lukács believes this to have been true of no precapitalist society. Only reification, the form of objectivity of capitalism, can be successfully mediated by members of the society it dominates. This is due to the fact that reification does not confound nature and culture in a single seamless web, impenetrable to those who live within it, as have all previous forms of objectivity. Second, in capitalist society itself it is necessary that the class in question participate in the central productive activities of the society so that its proximate objects correspond with the really determining forces in the social environment. This condition eliminates the petty bourgeoisie and the peasantry, classes of capitalist society not involved in large scale production. Third, for a class to be able to know the truth about its society, it must be, quite simply, in its interests to do so.

Every class consciousness is adjusted to the interests of the class. Where these interests are better served by a consciousness which remains in immediacy, class consciousness will be false consciousness. This is the case, claims Lukács, for the bourgeoisie which would discover in a true consciousness of society the limited and partial character of its domination as a ruling class. It must therefore systematically remain in the "necessary illusion" of reification, the better to believe in its universal mission. And where the limits of its pretensions are visibly manifest in the uprisings of the oppressed, the class nevertheless maintains itself in ignorance through the "falsity of consciousness," through the development of ideology in the pejorative sense. In the case of the bourgeoisie, class interest thus maintains the class in immediacy and represses any comprehension of the immediate manifestations of the class struggle.

Only the proletariat, the bourgeoisie's protagonist in this class struggle, has no interest in the maintenance of capitalism and therefore no need for illusions about the nature of society. As a class directly involved in large scale production, it can hope to understand the society as a whole. And, as I will show in the next section, it experiences reification not as a universal transhistorical horizon of knowledge, but rather as a historical barrier to its own self-actualization, a barrier it can attempt to overcome both in practice and in theory.

THE THEORY OF THE PROLETARIAT

Lukács' theory of proletarian class consciousness does not dogmatically assume that workers are frequently and spontaneously revolutionary; rather he is exploring the conditions of the possibility of workers acting in a truly revolutionary manner in *any* instance whatsoever, however unusual. Furthermore, as noted at the beginning of this chapter, Lukács' argument does not concern the motivations of revolt, but rather the degree to which it might be capable of effecting a profound cultural change. In sum, Lukács' theory of proletarian class consciousness is an attempt to show in principle that the class can make a revolution which does not merely replace one reified culture with another, but which overcomes the horizon of reification and alters the very foundations of social practice.

As I have shown, Lukács believes that the bourgeoisie and the proletariat stand in different, class determined relations to reification. This difference consists in the fact that the bourgeoisie accepts reification "immediately," whereas the proletariat is capable of mediating it. Lukács identifies some basic contexts within which, he argues, workers more or less spontaneously de-reify aspects of social reality. The worker himself is the proximate object of this initial de-reifying consciousness because he cannot accept immediately his own form of objectivity under capitalism as pure labor power. The capitalist, on the contrary, receives the worker at the factory gate as just such labor power and is not obliged to think beyond this immediacy for any reason of principle (although he might do so on occasion from a charitable impulse or from fear, of course). But the worker is constantly aware of the difference between his social form and his real content as a person.

Where, for example, a speed-up or lengthening of the working day is perceived by the capitalist as a simple matter of increasing the quantity of labor power purchased at a given price, for the worker this "quantity changes into quality." The worker cannot help but penetrate the reified quantitative determinants of this form of objectivity. He is inevitably aware of the real qualitative degradation of life and health associated with an intensification or extension of work activity. Thus, "the quantitative differences in exploitation which appear to the capitalist in the form of quantitative determinants of the objects of his calculation, must appear to the worker as the decisive, qualitative categories of his whole physical, mental and moral existence."[40]

For Lukács the proletariat is "always already" situated beyond immediacy in the simple act of becoming (socially) self-conscious. This self-consciousness begins to shatter the reified form of objectivity of its objects and penetrates to their "reality." In this sense, Lukács argues, the consciousness of the proletariat is *"the self-consciousness of the commodity;* or in other words it is the self-knowledge, the self-revelation of the capitalist society founded upon the production and exchange of commodities."[41] To this more or less spontaneous critique of reification will correspond everyday practices which, when extended in depth and breadth and systematized in the context of union and party activities challenge the most fundamental premises of capitalism and its culture. In sum, the addition of "consciousness" to the "commodity structure" adds up to a potentially explosive combination.

Lukács thus argues that proletarian class consciousness can de-reify its objects. This de-reification is not of course a pure thought process, still less a quasi-philosophical transcendence of opinion in knowledge. Rather, it must be explained as a socially immanent and class bound response to a particular situation in society. I would suggest that this response be understood as a systematic mapping of one set of rules into another set, a "transformation" according to quite specific determinations, in order to distinguish it clearly from the activity of a scientific *cogito*. In this case, it is the patterns of behavior which flow from and which reproduce reification that are altered in a rule governed operation which Lukács describes as "self-consciousness."

It is also important not to confound this "self-consciousness" with a phenomenological constitution. Lukács has in mind a socially specific operation which would consist in the juxtaposition of social form and content in everyday experience. In the terms of this book, proletarian class consciousness can be described as a meta-theoretical revision of abstractions at the level of lived experience. Social appearance—reification—and social reality are related here in social consciousness, and not merely in a scientific or philosophical theory. It is the discovery of this meta-theoretical critique in everyday life which promises not just the truth of social reality, but its transformation. Thus the life experience of the proletariat relates reified form and content and makes possible a unique revelation of the cultural limits of capitalism while at the same time promising a real transcendence of those limits.

It will be recalled that in his first attempts to find an agent of revolution, Marx surreptitiously made theory the subject of a historical change the proletariat itself would undergo rather than initiate and control. Marx found a solution to this problem through the meta-theoretical revision of the concept of reason: the demands of reason were shown to flow from the satisfaction of the human needs in function of which the proletariat itself would be moved to act. Lukács' theory of proletarian class consciousness is a response to a similar problem, and he arrives at a similar solution, although on the plane of methodology. To show that Marxism is not related in a merely accidental manner to the thought and action of proletarians, that it is not a scientific "consciousness from without" which the proletariat would serve as a "passive, material basis," Lukács demonstrates that Marxist method is itself an expression of proletarian class consciousness.

He argues that workers' everyday response to the reification of experience is the foundation on which Marxist dialectics arise. Marxism is thus, as theory, "adjusted" to the implicit methodological approach of proletarian class consciousness itself. In their daily experience workers relativize the given form of objectivity of capitalist society as a historically limited moment in a larger process that surpasses capitalist forms of life. It is this ability to transcend the given form of objectivity which distinguishes proletarian class consciousness from all previous forms of social awareness and makes it possible, in principle, for the entire structure of reified thought to be exposed to criticism from this class standpoint. A correct theoretical understanding of society is finally possible on this basis, as a critique of the economic and epistemological premises of capitalism. As Marx himself writes, "So far as such criticism represents a class, it can only represent the class whose vocation in history is the overthrow of the capitalist mode of production and the final abolition of all classes—the proletariat."[42]

BEYOND ONE-DIMENSIONALITY

How much reality remains to such a theory of the revolutionary proletariat? The whole Lukácsian approach seems to be suited for a period of capitalist social development long since transcended in most of the wealthiest countries of the West; even the very term "proletariat" now gives off the musty odor of old books. Furthermore, this theory does not seem immediately applicable to the study of those phenomena of focal concern to contemporary social theory, for example the emergence and effect of the culture industry and of mass markets in consumer goods under advanced capitalism.

However, Lukács' cultural approach to forms of consciousness does suggest the basis for an analysis of advanced capitalism. As class struggle in Western societies has diminished in intensity and become, consequently, a less central theme even of Marxist social theory, the power of the immediate form of objectivity of these societies has correspondingly increased. The proletariat, in Lukács' theory, is not automatically situated beyond the reach of this form of objectivity but, it will be recalled, is assured only of the "objective possibility" of transcending it on the basis of the gap between reification and reality which appears in its own initial self-perception. But it is a long way from this premise of de-reifying consciousness to a revolutionary political position. Lukács is fully aware of this, and himself prepares a study of the relative reification of proletarian *real* consciousness precisely in his analysis of its *class* consciousness.

As we have seen, Lukács considers the subversion of the functional autonomy of the various subsystems of capitalist society to be a *sine qua non* of revolutionary action. Yet nothing guarantees that workers will be able to carry the de-reification of social reality to this decisive point. Lukács envisages the failure of this operation, writing, for example, that the fragmentation of proletarian struggle and its corresponding theory into separate economic, political, and ideological spheres testifies to the low level of proletarian class consciousness.

The bare fact of separation itself indicates that the consciousness of the proletariat is still fettered by reification. And if the proletariat finds the economic inhumanity to which it is subjected easier to understand than the political, and the political easier than the cultural, then all these separations point to the extent of the still unconquered power of capitalist forms of life in the proletariat itself.[43]

The most important development in Marxist cultural theory after Lukács, the Frankfurt School's critique of modern forms of authoritarianism and mass culture, is rooted precisely in this Lukácsian cultural approach to the form of objectivity of capitalist society. Adorno himself acknowledged that Lukács' concept of reification was the initial breakthrough that opened the path to the Frankfurt School's study of modern capitalist culture.[44] A brief consideration of this matter helps to show the continuing usefulness of Lukács' approach to consciousness.

Insufficiently stressed in accounts of the Frankfurt School's theory of authority is the role of reification in founding a specifically modern type of authoritarianism. The Frankfurt School followed Marx in distinguishing between authority relations under capitalism, which are visibly rooted in relative economic power, and the similar relations which exist in precapitalist societies in which "the domination of the producers by the conditions of production is concealed by the relations of domination and servitude, which appear and are evident as the direct motive power of the process of production."[45] The problem the early Frankfurt School set for itself was to explain how new forms of authoritarianism, of psychologically introjected domination, had arisen from the capitalist system, contrary to the expectation of Marx and Engels that this system would promote, unwittingly of course, the mental independence and rationality of the producers.[46]

In their early studies of authority, Horkheimer and Marcuse both emphasize the transformation of capitalist rationality into the basis for these new forms of authoritarianism, an emphasis which is also apparent in the classic *Dialectic of Enlightenment*. Horkheimer writes that "The fullest possible adaptation of the subject to the reified authority of the economy is the form which reason really takes in bourgeois society."[47] Authoritarianism now arises not from atavistic respect for inherited privilege, but from "the fact that men regard economic data . . . as immediate or natural facts, and think they are adapting themselves to such facts when they submit to the authority relationship."[48] Marcuse summarizes this slide from the immediate acceptance of "facts" into unquestioning obedience to authority by saying that "reification is transformed into a false personalization."[49]

In analyses such as these the Frankfurt School used Lukács' theory of reification to explain how the increased rationality of capitalist society became the basis for its totalitarian perversion. I suppose one could claim that Lukács' influence was minimal, that ideas like his were "in the air." This may be true, and yet one should not underestimate Lukács' contribution to putting such ideas "in the air," where they could be picked up and developed in this striking and original manner.

In any case, this theory of authority is especially close to Lukács' approach because it does not subjectivize reification, but considers it as the stuff of capitalist social experience. In these discussions, reification is not deposited in the individuals in the first instance through ideology in the usual sense, nor through a psycho-dynamic ruled by the logic of the emotions, but rather in practical and perceptual dispositions.

This is not then a "culture and personality" approach, at least not yet, but still remains close to the Lukácsian way of understanding culture. Here culture is embodied proximally in the structure of the social world and the orientation of practice ("adaptation") toward that world.

Social "appearance," the form of objectivity of the social world, and not individual character structure, is the initial bearer of the general (culture) in the particular (psychology), the mediator between law and instance, collective and individual realities. Objective appearance, a concept basic to Lukács' Marxism, and not individual psychology links laws to their realization in the individuals and their activities. The concept of character structure has as yet only a derivative status as a mediation in this process. Later, under the increasingly strong impact of Freud and of American quantitative research methods, the Frankfurt School moved on to what I take to be a different position which is more psychologically oriented and bears less the trace of Lukács' influence. This later position is interesting in itself, but it is really incompatible with that of Lukács.

Yet, significantly, even as the Frankfurt School's theory of authority tends to become more psychologically oriented, in Marcuse's work the concept of "technological rationality" takes over the functions of the earlier concept of reification as objective social appearance determining the very paradigm of rationality in the culture of capitalism. A straight path leads from Lukács' theory of reification to Marcuse's theory of "one-dimensional" society. What is lost on the way is perhaps equally important, however, and this is the sense of immanent class-based contradictions in modern capitalism which can in principle lead to a radical break with its cultural forms. The attempt to reintegrate the very considerable theoretical advances of the Frankfurt School's study of mass culture into a class conception of modern capitalism would do well to look back to Lukács' own initial presentation of the problem.

This is what Stanley Aronowitz has done in a remarkable study of the shaping of American working class consciousness that exemplifies the kind of research that can be undertaken in the general framework of the Lukácsian theory. Like many Americans who participated in the new left, Aronowitz's political experience resonated positively with Marcuse's critique of advanced capitalism. Yet his experience of working class life indicated the necessity for a corrective to the Marcusian view of reification triumphant (or nearly so) in a one-dimensional society. Specifically, Aronowitz criticizes Marcuse's one-dimensionality thesis for underestimating the countertendencies in American culture, the submerged social resistance to reification that may still provide the basis for a socialist movement at some future date. The needed corrective is to be provided in the form of a theory of this prepolitical resistance to reification. Accordingly, Aronowitz emphasizes the dialectic of working class daily life, the constant tensions between workers and the institutions that are designed to shape them into passive social members. This is, then, an attempt to revive the theory of the immanently contradictory character of capitalism.

The adequacy of a theory of socialization that shows the possibility for liberatory self-activity by workers can neither rely on the pressure of external events nor on the reduction to biological urges. It must show that inside the structure of social life the activity pattern of the subjects (that is, the workers themselves) can produce values, norms, and ways of interacting that depart from the prescribed patterns of capitalist socialization as well as conform to it. It is the contradiction between the autonomous self-activity of workers . . . and the social constraints imposed by the capitalist mode of production . . . that constitutes the possibility of historical change. If the workers have no elements of their socialization that they can perceive as resistant to the economic role assigned to them by a relatively successful capitalism, neither economic crisis nor biological urges will suffice to change their responses to their life situation.[50]

Aronowitz sets out to apply such an approach to the study of working class life. He shares some explicit assumptions with Lukács in doing so: the belief in the intrinsic revolutionary potentialities of the working class; the denial that any automatic economic process can call this potentiality to life; and especially the theory of reification, which reveals the roots of working class *un*consciousness in the organization of labor, while providing also a basis for the study of the "commodification" of culture. But Aronowitz goes beyond Lukács toward a more concrete theory of the mediations shaping the real consciousness of workers. Specifically, he discusses the problem of the division of labor, not only in general, but in its historical connection with the development of the ethnically, racially and sexually differentiated labor force of American capitalism. "The roles of institutions, ideologies, and cultural influences," he writes, "must be explored as both products of this development and, in turn, determinants of the underlying social relations."[51] Most original is Aronowitz's extension of the theory of mediations beyond the political and economic arena into the institutions of daily life such as the family, schools, games, sports, religion and mass culture. "These institutions mediate between the social relations of production and individual consciousness. . ."[52]

To the extent that it is based on Lukács, Aronowitz's approach to the study of the American working class implies a different interpretation of the theory of class consciousness from that of the critics discussed above. Like Lucien Goldmann, Aronowitz uses the concept of class consciousness not just to refer to an ideal-typical model of the possible *beliefs* of a class, but also as the expression of the tendencies of its daily life, its behavior and its culture.[53] Class consciousness represents tendencies of action and thought that are *always* realized by the class at *some* level, even if it be only symptomatically in apparently unpolitical areas of "private" existence. The problem of relating the specific rationality of class practice to class beliefs and attitudes is solved here by the hermeneutic study of daily life, the analysis of the system of behavior characteristic of its situation in American society. Real consciousness is not juxtaposed abstractly to an ideal-typical model, but related to what the class *does* in function of the real determinants which the model reflects. The tension between thought and action identified in this manner is recognized, and it is shown that this tension is just as important as the explicitly formulated beliefs of the class.

Aronowitz's method illuminates an important implication of Lukács' theory, namely that by its very nature the working class is always already engaged at an elementary level in the practical critique of reification. This is what it means to say that its class consciousness is "revolutionary," not simply that it riots in the streets or is an easy mark for certain propaganda appeals. According to the logic of this position, for every reification of working class life there is an automatic response on the part of workers, a relatively de-reifying reaction which flows from their position in society. This reaction may not be politically effective; it may be confined to what are called personal affairs and it may leave untouched repressive structures of which workers are victims; and yet it is the concrete mediation in the life of the class between class consciousness and real consciousness.

Reification does not automatically provoke revolution, nor can reification automatically prevent it. What reification does produce by its very nature is some form of inevitable resistance by the human substance ground between the wheels of an inhuman system. This resistance can be conceived as a dialectically correlated counterposition to every reified position capitalism seizes from workers. Aronowitz traces this play of position and counterposition everywhere in workers' daily lives, in children's games, sports, schools, family life, music and mass culture, and, most importantly, in the workplace.

This may seem like a small gain for revolutionary theory against the massive forces that successfully contain working class resistance within tolerable channels. After all, how significant is it that certain children's games express an aspiration for equality and freedom, when grown-ups seem to be reconciled to inequality and unfreedom? Indeed, no necessarily revolutionary implications flow from Aronowitz's analysis any more than from that of Lukács. Yet in another sense, the gain is very great; it amounts to social theory's recognition of people in their working roles as individuals in the full sense of the term, and not merely as the outputs of a total programming radical theorists may witness with revulsion, but which they conceptualize as theoretically unsurpassable. Lukács' theory of class consciousness and its application to the study of the mediations in daily life may serve as a corrective to such a *systematic* pessimism, and open the field to a research which recognizes the historical limits of capitalism not only ideologically, in its general program, but also in its very methods of study of the present.

6

Cultural Marxism

THE MARXIAN SYNTHESIS

Lukács situates Marxism at the intersection of the two fundamental discoveries of modern social theory. The first of these, which he attributes to Vico, holds that society is a human product; from this idea derive all those later social theories which emphasize the creative power of man in history. The second discovery, attributable to Adam Smith if to anyone in particular, holds that in one of its dimensions—the economy—this product has a rational form willed by none of the actors, a form which can be described in universal, atemporal laws. Every later social or cultural determinism may be seen as stemming from this insight. These two discoveries compass what I will call the antinomy of process and system. (In Lukács' terminology, this is the antinomy of "historical production" and "categorial genesis.") This antinomy still divides social theory, which emphasizes now one, now the other of its poles, the constitution of history by a subject, or the logical structure of the social order.

As Lukács understands his work, Marx attempted to transcend precisely this antinomy. By Marx's day, the rapid prog-

ress of capitalism, which had subordinated all other areas of
social life to its exigencies, argued for an emphasis on the
dimension of system, the determining power of social structure over and against the will and intentions of human subjects. And yet the evidence of Vico—that history is a human
product—remained as strong as ever and was increasingly
confirmed by revolutionary movements and romantic cultural
protest against the deathless mechanism of capitalist social
life. Two heterogeneous strains run through Marx's work as
he attempts to recognize both these dimensions of social
reality. On the one hand, he insists that in history men are
"both the authors and the actors of their own drama."[1] On the
other hand, Marx also insists that social life be "viewed as a
process of natural history," in which men are "governed by
laws not only independent of human will, consciousness and
intelligence, but rather, on the contrary, determining that
will, consciousness and intelligence."[2] It is fair to state that
any interpretation of Marxism that fails to attempt a reconciliation of these opposing demands is alien to the spirit of the
theory.

Marx himself attempted to bridge the gap with two conceptual instruments: first, the thesis of historical materialism,
which was supposed to show the dependency of (social and
political) process on (economic) system; and second, with the
projection of a disalienating socialist revolution through which
humanity as subject would reassert its claims. Marxism's
aspiration to be a general social theory with implications for
the future of humankind depends entirely on these conceptual instruments. We have already seen in the previous
chapter how Lukács attempts to develop and apply them to
the theory of proletarian class consciousness, considered as
both socially determined and as agent of change.

Can both these dimensions of Marxism still be preserved
today, or must one be irrevocably subordinated to the other?
This is perhaps the central question of contemporary Marxism, distinguishing the two most influential contemporary

schools of Marxist theory, the Frankfurt School and the Althusserian school. Pierre Bourdieu has described the dilemma in terms not unlike those Lukács employed a generation earlier.

So long as one accepts the canonic opposition which, endlessly reappearing in new forms throughout the history of social thought, nowadays pits "humanist" against "structuralist" readings of Marx, to declare diametrical opposition to subjectivism is not genuinely to *break* with it, but to fall into the fetishism of social laws to which objectivism consigns itself when in establishing between structure and practice the relation of the virtual to the actual, of the score to the performance, of essence to existence, it merely substitutes for the creative man of subjectivism a man subjugated to the dead laws of a natural history. And how could one underestimate the strength of the ideological couple subjectivism/objectivism where one sees that the critique of the *individual* considered as an *ens realissimum* only leads to his being made an epiphenomenon of hypostasized structure, and that the well-founded assertion of the primacy of objective relations results in products of human action, the structures, being credited with the power to develop in accordance with their own laws and to determine and overdetermine other structures?[3]

In the conclusion to this chapter, I will return to a consideration of Bourdieu's solution to this dilemma, which has interesting similarities to Lukács'.

The theoretical and practical stakes in this debate are very high. The uniqueness of Marx's work lies in its attempt to combine a theory of system with a theory of process. The breakdown of the synthesis leads to the collapse of the mediations Marx proposed, his essentially programmatic suggestions for a theory of the superstructures and of socialist revolution. Where system is emphasized at the expense of process, the dependence of the superstructures on the base can be demonstrated, but no plausible account of socialist revolution can be offered. Where process is emphasized at the

expense of system, the theory can continue to explain historical agency in the revolution but it risks losing all connection
with a "material" base, a rigorous mode of economic analysis.
At issue practically is the famous antinomy of mechanistic
determinism and moralistic voluntarism which has haunted
Marxism from its origins. How can a society governed by laws
like those of nature be transformed by its members in the
course of history? On the other hand, if no science of society
offers insight into the actual moving forces of history, are we
not condemned impotently to will changes that may well be
desirable but which have no serious prospect of success?

These are some of the questions put to Marxism which are
widely regarded as unanswerable by contemporary social
theorists. The breakdown of the Marxian synthesis lies at the
origin of several important contemporary theories of culture,
which have attempted to salvage fragments from the debacle.
Among these I want to discuss briefly contributions by Jürgen
Habermas, Marshall Sahlins and Pierre Bourdieu. While this
chapter will not offer a full scale evaluation of their theories
in the light of Lukács' interpretation of Marxism, I do intend
to at least indicate the lines along which such an evaluation
could be made. In brief, it will be my contention that Lukács'
early Marxism provides the means to save far more of the
Marxist framework than is preserved by these authors.

MATERIALISM IN THE THEORY OF CULTURE

Marx's theory of ideology and the superstructures proceeds
from a very basic and specifically modern intuition about
social reality, the idea that there is a link between "higher"
and "lower" spheres, and a profound dependency of the
former on the latter, of what men think on what they do, of
what they believe on what they need, of ideology on interest
and of the alienated spheres of universality, such as religion
and politics, on economic realities and the conflict between
social classes. This general intuition we owe not only to Marx,

but also to Nietzsche, Freud and the tradition of the nineteenth century novel. I think we can call any theory of culture which embodies this intuition a "materialist" theory, in opposition to idealist theories emphasizing the predominant role of spiritual values in social life.

Not all materialist theories of culture are reductionist, but reductionism is a temptation and a danger they do not always successfully resist. The materialist insight into culture is itself reduced to absurdity where the higher spheres are not simply related to and rooted in the lower, but identified crudely with them. To give an example, Freud's theory of sublimation attempts to account for the sexual origin of artistic creativity, but it also maintains the distinction between the two domains, and recognizes that in its sublimated form the sexual drive opens up an original and relatively autonomous sphere of human potentialities. Had Freud confined himself to a cynical comment on the sexual frustrations of the artist, the theory would lack interest; it would be reductionist.

Similarly, Marx enjoyed making cynical observations on the interests hidden behind moral and religious pretensions, observations which in his day had something of the shock value of the assertion that man was descended from the apes. Hence such self-parodying examples of his theory of ideology as, "The English Established Church, e.g., will more readily pardon an attack on 38 of its 39 articles than 1/39 of its income."[4] It is of course a long way from such clearly reductionist pronouncements to an adequate theory of subjectivity and Marx himself was well aware of this even if many of his followers were not. In reaction to such crudity, much contemporary social theory attempts to recover the autonomy of the higher spheres. To the extent that Marxism confines itself to reducing these latter to economic interests that they are supposed to serve, it lends itself to precisely this sort of "transcendence" by non-Marxist social theory. Reductionist Marxism always falls short of explaining both the most general structural features of the cultural system it "reduces," and the creativity of the historical subjects it crudely identifies with positions in the production system. As a result of this failure, it is constantly challenged by independent sociological theories of culture which it can neither encompass nor refute.

In what follows, I would like to show how Lukács' construction of Marxism succeeds in retaining the Marxist emphasis on the determining role of the economy while avoiding reductionism. I will argue that Lukács' formulation, because it does work at the level of cultural forms, transcends this antinomy and brings Marxism into direct confrontation with alternative cultural theories. The starting point for this discussion must be Lukács' critique of the Marxist theory and social science of his own day. In both he identifies an over-emphasis on the moment of system which diminishes the role of revolutionary process. No matter that the one professes to be a materialist science of society, while the other reevaluates the role of "spiritual" causes in the framework of an original sociology of culture. They share a reification of society which obstructs conceptualization of social change.

The dominant tendencies in Marxism Lukács regards as mere reflexes of the triumph of bourgeois modes of thought in the working class movement. This reified standpoint leads to the quasi-naturalization of society, the interpretation of the social system through laws modelled on those of nature and which are therefore historically unsurpassable. Dialectically correlated with this mechanistic conception of society, a voluntaristic theory of action inevitably arises, which cannot in principle go beyond suggesting the desirability of moralizing the social world or of manipulating it technically according to its given laws. "Economic fatalism and the reformation of socialism through ethics are intimately connected."[5] Thus the great foes in the internal debates of German Social Democracy, the determinists of the orthodox "Center" and the neo-Kantian liberals of the revisionist right, appear to Lukács to occupy opposite poles of the bourgeois antinomy of fact and value. The Marxist movement merely recapitulates the an-

tinomies, especially those related to the opposition of reified
social law and individual action in history.

With the ideology of social democracy the proletariat falls victim to
all the antinomies of reification that we have hitherto analysed in
such detail. The important role increasingly played in this ideology
by "man" as a value, an ideal, an imperative, accompanied, of
course, by a growing "insight" into the necessity and logic of the
actual economic process, is only one symptom of this relapse into
the reified immediacy of the bourgeoisie.[6]

Methodological discussions in the bourgeois social sciences
reveal the real significance of this emphasis on social law in
Marxism. The then-dominant empiricist and neo-Kantian approaches agree in formulating the distinction of system and
process unhistorically as a distinction between the ontological
levels of their respective objects. The aim of cultural study in
this view is to arrive at generalizations which transcend
particular cultures and identify universal properties of social
life rooted in the nature of man in society. The concrete
substratum of these laws, the data they describe, appears
correspondingly as particular historical facts. Since these facts
are subsumed under the laws sociology derives, they offer no
basis for changing these laws but are merely instances of
them. The main difference between empiricism and neo-
Kantianism concerns the epistemological status granted to
these facts and the laws which describe them. But for both
methodologies, fact and laws stand in the same reified relation.

With this as a background, it should be possible to explain
why the mechanistic and reductionist Marxism of Social Democracy could offer no insight or leadership when the long
awaited revolution finally arrived. This version of Marxism
unwittingly places the laws of society beyond the reach of
historical action. It constructs its object, the mode of production, as a self-sufficient, unreflected thing. The mode of
production is distinguished by a process of abstraction from

the social conditions of its existence and reproduction, and from its own mode of appearance to the human beings who live and work within its confines. These other dimensions of society, the residue of the initial abstraction in which the concept of the mode of production is constituted, are then identified with another type of object, the superstructures. All the functions of relatedness, thought and action are deposited in the superstructures where they exist side by side with the mode of production which "determines" them.

This "determination" is extremely problematical. The concept of the mode of production, generated by scientific abstraction and analysis, is hypostasized as a real object and juxtaposed immediately with the residue of the process of abstraction in which it was constructed. The superstructures are simply the remainder of the whole from which the concept of the mode of production was first derived. The determination of the superstructures by the base thus involves a strange intercourse between an abstraction and its epistemological substratum. What began as a logical relation of abstraction is surreptitiously reformulated as a real causal relation. The result is a mechanistic and reductionist economic determinism.

The difficulties become still greater when an attempt is made to account for the revolution. Usually this is done by tossing in the idea of a "reciprocal action" of the superstructures on the base. Here the element of process is finally reintegrated as a self-evident dimension of revolutionary change. However, to explain revolution in this framework we are obliged to leave the clear air in which the laws of the mode of production float to descend to the level of particular historical data. These data appear to be superstructurally determined, for example by ideology, rather than economically determined by the mode of production. Hence the efficacy of the revolution implies the possibility of superstructural dominance. (*Marxisme oblige*, but keep it as brief as possible: socialism too is a mode of production with its laws, and so the reign of the superstructures is necessarily short, just long enough in fact to accomplish the impossible.) On this conception, the revolution is strictly inconceivable. Since the base has been constructed as the law of the superstructures, as, that is to say, the form of which the superstructures are merely the particular contents, this reversal in their relations of dominance is a methodological impossibility. No wonder, then, that a Marxism based on such theoretical foundations would tend to put off the day of the revolution indefinitely while suggesting, meanwhile, more or less principled opposition to the established system.

Lukács' alternative to this conception consists in interpreting the social laws as cultural forms, subject as such to historical change. Only as cultural forms can social laws truly be laws and yet be mutable by a collective practice. But if the social system is understood on cultural terms, then the revolution too must be reconceptualized. Its insurrectionary phase, which was such a stumbling block for earlier Marxist theory, is only a moment in a larger process of cultural change in which the transition to socialism consists. This transition is not primarily a political event, nor even an economic change, but the reconstitution of the cultural foundations of the social system. The transformation of culture, which earlier Marxist theory had imagined to be a rather secondary feature of the revolutionary process, turns out to be its central content.

Lukács argues that reified theory, including its Marxist forms, cannot transcend the antinomy of system and process because it cannot conceive of a collective subjectivity, a type of subjectivity capable of instituting and transforming the very forms of social action. Thus the systemic dimension of social life appears to be independent from and prior to the level of mere historical events, the correlated "content" of social life produced by the action of individual subjects. The study of culture misunderstands itself as the discovery of atemporal, universal laws divorced from the actual movement of events. Meanwhile, the individual activity which produces these events cannot institute culture, so understood, but is rather subsumed by it.

Lukács rejects the attempt to find mediations between such a separately conceived culture and history. Somehow, the two dimensions must arise simultaneously, as mutually necessary and mutually dependent aspects of the same basic substratum. This substratum is collective social practice which creates not only events but also their meaning. On this basis, Lukács repeatedly argues that history is no mere causal sequence but the production of the social world *in* a specific form of objectivity which has the (socially relative) universality of a cultural system. History is only comprehensible as a *cultural process*, in which practical activity generates not just events, but these events in a definite structural and functional order through which they take on meaning and coherence.

It is true that this order can be analytically separated from the events themselves, and the terms "culture" and "history" thereby distinguished. But for an individualistic concept of practice this distinction is inevitably more than analytic; it is ontological. The antinomy of system and process arises when these two dimensions of the historical process are hypostasized as independent realities; then formalism takes over in the study of culture and empiricism and in the study of history. Then too, it is discovered that once separated these two dimensions cannot be reunited by external mediations.

It is necessary to seek an entirely different starting point. This Lukács does by drawing on classical German philosophy, which confronted a somewhat similar problem at a much higher level of generality. Lukács interprets the philosophical concepts of "synthesis" and "mediation" of experience as the conceptual mythology corresponding to a real practical production of culture *as* history and *in* history. Demythologized, these concepts can be used to explain the dimension of system through the process of its real production in history, while process can be conceived not merely as a sequence of events in the narrative mode, but as the process of systematization, the construction and deconstruction of a cultural order. Lukács' originality lies in his attempt to conceive the priority of essence over appearance, of process over system, of history over culture, as a dialectical relation in a totality, without collapsing the second concept of each pair into the first, as in romantic and humanistic social theory.

Lukács' new social ontology is based on the idea of a collective activity that shapes the material of experience in function of universal forms in the very process of generating that material. There is a basis for this attempt in certain early texts of Marx, such as the "Theses on Feuerbach." In the *Manuscripts* Marx lays out the problem programmatically, saying, "It can be seen that the history of industry and industry as it objectively exists is an open book of human faculties, and a human psychology which can be sensuously apprehended."[7] But before Lukács, the only attempts to implement such a theoretical program are vague suggestions for an instrumentalist reduction of the forms of knowledge to practical needs, for example, Engels' hypothesis that geometry arose from the marking of boundaries when private property in land was introduced. For the first time in the history of Marxism, Lukács actually attempts to understand the being and the objectivity of social objects starting out from practice and not just from a pragmatic of belief.

We can advance further toward understanding this conception by comparing Lukács' view with that of Weber, whom he explicitly criticizes on methodological grounds. Weber assumes that social experience is worked up ("synthesized") by categories of the mind, a position obviously inspired by Kant. This methodology presupposes a sharp separation of the "facts," the immediate data of social experience, and their meaning for both participants and observers. As Weber puts it,

The transcendental presupposition of every *cultural science* lies not in our finding a certain culture or any "culture" in general to be *valuable* but rather in the fact that we are *cultural beings*, endowed with the capacity and the will to take a deliberate attitude towards the world and to lend it *significance*.[8]

For this neo-Kantian methodology, the meaning of social objects is constituted in a "deliberate attitude," that is to say in the theoretical standpoint of the observer. Social objects thus have no univocal inner meaning; rather, the subject is granted the power to "lend" them "significance" in a uniquely powerful glance. The interaction of subject and object envisaged here is located at the level of theory, as though culture itself were not constituted *practically* in its meaning as well as in its existence.

But what is true of the theoretical subject in its theoretical activity, Lukács insists, is all the more true of the individuals in their practical activity. Indeed, it is only because the individuals "practice" culture that it takes on a meaning for consciousness. Culture is not composed of what Lukács calls "fetishistic" facts to which a deliberate attitude might lend a meaning, as though conferring on them a dimension of which they were—in Kantian fashion—deprived "in themselves." Rather, culture is produced by practical activities which are fully as teleological as the thoughts of observers, activities which constantly structure and restructure social relations and lend them significance coterminously with bringing them into being. These activities are to be understood through the "*structural forms* which are the focal points of man's interaction with the environment at any given moment and which determine the objective nature of both his inner and his outer life."[9] Lukács thus arrives at an original position by translating the "transcendental presupposition" of the neo-Kantian view from theory into practice.

Pierre Bourdieu has expressed a similar point strikingly in a passage that contributes to understanding Lukács' approach.

The construction of the world of objects is clearly not the sovereign operation of consciousness which the neo-Kantian tradition con-

*

ceives of; the mental structures which construct the world of objects are constructed in the practice of a world of objects constructed according to the same structures. The mind born of the world of objects does not rise as a subjectivity confronting an objectivity: the objective universe is made up of objects which are the product of objectifying operations structured according to the very structures which the mind applies to it. The mind is a metaphor of the world of objects which is itself but an endless circle of mutually reflecting metaphors.[10]

What are the implications of this concept of culture for the idea of social scientific law? Both the laws of nature and those of society are ideal representations of their objects, formally identical with their essences. The object itself is self-evidently constructed in a process of abstraction from the raw materials of experience and observation. Lukács' distinction between natural scientific and social laws could be reformulated by reference to the different ontological status of these abstract models in the two domains. In sum, natural science assumes that its models are *approximations* to the real, whereas Lukács shows that the similar models of social science are also *moments* of the real.

The formal identity of law and object is a merely methodological and not an ontological feature of social science. Natural scientific laws *are* in some strong sense their objects; they have no *real relation* to these objects over and above this ideal one. On the contrary, the economic laws do have a real relation to their objects as well as an ideal-theoretic one. The mechanisms by which human beings become the bearers of these laws are open to explanation. These mechanisms are the cultural processes which are described in Marxist theory by the concept of "social reproduction."

This difference between natural and social scientific law is due to the fact that the object of Marxist theory is not a thing but a system of human practices, of regularies of behavior which "realize" or "manifest" the rules governing them as the law of their appearance, enacting these rules and reproducing the conditions for their reenactment. Thus human beings "obey" the laws which govern them in a very different manner from the things of nature. They may, indeed, cease to obey a given set of laws and begin to interact in fundamentally new ways, whereas no similar statement about the objects of natural scientific laws would be meaningful.

These observations suggest the need for a historical approach to the concept of economic law, like the approach Lukács takes in his theory of reification, rather than one derived from a general materialist ontology. It is not some universal principle such as the "lawful character of history" which explains why it is possible for Marxism to arrive at a conception of the capitalist economy as a system, an autonomous sphere governed by quantitatively precise laws. Rather, Marxism points to the existence of specific social processes, open to historical analysis and explanation, that tend unconsciously to constitute the capitalist economy as a sphere of law; it is this which makes it possible for the economy to be increasingly autonomized, for it consequently to take on the character of a domain of appearance with a lawful form, and thus for it to be abstracted as a special object of scientific study.

Explanation of the social relations through which the economy takes on a lawful form is possible, contrary to the case of the natural sciences. These relations do not appear in precise quantitative lawful forms, but they can still be integrated to the social totality as nonquantitative moments. Understanding these social relations in any given concrete instance requires a different method from that which Marx applies to the economy. The economy can be constructed as an ideal type at a high level of abstraction precisely because it has been autonomized to a considerable degree. These other moments of the totality cannot, however, be studied at the same level of abstraction. Or rather, more accurately, the analysis of these social relations requires not simply a level of abstraction less than that of economics, but the specification of a different type of object corresponding to the total social process, to all the concrete mechanisms by which social reproduction is assured, including the reproduction of the lawful course of economic development. The implications of these methodological innovations for revolutionary theory will be developed in what follows.

SYMBOLIC PRODUCTION

I would like to introduce the consideration of Lukács' theory of revolution by contrasting his position with that of Habermas, one of the most important contemporary social theorists to discuss the theory of culture at least partially in the light of Marxism. Unlike Lukács and Marx, Habermas sets out to explain society not on the basis of the economy, but in terms of an independently conceptualized communicative function. In Habermas the distinction between the instrumental domain of work and the cultural sphere of communicative interaction and meaning is sharply drawn. Habermas considers Marxism to be "positivistic" to the extent that it reduces the latter to the former.

The Marxist thesis of historical materialism most clearly exemplifies this positivistic reduction. As I have argued in the first chapter of this book, Habermas claims that there is a link, established in reflection, between the various types of rationality and very general transhistorical interests which they serve. Positivism arises from the reduction of the non-technical interests and their corresponding fields of rationality to the technical one. An adequate social theory would have to approach each interest and form of rationality on its own terms in order to bring them correctly into relation.

It is significant that Lukács himself is a distant influence on this theory, his own early Marxist work having shaped many aspects of the Frankfurt School's interpretation of Marxism, and through the latter if not directly, Habermas' views as well. Habermas' project, reformulated in the more traditional

Marxist language of Lukács, consists in saving the sphere of "consciousness" from its reductive assimilation to the mode of production. The Frankfurt School followed Lukács in making this a central methodological task. Habermas changes the terms of the problem by substituting concepts of anthropological generality for the historical concepts of Marxism.

On this basis some important advances have been made, including the opening of a line between Marxism and communication theory. However, from a Lukácsian perspective there are also corresponding losses. The split in human nature Habermas posits between its instrumental and communicative dimensions seems to restrict the critical import of the theory to the latter while neutralizing the former. As a result, Lukács' critique of reification as a cultural formation, affecting technology, economy and consciousness, is now abandoned for a much narrower critique of positivism as a mode of thought, an ideology. Similarly, the Lukácsian concept of practice, which bridged the gap between labor and culture, is abandoned for a differentiated concept of practice which separates technical and cultural activity. However, Habermas does remain closer to Marx than most of the new theories of culture with which he shares these assumptions because he recognizes that the economy has certain cultural functions under capitalism.

Nevertheless, Habermas brings out very clearly the common denominator of most recent non-Marxist theories of culture, the view that the level of the economy, of instrumental action, must be distinguished sharply from the cultural dimension of society, and that therefore, far from being determining, the economy draws its meaning from outside itself, from more fundamental processes than those of labor and production.[11] These theories today, like Weber's and sociological functionalism in an earlier period, have their relative justification in the reductionist excesses of the dominant Marxist formulations.

In addition, however, the new cultural theories draw strength from some of the most important historical phenomena of the twentieth century, and for that reason their challenge to Marxism goes very deep. We have learned from the socialist countries themselves just how narrow are the limits of the cultural changes that can be effected through a certain type of economic reform, however revolutionary the mode of its implementation. Indeed, some of the worst aspects of capitalist culture seem to have been reproduced rather than overthrown by the great revolutionary political and economic transformations of this century. What is more, the capitalist social structure has evolved since the days of Marx and Lukács; now the weight of its reproductive, legitimating and ideological institutions is proportionately much greater in the system. This too suggests a social basis for more clearly distinguishing the cultural from the economic and granting the former a larger measure of independent significance. To this extent, the new theories, with their sharp separation of culture from economics, resonate with important contemporary realities.

It has been suggested, notably by Habermas and following him by Marshall Sahlins, that Marx himself failed to make this clear separation because he tended to see culture as rooted in human nature. If in fact Marx's thought was haunted by naturalistic and utilitarian assumptions of the sort to which these critics refer, then this would indeed explain why he took it for granted that the economy was determining for all of social life. Sahlins argues that once we have achieved a better understanding of the cultural relativity of the economy, then the privilege of production as a principle of social explanation vanishes *ipso facto*.

The point is that material effectiveness, practicality, does not exist in any absolute sense, but only in the measure and form projected by a cultural order. Selecting its material means and ends from among all possible ones, as well as the relations under which they are combined, it is society which sets the productive intentions and intensities, in a manner and measure appropriate to the entire structural system. There remains, as *logic*, only the meaningful system of culture. Historical materialism installs one such cultural logic as the definition of everyone's material necessity.[12]

For all its merits as a critique of reductionist tendencies in Marx and Marxism, this passage raises other problems that are typical of the new theories of culture. Sahlins posits "society" as the subject of the new determining social instance, which is "culture," in order to put production in its proper place as one sub-system among many. The argument would seem to rest on a fallacy of misplaced concreteness, "society" itself being an abstract theoretical construction and not a real subject. Unless we are to return to a theory of culture like that of Hegel, in which abstract "*Gestalten*" are treated as the foundation of cultural systems, we must find culture's source in concrete dimensions of the social system, real subjects and objects such as groups, classes, institutions, and so on. Only on these terms can one hope to explain the dimension of conflict and change, as well as the very relative unity exhibited by social systems.[13]

Sahlins himself would seem to agree with this for, at a later point in his discussion, he qualifies his argument, suggesting further that while production is not the source of culture in all societies, it does play such a role under capitalism. He writes, in fact, that "In bourgeois society, material production is the dominant locus of symbolic production."[14] Thus in this case, at any rate, not society in general but production is determining in something like the Marxist sense. Is this a return to the reductionist model? I think not, for Sahlins does not reduce the superstructures to economic interests or to mere instruments of class struggle, but rather points to the predominant role of production in instituting the logic of a specifically capitalist culture. The determining role is thus assigned to the economy in its symbolic significance and not in its natural-utilitarian function. This formulation suggests the possibility of bridging the gap between economics and culture without reducing the one to the other.

As I have interpreted it, Lukács' theory of reification bridges the same gap in a generally similar manner. Lukács' theory, like Sahlins', is based on the double character of the capitalist economy, as means of life and form of life, utilitarian instrumentality and foundation of a cultural system. For Lukács, the system of economic categories is the paradigmatic order in which formal rationality emerges from social practice to become the general cultural form of society as a whole. The theory of reification thus attempts to explain how the mode of production becomes the bearer of a way of life, how the cultural pattern of capitalism is derived from its economic system. For Lukács too, then, material production gives rise to the production of meaning, at least in capitalist society.

Is this still a Marxist position, rooted in Marx's own self-understanding? I think it can be shown that this is at least *one* possible Marxist position, one way in which Marx understood his own theory programmatically, although it is true that Marx himself never really worked out the implications of this program. There are a number of passages in his work which authorize this interpretation, the most important of which is in *The German Ideology*. There Marx writes that:

This mode of production must not be considered simply as being the reproduction of the physical existence of the individuals. Rather, it is a definite form of activity of these individuals, a definite form of expressing their life, a definite *mode of life* on their part. As individuals express their life, so they are. . . . What they are therefore coincides with their production, both with *what* they produce and with *how* they produce.[15]

Here Marx clearly expresses that same double character of the economy found in Lukács' theory of reification. As Marx puts it once again in another context, "Production thus produces not only an object for the subject, but also a subject for the object."[16]

CULTURE AND REVOLUTION

I argue above that traditional interpretations of the Marxist thesis of historical materialism are reductionist and rigidly determinist. The previous section has indicated a way of reconstructing the thesis to avoid reductionism; the goal of this section is to show how determinism can also be avoided and the thesis of historical materialism reconciled with the Marxist theory of socialist revolution. This is by no means an easy task, and the substitution of a cultural for a reductionist interpretation of the thesis appears to make it more rather than less difficult. Most recent theorists of culture—e.g. Winch, or Lévi-Strauss—emphasize the determining role of culture as the prior condition for the beliefs and actions it shapes. Culture is conserved and reproduced by the performances it inspires, not subverted and transformed. To culture's action on society there seems to correspond no equal and opposite reaction of society on culture. Thus we may well ask whether a cultural Marxism is not just another, perhaps more sophisticated version of determinism. How, after all, can we imagine individuals standing within a given culture overreaching it and transforming it in line with their conscious intentions? How can the actors of history produce a system corresponding to their collective will and real potentialities, gaining thereby control of the very logic of the culture to which they belong?

These questions can be answered by reference to Lukács' idea that the immediate reified form of objectivity arising from the capitalist economy itself plays the chief role in the reproduction of the cultural structures governing the social system. This distinguishes capitalist society from all precapitalist social systems, in which reproduction is secured through cultural mechanisms less directly rooted in the economy. In these other systems, therefore, class struggle is not functionally inserted in a position from which it can threaten the overall survival of the mode of production, even if it can still threaten particular institutions, laws and rulers. Under capitalism, on the contrary, class struggle has devastating cultural implications because it directly affects the most basic cultural foundations of the society. The de-reifying class consciousness of the proletariat, arising in the context of economic struggles, can have the same sort of general cultural impact as reification itself. This is why Lukács says that "The process of the revolution is—on a historical scale— synonymous with the process of development of proletarian class consciousness."[17]

This interpretation of Marxism unites the thesis of historical materialism and the theory of socialist revolution as two sides of the same coin. It is no longer necessary to make *ad hoc* claims to defend the theory, for example, explaining that the normal dominance of base over superstructure may be exceptionally reversed in the revolution. The revolution is no longer conceived here as a superstructural reaction on the base, nor is the base conceived in narrow economic terms. Base has been implicitly redefined as the instance founding for the cultural system and superstructure as what is derivative from the the base. In this way, Lukács can freely admit that the economy may not have been determining in precapitalist societies, while also claiming that the revolution is no merely political intervention into the normal course of the economy but rather activity at the base itself. It will be recalled that the early Marx also made some such claim in distinguishing a merely political from a social revolution.

This redefinition of the concepts of base and superstructure is suggested by Lukács' discussion of violence in his essay on "The Changing Function of Historical Materialism." Still more significant is a short passage in which he explains why Marxist economic theory is primarily focussed on the relation of capital to labor. In this passage Lukács presents an argument which might equally be generalized to explain the relation of base to superstructure.

The difference between "fact" and tendency has been brought out on innumerable occasions by Marx and placed in the foreground of his studies. After all, the basic thought underlying his *magnum opus*, the retranslation of economic objects from things back into processes, in the changing relations between men, rests on just this idea. But from this it follows further that the question of theoretical priority, the location within the system (i.e. whether original or derivative) of the particular forms of the economic structure of society depends on their distance from this retranslation.[18]

This approach to the Marxist concept of revolution makes it possible to reformulate the antinomy of system and process as a problem to which a solution might actually be found. This problem concerns the means of "retranslating" cultural objects "from things back into processes." From the beginning, Marxism implied a solution to this problem which Lukács' theory finally elucidates. Traditional Marxism, it is true, lacked the modern concept of culture, but it did discuss many of the objects to which that concept refers, for example, ideology and human "nature" in its socially determined aspect. Traditional Marxism recognized, furthermore, that socialism was in one significant dimension a process of cultural change. It argued, according to the thesis of historical materialism, that such cultural change could be achieved indirectly, by altering the economic basis of the superstructures. The economy, in turn, was to come under social control through a political process. Here we have the structure of classical Marxist practice: politics plays a pivotal role not because socialism is primarily a political project but because political action is the Archimedeian point for those larger economic and cultural changes in which socialism actually consists.

In spite of the danger of crude economism which threatens this approach to social transformation, it contains a deep insight and represents an enormous advance over earlier theories of social change, for example, those of Rousseau or Hegel. Marx and his successors finally understood that culture, as the most durable and intractable object of the process of social transformation, must be approached through complex mediations to be changed at all. This conception of Marxist practice is well described by Gramsci, who always knew better than anyone else how to recover the insights of Marxism, banalized and vulgarized by the socialist movement itself.

Can there be a cultural reform and an uplifting of the civilisation of the depressed strata of society without there first being an economic reform and a change in their social position and place in the economic world? Intellectual and moral reform must be tied to a programme of economic reform; moreover, the programme of economic reform is precisely the concrete way in which every intellectual and moral reform is presented.[19]

Can this theory of revolutionary social change answer the objections of the new theories of culture discussed above? I think it can at least allay the fear of reductionism and accomodate some of the methodological innovations of recent cultural theory. In addition, it may have a certain value in the discussion of the political experience of the 1960s, which forms the background to the more politically conscious formulations of the new theories. These formulations imply a politics of culture focussed on the direct transformation of communication systems and character structure, at first on the left itself and then in the larger society. To a certain extent the 1960s saw actual experiments with such innovative political methods.

This is not the place to attempt an evaluation of those experiments; they contributed to breaking the reified limits of traditional Stalinist and social democratic practice, but they also encountered certain limits of their own. The attempt to make a new type of revolution without class struggle proved as unsuccessful as the parallel attempt to rekindle revolutionary class struggle without new ideas. The inability of the organizers to find a link between "moral reform" and "economic program" condemned them all too often to moralism or economism. Yet it is true that under the new conditions of advanced capitalism, the direct practice of cultural change revealed itself to be far more effective than anyone would have suspected from reading the classics of Marxism. In a surprising number of areas, the cultural system proved vulnerable to de-reification, to a dissolution into process, as Lukács would call it. Yet the economy still seems to have set the limits of change and, with the coming of the great economic slowdown of the 1970s, to have arrested it.

Lukács' argument shows that in Communist countries traditional Marxism scarcely began to exhaust the cultural potential of the economic transformations it set in motion. Slavish obedience to the laws of economic modernization confirmed reification rather than taking it as the premise of a dialectical transcendence. The movements of the 1960s brought about mass awareness of the limits of traditional strategies. Yet the 1960s did not succeed in getting beyond the old world of political economy into a new one of purely cultural concerns. In the next section, I will consider how Lukács' reinterpretation of historical materialism can contribute to the elaboration of a much-needed synthesis.

THE SOCIAL CONTROL OF CULTURE

What kind of politics is implied by the Lukácsian theory? In the early 1920s, Lukács himself conjoined his theory to the practice of the Third International; when, shortly thereafter he was obliged to choose between his theory and this practice, he opted for the latter, abandoning his early Marxism. As we have seen, Lukács' most recent critics have argued that his theory was after all fully compatible with the practice of Stalinism. Both Lukács and the Stalinists of his day would have been surprised to learn this. Lukács himself, in any case, was never able to convince anyone of this compatibility when it really counted to do so.

I think there is a good reason for his failure. The Stalinists made no mistake in demanding that Lukács abandon his theory as the price for participating in the movement they controlled. They perceived quite accurately that he was arguing for what they considered an "idealistic" politics emphasizing cultural action at the expense of the administrative and paramilitary practices privileged by the Third International.

Indeed, Lukács himself says as much in a provocative passage of *History and Class Consciousness* which did not go unnoticed at the time.

The coercive measures taken by society in individual cases are often hard and brutally materialistic, but the *strength of every society is in the last resort a spiritual strength.* And from this we can only be liberated by knowledge. This knowledge cannot be of the abstract kind that remains in one's head—many "socialists" have possessed that sort of knowledge. It must be knowledge that has become flesh and blood; to use Marx's phrase, it must be "practical critical activity."[20]

What Lukács calls for is thus a politics of cultural change that would challenge capitalist society at its "spiritual" roots, that is to say, in its most basic definition of reality, in its paradigm of rationality, in its founding practices.

This Lukácsian conception of politics went ignored in his day. But recently, as Stalinist political parties lose control of significant portions of the left and new social movements emerge, cultural politics has begun to appear as a practical force. The experience of the new left focussed attention on culture to an unprecedented degree and stimulated new attempts to theorize politics in cultural terms, independent of Lukács no doubt, but converging in interesting ways with his original formulation of the problems.

New theoretical approaches to understanding the relation of culture and politics are especially influential today in France, perhaps because of the early contribution of Sartre and his school to elaborating a non-Stalinist radical theory.[21] Most recently, Jean Baudrillard and Pierre Bourdieu have both, in very different ways, formulated striking and original theories of cultural action.[22] I would like to examine Bourdieu's formulation briefly for the light it can shed on Lukács' original attempt to articulate a politics of culture.

Bourdieu suggests that the decisive reproductive mechanism of society is control over the definition of reality, the ability to draw the boundaries between what is generally understood to be permanent and real, and what is subject, on the contrary, to debate and change. What Bourdieu calls the "doxic" relation to reality is that relation in which social determinations are simply taken for granted as uncontestable realities. The doxic relation to reality is the foundation of practices that reproduce precisely that relation, and with it the corresponding reality. The most familiar examples are such well known phenomena as "labeling," in which individuals treated in function of the label they have been assigned learn to produce the behavior that corresponds to their label, thereby justifying and reproducing the initial definition under which they labor. Bourdieu generalizes this problematic to make of it a fundamental mediation in the dialectic of social practice and reality. From this standpoint he proposes a cultural interpretation of class politics, remarkably similar to that of Lukács.

In class societies, in which the definition of the social world is at stake in overt or latent class struggle, the drawing of the line between the field of opinion, of that which is explicitly questioned, and the field of *doxa*, of that which is beyond question and which each agent tacitly accords by the mere fact of acting in accord with social convention, is itself a fundamental objective at stake in that form of class struggle which is the struggle for the imposition of the dominant system of classification. . . . It is only when the domi-

nated have the material and symbolic means of rejecting the definition of the real that is imposed on them through logical structures
reproducing the social structures, . . . i.e. when social classifications
become the object and instrument of class struggle, that the arbitrary principles of the prevailing classification can appear as
such. . .[23]

How close this analysis is to that of Lukács can be shown by
recalling the structure of the latter's theory of reification.
Bourdieu's *"doxa"* is similar to what Lukács calls a "form of
objectivity," that is to say, a schema of the practical synthesis
of the real. The *"doxa"* appears as a fact or a law of social life to
those who stand under it and who unconsciously reproduce it
through their action. So too, in Lukács the form of objectivity
is an "appearance," the efficacy of which lies precisely in the
fact that it is confounded with reality, and on that basis
perceived as prior to and founding for the practices which
unconsciously produce it. In Lukács' view class struggle is the
practice of de-reifying capitalist social reality by apprehending
this appearance as such, in practice and in thought. Just so in
Bourdieu does class struggle proceed by challenging socially
accepted significations. In both cases, it thus consists in
raising the unconscious horizon of practice to consciousness
where it can be criticized and transformed.

This unique conception of class struggle helps to understand Lukács' identification of the proletariat with the identical subject-object of history, discussed at some length above.
It will be recalled that Lukács employed this concept to fulfill
the demand of reason for a subject of practice which is also an
object, a subject which creates itself through its own action, a
subject which, furthermore, acts on both form and content
and which encounters neither eternal laws nor a Kantian thing
in itself at the horizon of its practice. The proletariat is this
subject because it is capable in principle of acting on its own
social definition and that of social objects generally, thereby
overcoming the contemplative standpoint of reification and,
in Lukács' phrase, "penetrating" its objects.

This action directed at the function and meaning of objects, this "practical-critical activity" transcends the usual dichotomy between theory and practice. It is a specifically *cultural practice*, a knowledge that has "become flesh and blood," transforming its objects in the act of knowing them and knowing them through submitting them to new forms of practical manipulation hitherto forbidden by their accepted social signification. Proletarian class consciousness is thus "already practical. That is to say, this knowledge brings about an objective structural change in the object of knowledge."[24]

This is true in the first instance of the proletariat itself. The class conscious proletariat is more and other than the proletariat bound by its official social definition. This appears in the ability of the class to suspend the operation of the reified laws of the market that divide it, to unify around conscious common goals, and to break down the compartmentalizations of reified society, exposing its partial sectors to radical transformation by shifting their social signification for the lives they fragment and constrain. A new kind of social practice appears in these de-reifying operations, a practice which is conscious in its very principle and which transforms reality precisely in the act of becoming conscious. This practice is thus the very "intellectual intuition" with a finite subject which the metatheory of philosophy demands as a foundation for its dialectical paradigm of rationality.

Lukács' argument might be usefully reformulated in somewhat less abstract terms to conclude this discussion. In sum, the politics of *History and Class Consciousness* consists in the demand for the social control of culture, for conscious action to bring the cultural structures governing human life under human control. The mediation of capitalism's reified form of objectivity in which the class conscious proletariat engages daily is an example of such social control of culture. This process of mediation is itself a new cultural formation in emergence, a culture which is integrally conscious of its own historical premises, and which no longer, therefore, encounters these premises as a horizon, an unconsciousness under-girding its every conscious act.

A social practice which is in essence the practice of trans-forming culture generates a new type of cultural world. In his earliest conception of socialism, Marx explained it as human-ity reclaiming its *"forces propres,"* the common powers gen-erated by its alienated cooperation in class society. Lukács' cultural Marxism radicalizes this definition to include the dimension of culture itself as an alienated objectivity which humankind must bring under its conscious and free dominion. For Lukács the "social construction of reality" is thus not something that happens only unconsciously in the minds of individuals; it is the real creation of a social world by subjects who are themselves its products. When this creative activity finally becomes conscious, it will be possible for human beings to make a servant of culture instead of themselves serving an alienated cultural order that dehumanizes and destroys its creators.

7

History and Nature

THE ANTINOMY OF HISTORY AND NATURE

The intellectual environment in which *History and Class Consciousness* was written was hostile to naturalism and favored the idea of an independent *Geisteswissenschaft* based on methods different from those of the natural sciences. Lukács himself can fairly be described as a product of this environment, its representative on the left, defending the validity of *Geist* against theoretical reification by vulgar Marxism. His philosophy of praxis is thus very different from Marx's, in that it rejects the "naturalization of man" for an insistent emphasis on the originality and autonomy of the human phenomenon.

Nevertheless, Lukács' doctrine is not to be confounded with that of Dilthey or Heidegger, if only because Lukács is a much less consistent historicist than are they. While the logic of his position seems to demand that he give history a privileged place at the expense of the traditional Marxist faith in the natural sciences, in practice he never goes so far. There result contradictions in his philosophy of praxis on which his critics have focussed ever since the first appearance of *History and Class Consciousness*. This chapter will consider some of the implications of these problems for Lukács' early Marxism, and once again relate his position to that of the young Marx who, in contrast with Lukács, affirmed the unity of history and nature. In conclusion I will sketch a synthesis of ideas drawn from both Lukács and Marx which resolves certain problems in the philosophy of praxis.

Lukács' early philosophy of praxis has been criticized most often for its inability to give a consistent account of the concept of nature and the truth value of the natural sciences. I will review here three types of arguments in support of this criticism, arguments against Lukács' supposed idealism, the false identification of objectification and alienation in his concept of reification, and the unacceptable dualism of history and nature that haunts his theory. I will argue that the first two criticisms are wrong, but that they do point to serious and unresolved problems discussed under the last heading.

Deborin wrote the major early critique of *History and Class Consciousness*, accusing it of idealism from a Leninist perspective. His approach continues to be typical of "orthodox" criticism of Lukács.[1] Deborin begins by accusing Lukács of setting Engels against Marx in order to oppose the former's materialistic dialectic with his own idealistic dialectic, falsely imputed to the latter. Deborin is especially troubled by Lukács' rejection of Engels' dialectics of nature, a position which is in fact central to all of Lukács' difficulties, although not for the reasons Deborin suggests. In the first essay of *History and Class Consciousness*, Lukács does actually reject the application of dialectics to nature, and offers an interpretation of historical dialectics which he distinguishes rather sharply from that of Engels. Deborin calls this "a new conception of dialectical method, . . . a conception which contradicts that of Marxism. . . ."[2]

Deborin goes on to argue that Lukács is an idealist who "sees in the category of *knowledge*, in a certain sense, the substance or truth of reality."[3] In Lukács' dialectic, practice and historical reality are supposedly *aufgehoben* in the knowledge of a knowing subject. Hence, "According to

Lukács 'praxis' is *overcome* only through theory, only through knowledge, and not through the self-development of reality, of which knowledge is simply a part."[4] Deborin interprets the Lukácsian theory of subject-object identity as though it were a traditional idealist position, completely overlooking Lukács' meta-theoretical revision of the subject-object concept. "The object," Deborin declares, "is swallowed by the subject."[5] Clearly then, since Lukács does not intend for humanity to swallow the whole of nature, the natural world must be excluded from this subject-object identity, and forthwith from the dialectic itself.

Deborin concludes by contrasting Lukács' theory with that of orthodox Marxism. For Lukács the identical subject-object is the conscious proletariat, as knowing subject, oppressed object, and driving force of historical development. Deborin objects to this formulation. Knowledge, he affirms, is never identical with its objects but tends asymptotically toward an accurate picturing of them. The true unity of subject and object is to be found in the domain of labor practice, not in revolutionary class consciousness. He argues that the object with which Marxism is specifically concerned is nature, which is the substratum of human life, the subject is labor, and their unity (not identity) is the process of production.

Like many later Lukács critics, Deborin misses the point because he does not grasp the originality of Lukács' concept of class consciousness. In Lukács' sense of the term, "consciousness" is not identifiable with a "knowledge" of the sort to which Deborin refers. I have argued this matter at length above. Merleau-Ponty would seem to be the first to clarify the distinction between consciousness and knowledge in Lukács. His interpretation, which I take to be the correct one, holds that, "In the proletariat, class consciousness is not a state of mind or a knowledge, nor yet is it a theoretical construction, because it is a praxis, that is to say less than a subject and more than an object . . ."[6] It is, on these terms, absurd to argue that for Lukács consciousness "transcends" practice, or that the subject "swallows" the object. The goal of Lukács'

204 Lukács, Marx and the Sources of Critical Theory

dialectic is to overcome the opposition of theory and practice, subject and object in a region of historical reality where they stand in essential and necessary relation. But by defining the Lukácsian subject as a subject of thought, of knowledge, Deborin forces Lukács' theory back into a traditional idealistic framework which it is designed precisely to transcend.

In spite of these errors, Deborin's critique does strike tangentially at some of the real problems. It is true that Lukács' fundamental difficulty is with nature. His dialectic is a dialectic of consciousness—better, of cultural practice—different in important respects from Marx's own dialectic of the labor process. Furthermore, Lukács does not have a fully coherent theory of either nature or natural science. These things Deborin notes, without succeeding in developing a useful account of them.

In his new foreword of 1967, Lukács himself discusses these problems, and suggests another line of criticism which is surely unique as an example of philosophical self-misunderstanding. Lukács describes how the reading of Marx's 1844 *Manuscripts* finally convinced him of the ontological priority of objectivity and the universality of objectification; therewith, says the older Lukács, his early Marxist work became completely "foreign" to him.[7] Many other critics have similarly charged the early Lukács with confounding, as did Hegel, objectification with alienation in the concept of reification.[8] This would indeed be a powerful critique, if it were true. But does Lukács actually use the term "reification" to refer to being in general; does he identify in it "alienation" and "objectification"; does he, in sum, believe the historical transcendence of reification to be the *Aufhebung* of objectivity in general, as does Hegel?

The stumbling block to such an interpretation remains Lukács' refusal to apply the dialectic to nature which so troubled Deborin from an orthodox standpoint. For this refusal surely indicates that nature forms a sphere of objectivity which is not transcended in revolution, and which does not form a mere moment in the dialectic, as it does in Hegel. Still, there are occasional passages in *History and Class Conscious-ness* which seem to point in the opposite direction. Some-times the critique of reification seems to extend to the reified form of objectivity of nature, and there are passages which look like a critique of natural science. Some critics have lept at the bait and argued, with Alfred Schmidt, that nature in Lukács is "totally dissolved into the historical processes of its appropriation in respect of form, content, extent and objec-tivity."[9]

For some reason, no one has gone on to complete the critique of Lukács implicit in these assertions. For, if Lukács really believed that the revolution would overcome all objec-tive being in overcoming reification, his theory would be both rigorously consistent and obviously absurd. Then nature would be "posited" by the identical subject-object of history, and in overcoming social reification the proletariat would transform nature itself. The result would be, as Lukács him-self suggests in his new foreword, rather more Fichtean than Hegelian, but clearly idealistic.[10] Without elaborating further on the views of particular critics, I would like to construct a brief sketch of a consistent version of this Fichtean construc-tion of Lukács' theory. It rests on the following propositions, which outline an ontology and epistemology in conformity with the critics' image of Lukács, if not with Lukács' actual views.

1. Nature is a purely social category, and the natural world therefore has no independence of humanity and the human understanding of it.

2. Reification is a capitalist category, in terms of which the whole of being, including nature, is "posited" by capitalist society.

3. Proletarian revolution suppresses the reified objectivity of nature in suppressing capitalism.

4. Since the existing natural sciences are reified, and therefore conditioned by capitalist society both in their

genesis and their validity, proletarian revolution also suppresses these sciences in suppressing capitalism.

5. In sum, the identical subject-object of history is also the identical subject-object of nature.

This image of Lukács' theory is immensely overdrawn, but it has the virtue of rendering one commonplace interpretation of it rigorously consistent. If the critics are correct in attributing some such views to Lukács, then they are also right to tax him with idealism: in this form his theory holds that the entire existing world is a product of human activity. All that would distinguish Lukács' "Marxism" from other forms of idealism would be his insistence that this constituting activity is social in character.

But does this construct, which various critics have to one degree or another identified with Lukács' position, really concern theses sustained in *History and Class Consciousness?* Or even distant implications of the book? The careful reader of Lukács discovers no significant support for such an interpretation, while there are numerous positive statements to the contrary. This is, in fact, the "myth" of Lukács' famous book, which hovers over it as an atmosphere and prejudices the very reading of its text. It might have been appropriate had Lukács actually argued such a position, in terms of filling a niche in the gamut of radical post-Marxist philosophy; but in fact, he did not.

Which is Lukács' concept of nature? Let us begin with the passage usually cited in support of the interpretation sketched above. It is true that Lukács does say, in an oft-quoted phrase, that "Nature is a social category." But he proceeds immediately in the following sentence to qualify this statement. The entire passage reads:

Nature is a social category. That is to say [*D.h.*], *what passes for nature* [*als Natur gilt*] at a determinate stage in social evolution, the constitution of the relation between *this* [*dieser*] nature and man and the form in which the confrontation of man and nature takes place, in short, what nature *signifies* [*bedeuten*] in its form and its content, its range and its objectivity, are all socially conditioned.[11]

The opening sentence of this passage is often quoted to show that Lukács believed nature in itself, without qualification, to be a social product. But the second sentence is quite careful to discuss not nature as such, but only "what passes for nature." And surely Lukács intends us to understand this qualification, since he introduces the second sentence with "that is to say," as equivalent to but more precise than the preceding one.[12]

Already the first two theses of the construct have fallen, for now nature in itself, if not the knowledge of it, is independent of man and cannot possibly be "posited" by capitalism. And then, of course, the third thesis is also untenable, for under these conditions nature cannot be suppressed and transformed by proletarian revolution, not can it appear as a social product. Lukács says as much himself, clearly and without equivocation. Speaking of the process in which the proletariat suppresses reification, he remarks that "there can be no single act that will eliminate reification in all its forms at one blow; a whole host of objects seem to remain more or less unaffected by the process. This is true in the first instance of nature."[13] The use of the word "seem" in this passage does not introduce an antithesis in which it would be shown that the reification of nature is transcended somehow despite appearances; on the contrary, it introduces a discussion of the dialectics of nature as a possible articulation of Marxist dialectics, somewhat along the lines suggested by Engels.

Nevertheless, Lukács continues to affirm, if not exactly the fourth thesis, something quite similar. He says, "it cannot be our task to investigate the question of the priority or the historical and causal order of succession between the 'laws of nature' and capitalism. (The author of these lines has, however, no wish to conceal his view that the development of capitalist economics takes precedence.)"[14] In addition, after distinguishing the objective dialectic of nature from the dialectic of subject and object in history, Lukács notes that "the growth of *knowledge* about nature is a social phenomenon and therefore to be included in the second dialectical type."[15] Thus the fate of the natural sciences and that of capitalism would still seem to be intimately intertwined.

These statements, combined with the critique of reification, have been used by Colletti and others to build an image of an irrationalist, "Bergsonian" Lukács.[16] Yet Lukács himself rejects irrationalism as an immediate reflex of reification. "The value of formal knowledge in the face of 'living life' may be questioned (see irrationalist philosophies from Hamann to Bergson)," but, Lukács writes, reification is not thereby transcended: "Whether this gives rise to ecstasy, resignation or despair, whether we search for a path leading to 'life' via irrational mystical experience, this will do absolutely nothing to modify the situation as it is in fact."[17] Another significant passage makes clear Lukács' disagreement with the irrationalist attack on the natural sciences. After a lengthy and apparently "Bergsonian" critique of the application of natural scientific method to society, a critique that seems at points to cast doubt on the validity of science in general, Lukács states: "When the epistemological ideal of the natural sciences is applied to nature it simply furthers the progress of science. But when it is applied to society it turns out to be an ideological weapon of the bourgeoisie."[18]

Lukács' precise attitude toward the fourth thesis can now be summarized. He does believe the rise of capitalism to have been a condition for the growth of natural scientific knowledge, but he nowhere proposes that these sciences are therefore false, that proletarian revolution will abolish them or transcend the reified form of objectivity of nature. The validity of the natural sciences and of the reified concept of nature on which they are based seems to be independent of the conditions of their creation. Here Lukács is in agreement with Marx and Engels, both of whom attribute the emergence of modern science to the capitalist revolution in production, while affirming also the independent validity of that science.

The interpretation of Lukács' philosophy as a form of idealism is summed up in the final thesis, according to which the identical subject-object of history is also the identical subject-object of nature. This thesis Lukács explicitly rejects early in *History and Class Consciousness*. In a famous note he writes:

It is of the first importance to realize that the method is limited here to the realms of history and society. The misunderstandings that arise from Engels' account of dialectics can in the main be put down to the fact that Engels—following Hegel's mistaken lead—extended the method to apply also to nature. However, the crucial determinants of dialectics—the interaction of subject and object, the unity of theory and practice, the historical changes in the reality underlying the categories as the root cause of changes in thought, etc.,—are absent from our knowledge of nature.[19]

Even when, later in his book, Lukács reverses his position on the dialectics of nature, he continues explicitly to distinguish dialectics in that domain from historical dialectics by the absence of subject-object interaction.[20]

After examining all these passages in detail, one is astonished to discover that nothing remains of the image of Lukács as a subjective idealist at the level of the collective "I" of the proletariat, Lukács the Fichtean, the irrationalist, the Bergsonian, the antiscientific cryptoexistentialist *avant la lettre*, an image which begins with Deborin in 1924 and continues to contemporaries such as Colletti. In fact the Lukács of *History and Class Consciousness* has a quite banal respect for the sciences of nature. He nowhere denies the independence of nature nor the validity of the sciences which study it. Nor, *pace* Colletti, is his denunciation of modern technology so very different from Marx's that it would justify the label of "romantic" it has acquired in the course of numerous polemics.

Some critics have understood this and noticed the dualism which it introduces into Lukács' theory. There is in fact a clear methodological split between history and nature in the theory, and it is only this which saves Lukács from the type of attack discussed at length above. Most of those who recognize this split argue, I think correctly, that it gives rise to serious problems for Lukács' philosophy of praxis. However, it is not uncommon for critics of Lukács' dualism to fail to notice that it renders the identification of his concept of reification with Hegel's concept of alienation quite futile. For, if nature is reified and undialectical in essence, as Lukács seems to assert, and if it is not transcended in the revolution, then clearly Lukács' philosophy is not hostile to objectivity *per se*, and to that degree it is quite different from Hegel's. These critics produce an empirically accurate image of the various strands of Lukács' thought, but a theoretically inconsistent critique of them. Poor Lukács is charged with the contradictory vices of identifying what should be separated (alienation and objectification) and separating what should be identified (nature and history).[21] The resulting critique is hardly more satisfactory than the positions surveyed above.

This self-contradictory critique of Lukács is nevertheless useful because it points to the real contradiction in his thought. It may well be asked whether Lukács' philosophy of praxis can survive the acceptance of the general validity of the sciences of nature and the independence of their objects. The ambition of this theory is to demonstrate that "the core of being [is] social becoming."[22] Lukács' theory can only achieve consistency if he, as classical German philosophy would have it, can fulfill the "exigency of understanding . . . every givenness as a product of this identical subject-object, every duality as a special case derived from this original unity."[23] How can this be accomplished if nature and the knowledge of it remain as a reified residue? How can reason be founded on the identity of subject and object in history when such identity cannot be achieved in the sciences of nature? To the extent that nature is conceived as an irreducible and unhistorical reality in a dualistic worldview, the whole theoretical superstructure collapses. It would seem that Lukács is saved from his critics only to fall into self-contradiction.

The ambition of identity philosophy from Descartes to Hegel is to validate the power of reason by showing that the laws of thought and those of things are one in principle. Whether this identity is guaranteed by God, demonstrated in phenomenology, or, as in Lukács, established by historical practice, identity in some form is required by a "heroic" rationalism that accepts no boundaries. This, I believe, is Lukács' goal: to overcome every barrier to the development of reason, not only in theory as for his predecessors, but also in practice. But the dualism of history and nature he admits is incompatible with this goal.

At the end of the discussion of Lukács' meta-theory of philosophy, I summarized the theoretical exigencies which the identical subject-object of socialist revolution is supposed finally to satisfy: the principle of practice; history as reality; dialectical method. The identical subject-object is supposed to satisfy the demand of the principle of practice that the action of the subject "penetrate" the object; the demand that history be reality in the specific sense that all subject-objects are explained through their historical insertion; and the demand for dialectical method, insofar as subject-object identity in history is understood not as immediate but as mediated in an interaction of theory and practice, subjectivity and its objectifications.

These demands are not, however, compatible with Lukács' concept of nature. The "positing" of nature by society, its reduction to an object of social practice, is unthinkable except in the context of a speculative philosophy of nature such as Lukács rightly rejects. Yet if there is something in nature which is not produced in history, then history is not the fundamental ontological domain from which all others are derived. What is more, unless the identity of subject and object in nature can somehow be established, its identity in history appears as a purely contingent feature of the universe.

Lukács stops short before having founded reason in history; nature appears once again as the sphere of true being, as in the naturalistic philosophies he rejects. Another type of rationality with its own objectivity arises alongside history, and there subject and object can never be united. Reason remains permanently caught in the antinomies of reified thought in relation to nature, which persists as an impenetrable thing in itself. The Kantian construction of rationality now returns in full force, bringing in its train all the untranscended antinomies Lukács set out to resolve. Unless some solution can be found, Lukács' philosophy of praxis will collapse into a far more limited methodological preliminary to historical research. It could then no longer pretend to solve problems of ontology, but only certain epistemological problems relating to historical knowledge. Reason would not be implicated in revolution, only social theory. This is in fact the position adopted by Lucien Goldmann, Lukács' most important follower.[24]

MARX'S CONCEPT OF NATURE

In 1844 Marx encountered somewhat similar problems in his philosophy of praxis, which he attempted to resolve with the idea of a dialectic of the natural subject and object of labor. (Of course the relevant texts were unavailable to Lukács in the early 1920s.) Marx too sought to transcend philosophy and to develop a new concept of reason based on the practical identity of subject and object, just as did Lukács in a later period. However, Marx starts out not from historical practice as the proximate domain of identity but from the labor process, and he is therefore able to grasp the natural subject and object in a dialectical interaction.

Alfred Schmidt summarizes Marx's conception as follows:

The hidden nature speculation in Marx [holds that] the different economic formations of society which have succeeded each other historically have been so many modes of nature's self-mediation. Sundered into two parts, man and material to be worked on, nature is always present to itself in this division. Nature attains self-consciousness in men, and amalgamates with itself by virtue of their theoretical-practical activity. Human participation in something alien and external to them appears at first to be something equally alien and external to nature; but in fact it proves to be a "natural condition of human existence," which is itself a part of nature, and it therefore constitutes nature's self-movement. Only in this way can we speak meaningfully of a "dialectic of nature."[25]

This description makes clear the difference between Marx's materialism and all previous forms of materialism, which lies in Marx's belief that human consciousness is a moment in nature's self-development and not an external spectator on the latter.

Marx's theory suggests a solution to some of the problems in Lukács discussed above. Specifically, Marx's way of conceiving the relation of man to nature promises to overcome the split between history and nature which mars Lukács' theory. However, the Marxian solution is not without very serious problems of its own. Throughout the *Manuscripts* one senses that there is something very wrong with Marx's concept of subject-object identity. In the following passage, to cite but one example among many, Marx seems to hover between metaphor and absurdity:

It is only when objective reality everywhere becomes for man in society the reality of human faculties, human reality, and the reality of his own faculties that all *objects* become for him the *objectification of himself*. The objects then confirm and realize his individuality, they are *his own* objects, i.e. man himself becomes the object.[26]

Reading such passages, one wonders if Marx can really

mean it. Under what conditions can "man himself become *the* object?" Will not the realm of independent nature always transcend society, hence the human subject? In short, will not man always be a stranger in the universe, whatever the form and content of his social interactions? Marx seems to argue the contrary, that under the appropriate social conditions it will be possible to recognize the essence of nature as human activity. Formally, this recognition would exactly parallel Vico's discovery, discussed in the previous chapter, according to which history is a human product, an objectification of human activity. Just as this discovery opens the way to the de-reification of history and the recognition of human creative power in the historical domain, so Marx wants to de-reify nature and to attribute to human beings a comparable creative power in the natural domain. As we have seen, Lukács stops short of such a claim and accepts the reification of nature as an insuperable ontological condition.

Marx's concept of nature as human activity has three somewhat different dimensions which he does not distinguish clearly. At the simplest level Marx's claim that man and nature are consubstantial reduces to a conundrum, as when he writes that "the physical and mental life of man, and nature, are interdependent means simply that nature is interdependent with itself, for man is a part of nature."[27] By itself such a statement only classifies man as a natural being without elucidating the essence of nature or establishing man's active powers in the natural world. However, Marx aims to prove more than this; he wants to convince us that human being *qua* social being, with all the subjective capacities of the fully developed human personality, can recognize its consubstantiality with "objective reality everywhere" as "the reality of human faculties." This more ambitious claim points to a second level of the theory.

In a previous chapter I discussed at some length Marx's theory of need. According to that theory the interdependence of man and nature can be demonstrated in the essential internal relation between human need and the natural objects of satisfaction. Marx explicitly affirms that this is an ontological relation, and not merely a fact of physiology. What is more, Marx proposes a theory of the historical evolution of human need which indicates that it is not only hunger which is objectified in food, but the higher needs of the social human being which find their essential object in the natural world. In this sense the unity of man and nature takes on a larger metaphysical significance which I will call the "participatory identity" of man and nature and discuss in more detail in the conclusion to this book.

This second dimension of the theory of nature does not stand alone in Marx's text but is always related to a third in which the idea of a de-reification of nature is given a more active character. At this third level, the unity of man and nature is a result of human labor, which really objectifies human faculties in the transformed natural objects of human need. This third level of the theory presupposes the first two and, in a sense, supersedes them as the fully realized form of the unity of man and nature, the form in which human creative power in nature is most completely expressed.

The grandeur but also the paradox of this culminating aspect of the theory consists in the universality of Marx's claims for human labor. He is not content to confine human creative powers to the narrow domain that mankind actually and potentially transforms in an imaginable labor process, but wants to extend those powers to "objective reality everywhere." One may well ask why he should formulate his theory in such a way that it would seem to incorporate all sorts of natural objects which cannot be imagined as objects of labor. After all, objective reality *everywhere* includes the entire universe! In what sense can we really conceive such an immensity as "the reality of human faculties?"

The paradox results from casting the dialectics of the labor process in the *form* of identity philosophy, meta-theoretically redefining the subject and object in terms of labor and raw material. Sense might be made of such a bizarre procedure somewhat along the lines later sketched by Heidegger, by claiming that being is primordially given to the human subject through its *potentiality* for manipulation. One might then ignore the problem of whether such a potentiality is really ever actualizable in the case of the objects most distant from human concern. Furthermore, while it is true that the labor process presupposes the independent existence of untransformed nature against the background of which it arises, yet it is possible to argue that nature in that untransformed condition is at least potentially an object of labor and hence incorporated in essence, if not in existence, into the sphere of human creative activity.

However, even in this formulation the theory is profoundly unsatisfactory. It is not only that some natural objects are unimaginable as objects even of potential labor; equally questionable is the narrowness of any definition of the fundamental human relation to nature which focusses so exclusively on labor. It is by no means self-evident that the transformative impulse is the primary one through which being is disclosed. In play, aesthetic appreciation and contemplation humans relate to being perhaps just as fundamentally as they do in labor without attempting to remake objects in their own image. And to these less active modes of involvement in the world there correspond objective dimensions of the real perhaps just as fundamental as any revealed to the laboring subject. How then can the philosophical functions of subject-object identity devolve onto the labor process when in that domain the object seems necessarily to overflow the subject in every direction?

Marx is of course reacting against what he considers the unilaterality of traditional philosophy, which attempts to sum up the human relation to reality in the concept of consciousness. And he may well be right to protest that other and perhaps more fundamental relations to the real should have priority over that one. Yet the imaginable extension of the concept of an object of consciousness is in truth far greater than that of an object of labor. Thus if a Fichte or a Husserl were to declare that "consciousness itself becomes the object," we might disagree with the philosophical premises that lead to such a conclusion, but at least the notion of "consciousness" refers potentially to every possible object. The idealistic conclusion need not be rejected out of hand because consciousness self-evidently and in principle *requires* an object irreducible to it. (This is, of course, Sartre's thesis, but it is by no means self-evident.)

Just as Lukács encountered an insuperable barrier to applying his concept of historical practice to nature, so Marx seems to encounter a similar barrier to generalizing his concept of labor from the human scale to the totality of nature. Marx needs to unify man and nature extensively, in relation to any *possible* object if "man himself" is really to "become the object." But the universe is not, in principle, mere raw material for labor: the very idea is either absurd or abhorrent. Even admitting that in some partial domains labor achieves subject-object identity, this identity still falls short of that required by a philosophy of praxis. As a result, the whole Kantian problematic of the thing in itself returns, for alongside history, in which subject and object are one in labor, another sphere of nature and natural science must be distinguished in which man is *not* the object.

So compelling is this conclusion that Habermas and several other interpreters of the early Marx attribute it to him. But, as I have argued in the first chapter of this book, such an interpretation of Marx contradicts the letter and the spirit of his text. Instead of accepting a Kantian resolution of the difficulties, I believe that Marx attempted to turn them by elaborating a remarkable new theory of sensation in which the senses "become directly theoreticians in practice," acting on their objects as does the worker on his raw materials.[28] The senses, unlike labor, have traditionally been conceived by philosophy as a potentially universal mode of reception, relating to all possible (real) objects. The senses can therefore take over where actual labor leaves off, supporting the assertion of a universal identity of subject and object in nature.

Marx's theory of sensation is distinguished from all previous ones by his meta-theoretical reconstruction of sense knowledge as a historically evolving dimension of human being. Marx argues that the object of sensation contains a wealth of meaning available only to the trained and socially developed sense organ. In alienated society man experiences nature as a dog or cat might experience a symphony. And, as the "musical" ear recognizes itself "affirmed" in the music it hears, so will liberated humanity recognize itself affirmed in nature. "The distinctive character of each faculty is precisely its characteristic essence and thus also the characteristic mode of its objectification, of its objective real, living being. It is therefore not only in thought, but through all the senses that man is affirmed in the objective world."[29] On these terms, the emancipated senses are active transformers of their objects and not mere passive receptors; they can be understood on the model of the labor process as engaging in a theoretical-practical activity, objectifying human nature and releasing the implicit potentialities of the material on which they work.

For the early Marx, the senses are alienated in the alienation of labor. The liberation of labor is thus the condition for the training of the senses to their highest pitch of perfection. In transforming the senses by abolishing alienation historical action attains the core of being itself, as required by the philosophy of praxis: "The supersession of private property is, therefore, the complete emancipation of all the human qualities and senses. . . . The eye has become a human eye when its object has become a human, social object, created by man and destined for him."[30] Revolution unites subject and object in liberated sensation and thereby reveals the truth of nature.

But can one really speak of "truth" in this context? Has not Marx simply arrived once again by a different route at the very difficulty Lukács encountered? Conceivably, the histori-

cally evolved senses of communist man are different from
those of man in class society, but are the senses in any case
significantly related to the truth about nature? Is it not natural
science which discovers this truth, and often by the most
arduous effort to transcend the given social-sensory horizon
toward deeper representations? In the *Manuscripts*, Marx
explicitly rejects the epistemology implied by these questions, and with it, the existing natural sciences as well.

Marx insists that he is seeking the "unifying truth" of "both
idealism and materialism."[31] He therefore argues, on the one
hand, that the sense object is real and not simply a product of
consciousness. Given his quasi-naturalistic assumptions, he
cannot claim that the senses "posit" their objects in some sort
of prior constitution. This would be to deny the reality of
nature while affirming the natural, sensory character of man,
an obvious contradiction. On the other hand, Marx rejects any
notion of a thing in itself transcendent to perception in
principle. Neither realistic epistemology nor the Kantian
critique that corresponds to realism is compatible with his
position. Marx cannot allow, as does British empiricism, that
the sense object is merely a sign, causally (or otherwise)
connected with a "real" object that would be only accidentally
related to sensation. If the sensed object is only a sign or
image, then no real unity of subject and object is achieved in
sensation, as Kant's first *Critique* makes abundantly clear.
The "real" object is not "humanized" by sensation in realistic
and critical epistemology, but flees behind the senses to
where it can be reached through thought alone, if at all. Marx
therefore rejects the attempt to conceive nature as a reality
transcendent to sensation: "Nature too," he writes, "taken
abstractly, for itself, and rigidly separated from man, is nothing for man."[32] And to this "abstract" nature, he opposes the
concrete, living nature of direct sensory experience. Marx's
synthesis of idealism and materialism thus culminates in a
unique form of phenomenalism.

Marx's theory of sensation leads him to reject the natural

sciences for their "abstract materialist, or rather idealist orientation."[33] His critique might be elaborated more fully as follows. The materialist interpretation of science asserts the reality of the ideal objects of scientific laws, in contrast with the mere appearances perceived by the senses; but the ideal objects of science are objects of thought, and so via materialism we return to the basic premise of idealism, the notion that in its essence being is an object of thought and not of a natural, sensuous subject. For Marx such a conclusion is to be understood as a secularized version of the theological priority of spirit over matter. Marx's own radical epistemological atheism insists on locating both appearance and reality in the sphere of sensation, as levels or degrees in the unveiling of what is perceived. The truth of the object does not lie beyond sensation in thought but in truer and deeper sensation itself, in the developed and liberated senses of social man. Only on this assumption can Marx overcome the split between man and nature which threatens his philosophy of praxis at every turn.

Now science must be transformed in its methods and its structure. Following Feuerbach (and definitely not Locke), Marx states: "Sense experience . . . must be the basis of all science."[34] Presumably, the perceptions of the liberated senses can be raised to consciousness by a new science, although it is difficult to imagine in what form. Furthermore, the division of natural and social science must be overcome: the very object of natural science has been *aufgehoben* and in its place stands the "humanized" nature disclosed to liberated sensation. "There will be," Marx prophesizes, "a single science."[35] Marx seems to be saying that a reformed science will, in studying nature, really be studying the objectifications of man's socialized senses, hence man himself.

The first object for man—man himself—is nature, sense experience; and the particular sensuous human faculties, which can only find objective realization in natural objects, can only attain self-knowledge in the science of natural being. . . . The social reality of nature and human natural science, or the natural science of man, are identical expressions.[36]

In these passages, Marx takes the step that Lukács later refused to take: the rejection of the existing natural sciences as the precondition for a radical historicization of the concept of nature. Undergirding the "abstractly conceived" nature of the existing sciences, Marx seems to say, there is a primordial practical relation of human subject to natural object. This practical relation cannot be explained as external interaction between the sort of objectivities conceived by natural science, but rather founds those very objectivities in a prior reality. In his critique of natural science, the early Marx can be seen to approach and anticipate the phenomenological concept of a "pre-reflexive" unity of subject and object from which the contemplative conception of their independent existence would be derived by an objectivistic misconstruction. Here, if not in Lukács' case, it might be shown that philosophy of praxis leads to a romantic and antiscientific doctrine.

The next step, which Marx did not take, would be the development of a philosophy of nature based on a teleological concept of being as in essence subordinated to human aims. Rather than go this route, Marx rejected his entire early philosophy. In the works immediately following the *Manuscripts*, particularly in the "Theses on Feuerbach" and *The German Ideology*, Marx began to backtrack. He first rejected not so much the premises of the *Manuscripts* as the conclusion they were supposed to establish, the identity of subject and object. In *The German Ideology*, for example, Marx sets out at one point to prove that the entire universe is a product of human sensuous activity. But, in the very middle of a passage that could have been lifted from the *Manuscripts*, he suddenly notes, "Of course the priority of external nature remains, and all this has no application to the original men produced by *generatio aequivoca*." This is a damaging admission from the point of view of his earlier philosophy of praxis: it presupposes that nature can be meaningfully conceived apart from man, and so presumably, comprehended in abstraction from its sensuous appearance. Perhaps this implication still made Marx a bit uncomfortable, for he immediately tries to patch things up. He continues, "But this differentation has meaning only insofar as man is considered distinct from nature," a perspective which, Marx assures us, is irrelevant in the modern world where industry has transformed nature except "on a few Australian coral islands of recent origin."[37]

These are school boy squirmings compared with the daring and rigor of the *Manuscripts*, and show to what extent Marx has abandoned his philosophy of praxis even though some of his arguments still *tend* toward establishing his old conclusions. This hesitation and wavering occurs several times in the first part of *The German Ideology*, where occasional passages prepare proofs of the identity of subject and object despite the fact that Marx now ridicules the very terminology in which such a conclusion would have to be stated. Soon even this backhanded reference to the philosophy of praxis of the *Manuscripts* is dropped, and Marx plunges into economic and historical research without philosophical afterthoughts such as those which troubled him in the early 1840s.

The mature work of Marx and Lukács is not based on a philosophy of praxis but on a materialistic faith in science. Yet, as I have argued at length in earlier chapters, some important aspects of the philosophy of praxis survive the abandonment of its most daring theses. The meta-theory of philosophy of the early works continues to influence Marx and Lukács in the later ones. It will be recalled that this meta-theory has three moments, the first two of which reconstruct the categories of identity philosophy in social reality, while the third resolves the philosophical antinomies of that philosophy through the demand for the historical transformation of the reconstructed terms. Now the third moment of the meta-theory of philosophy is abandoned, and the first two survive as a negative critique of reified forms of social thought. The meta-theoretically reconstructed categories still interact dialectically in history, but their ultimate identity in a synthesis is denied. This is also the basis of the "negative dialectics" of the Frankfurt School.

It was left to Engels to elaborate an ontology corresponding to this social theory. He did so in numerous articles and books which espouse an unabashed naturalism. Marx himself seems to have accepted this as a satisfactory substitute for the philosophy of praxis. However, a discussion of Engels' naturalism would bring us full circle: Lukács was, of course, aware of Engels' views which he condemns as precritical, still unawakened from the "dogmatic slumbers" Kant interrupted for all time. On this point Lukács is undoubtedly right.

In view of the superficiality of the naturalism stemming from Engels, I think it is worthwhile reexamining more carefully the early work of Marx and Lukács in search of the conceptual bases of an original solution to the problems, perhaps not as radical as that which these thinkers at first envisioned, but nevertheless more challenging than what currently passes for "orthodoxy."

EXISTENTIAL MARXISM

Central to philosophy of praxis is the idea of revealing the truth of being as historical becoming; but it is also from this idea that the antinomy of history and nature arises. The project of this philosophy is to transpose the concept of subject-object identity from the domain of metaphysical theory to that of real social practice. In support of this project, philosophy of praxis argues that being is first disclosed to the subject in a practical relation such as needing, laboring, or historical action. The dialectical interdependence of the practically related subject and object is then taken as paradigmatic for subject-object relations in general. Objectivity and its corresponding theoretical knowledge is not denied but is comprehended as a derivative category, based on this more fundamental practical relation to being. The antinomy of history and nature arises from difficulties in understanding the concept of nature on these terms.

The methodological dimension of this antinomy concerns the relation of theory to practice. So-called "external" nature is a privileged object of theoretical contemplation; as Lukács shows, even the corresponding technical practice in which nature is manipulated is basically "contemplative," in the sense that it follows the lead of theory and cannot alter the laws disclosed to theory. The matter stands quite differently with society and history, which are humanly created objectivities in their very being. Practice actually produces the objects that appear in their (created) independence as objects of social theory and which in turn reproduce the practice that produced them. Here the objects of theory are objectifications of practice, which latter is therefore no merely derivative function of theory. Lukács' theory of reification shows that the dependence of historical objects on a founding practice sets certain limits of validity on the terms of their theoretical comprehension. In particular, the historical contingency of the laws of historical objects is without parallel in the domain of natural science. The specificity of the historical sciences is based on this methodological principle.

At issue in the ontological question of whether "external" nature has priority over historical reality or *vice versa* is the methodological question of whether theory or practice has epistemological priority. On this in turn depends whether or not subject and object can be united. In the customary representation of theory, subject and object are not identical, but distinctly separate. As Lukács argues in his discussion of contemplative thought, the ideal of a pure theoretical subject-object identity presupposes the separation of the terms it brings into relation. The subject of theory occupies a "systematic locus" beyond all but cognitive connection with its objects, and unites with them not in reality but in knowledge, in a specular relation of correspondence or reflection.

For contemplative theory, the position of truth is attained by abstracting from the concrete position of the subject in existence. The ideal knower would thus be a subject without objectivity, uninvolved in the vicissitudes of existence on which it would be a pure spectator. Human beings are, of course, physical things and this is their epistemological impediment; yet traditional philosophy assigns them a spark of divinity, admitting the capacity of finite subjectivity occasionally to achieve the position of truth in objective knowledge. By letting things be as they are, the human subject can coincide momentarily with the hypothetical absolute spectator and know the truth of the real.

This tenuous subject-object relation in which truth is revealed to theory is utterly unlike the principle of practice required by Marx and Lukács. They insist that subject-object identity be demonstrated by explaining the real process of production of the objects of theory. This involves no merely reflexive correspondence of thought and things, but an active creating. It is only on such a basis that subject-object identity can be anything more than a speculative mythology. It may now be somewhat clearer why the admission of the "priority of external nature," which is of course not humanly created, is so damaging to the philosophy of praxis. If the fundamental reality is nature, then the primordial relation of subject to object is theoretical, and the sort of identity on which Marx and Lukács insist is impossible.

Some Marxists have concluded that only a speculative nature philosophy can complete the philosophy of praxis, once and for all subordinating nature and the theory of it to historical practice.[38] They attempt to conceive a "practice" prior to and founding for the objectivity of nature, either in the form of a transcendental constitution or a pantheistic providentialism. In such theories, society's meaning-positing functions are mythologized as a generative principle for nature, or nature itself is mythologized as a living organism of which man would be the conscious faculty. Yet even here, in the context of the most ambitious attempt to found philosophy of praxis, the antinomy of history and nature reappears. The historical practice which, for Marxism, founds the objectivity of social objects, is the "real" practice of identifiable human subjects and social groups. The practice in which speculative philosophy conceives nature to be constituted does not have this "real" character, but is a conceptual mythology.

In spite of terminological similarities, there is no comparison between the mythic practice of such a nature philosophy and the real historical practice to which Marx and Lukács refer. Both prefer to accept the insuperable split between nature and history, at the risk of inconsistency, rather than to unite them through speculative mediations. This is the dilemma of a philosophy of praxis that remains on materialistic ground, preserving the independence of nature and the reality of practice, and yet simultaneously affirms the philosophical pertinence of historical action. Somehow, Marx and Lukács need to subordinate objectivity to a more dialectical, practical relation to being in which the identity of subject and object can be established, without for that matter reverting to the methods of traditional philosophical idealism.

There is a difficult ambiguity in their attempts to achieve this goal, an ambiguity which leaves them exposed to misinterpretation and inconsistency. Marx, for example, argues that only "real" objects can exist in practical relations. But by "real" objects we usually mean objects that have their being in their objectivity and not in a relation to a subject; it is thus that we distinguish a real thing from an imaginary one that can only exist "in the mind." Now, our ordinary conception of practice presupposes the objectivity of its moments, in this usual sense of the term. But this objectivity is first revealed not to practice, but to theory; it involves not the strong dialectical interrelatedness of a doing, but the weak and contingent relation of a knowing. Hence the very attempt to make practice primordial appears to be self-contradictory since before practice acts on objects they must be known, and it is customary to assign to theory the role of accomplishing this epistemological preliminary to action.

This contradictory result is reached because philosophy of praxis rejects idealism and insists on defining the subject-object relation as a "real" practical relation between "real" objects, without sufficiently clarifying its concept of reality. It intends for practice to found objectivity, and yet it implies the contrary, that objectivity is independent of practice and founding for it. Philosophy of praxis would thus be bounded by traditional objectivity and its corresponding form of contemplative rationality. This boundary is reached as soon as it becomes apparent that for this philosophy nature is a thing in itself, beyond the horizon of social practice, a permanently reified, external substratum of history which social practice can never touch in its being, but which that practice must always presuppose as its own ontological foundation.

The demand for identity that is characteristic of philosophy of praxis cannot be satisfied where the reality of the practical moments is interpreted in terms of the usual concept of objectivity. To the extent that Marx and Lukács hint at a solution to the problem, they therefore look to a revision of the concept of objectivity as the precondition for conceiving subject-object identity with real subjects and objects. Unfortunately, neither Marx nor Lukács follows through adequately on this requirement of a consistent philosophy of praxis. Marx offers daring suggestions for transforming the concept of nature, but he barely sketches the meta-theoretical revision of the concept of objectivity on which such an enterprise depends. Lukács develops an elaborate framework for revising the concept of objectivity, but then draws back from applying it to nature and natural science. It is still remarkable, despite these hesitations, that both Marx and Lukács arrive independently at a similar radical break with the traditional concept of objectivity. I would like now to review their discussion of these matters, to measure the extent of their innovation, and to attempt to explore some of the possibilities it opens.

The position which Marx and Lukács share is based on the rejection of the hypothetical absolute subject which serves as an epistemological model for traditional reflection on the problem of knowledge. The absolute subject always has it in its power to shatter the hard won unity of subject and object by positing external nature as reality. They therefore deny that it is meaningful even to imagine an observer that could perceive and question the universe from "outside," from a disincarnated position of pure theory. They regard this hypothesis, even in its regulative employment as an ideal of knowledge, as an ultimate theological postulate that escapes the critique of their philosophical predecessors, and which they must expunge from theory.

The epistemology which derives from their critique is closer to Nietzsche's than it is to Hegel's, with whom Marx and Lukács are usually compared. It is true that, like Hegel, they regard knowledge as a historical outcome, but they deny the possibility of a final synoptic wisdom such as that in which Hegel's philosophy of history culminates. The tendency to which they belong would say, rather, with Nietzsche:

Let us, from now on, be on our guard against the hallowed philosophers' myth of a "pure, will-less, painless, timeless knower"; let us beware of the tentacles of such contradictory notions as "pure reason," "absolute knowledge," "absolute intelligence." All these concepts presuppose an eye such as no living being can imagine, an eye required to have no direction, to abrogate its active and interpretive powers—precisely those powers that alone make of seeing, seeing *something*. All seeing is essentially perspective, and so is all knowing.[39]

This reference to existentialism is not arbitrary, for at least in their critique of objectivism, Marx and Lukács are "existential" Marxists. Both assert the inevitable existential involvement of a finite subject of knowledge in the object of its discourse; and both reject the sceptical consequences that usually derive from this premise in order that they may revise the concept of objectivity meta-theoretically in accordance with the epistemological potentialities of a finite being.

There is a brief argument in Marx's *Manuscripts* which makes these points with startling effect. In a discussion of the cosmological proof of the existence of God, Marx demands that his imaginary interlocutor, who questions the source of the universe, reflect on his own position in relation to the question:

If you ask a question about the creation of nature and man you abstract from nature and man. You suppose them non-existent and you want me to demonstrate that they exist. I reply: give up your abstraction and at the same time you abandon your question. Or else, if you want to maintain your abstraction, be consistent, and if you think of man and nature as non-existent, think of yourself too as non-existent, for you are also man and nature. Do not think, do not ask me any questions, for as soon as you think and ask questions your abstraction from the existence of nature and man becomes meaningless. [40]

At issue in this passage is not just the problem of the existence of God, but also the very nature of objectivity. For, in denying his interlocutor the right the abstract from his position in existence in order to pose a question about existence, Marx denies that thinking can go on in what Lukács calls a "systematic locus," an absolute position of truth beyond all real connection with its objects.

The student of existentialism may recognize the formal similarity of Marx's argument and certain arguments in Kierkegaard. Independently of both Marx and Kierkegaard, Gabriel Marcel developed this type of argument into a well defined methodology. (This rather surprising convergence between thinkers as different as Marx, Kierkegaard and Marcel is explained in part by a common reference to and reaction against Hegelian rationalism on certain key points.)[41] Like

Marx, Marcel also questions the legitimacy of interrogating being as a whole, and for the same reason, because it involves abstracting from the position of the questioner in being. A problem like that posed by the cosmological proof is simply insoluble because it is not a legitimate problem at all.

The comparison of Marx and Marcel is worth expanding briefly, for both are concerned to demonstrate the ontological priority of lived experience over its objectivistic representation. For Marcel, lived experience is "meta-problematical," a domain of "mystery" which can only be explored from within. Marcel's term "mystery" is ill-chosen, because it does not refer to a numinous reality. As he defines it, "A mystery is a problem which encroaches on its own data, invading them, as it were, and thereby transcending itself as a simple problem."[42] Just so, in Marx the "problem" of the existence of the universe "encroaches" on the subject who poses it as a problem. Marcel concludes, again along lines anticipated by Marx, that "To postulate the metaproblematical is to postulate the primacy of being over knowledge; . . . it is to recognise that knowledge is, as it were, environed by being. . . ."[43]

In his later writings, Marcel discussed the methodological implications of this conception in terms of the distinction between "primary" and "secondary" reflection. Primary reflection of the objectivistic, analytic sort, abstracts from the relation of subject to object. It is the proper mode of reflection on problems which do not implicate the subject. Secondary reflection has an exploratory, synthetic character that comes from the recognition of the involvement of the subject in the object of its inquiry. Secondary reflection arises from the methodological refusal to pursue certain types of inquiries at the level of ordinary analytic reasoning, which cannot account for the position of the subject in the discourse it employs to account for the object.

Marx's argument against the cosmological proof is part of a larger attempt to establish the ontological priority of the living nature of which we are a part over the objective nature of the natural sciences on which we are only a spectator. To accomplish this he interrupts the "primary reflection" of his imaginary interlocutor with the phrase, "Do not think, do not ask me any questions. . . ." He seems to be operating here with a unique criterion of meaning, which restricts propositions about reality to those that can be accounted for in a dialectic of subject and object. His aim is to deny ontology access to the object "in itself," as it would appear to a contemplative subject, apart from its relation to man in labor and sensation, in order to defend his philosophy of praxis from the incipient objectivism which threatens it. Otherwise, stated, Marx attempts to found his theory on the "real" or "concrete" relation of man to nature, subject to object which, in labor, has the form of an essential interdependence, rather than founding it on the mathematicized model of objective nature which we owe to the sciences and which bears no essential relation to humanity. In effect, Marx wants to show that nature as it really is can only be conceived in dialectical interaction with man, while "abstractly" conceived, merely "external" nature must be excluded from philosophical consideration as a meaningless construction.

This interpretation of Marx's argument suggests yet another similarity between his early thought and existentialism. Marx's criterion of meaning resembles the phenomenological concept of "horizon." Heidegger's American translators define that concept usefully for our purposes:

Throughout this work the word "horizon" is used with a connotation somewhat different from that to which the English-speaking reader is likely to be accustomed. We tend to think of a horizon as something which we may widen or extend or go beyond; Heidegger, however, seems to think of it rather as something which we can neither widen nor go beyond, but which provides the limits for certain intellectual activities performed "within it."[44]

The discussion above shows Marx too involved in prescribing such limits, and identifying them with the limits of the finite, natural subject of experience.

Kant would seem to be the primary reference for this

approach to the problem of meaning. It was he who first suggested that there are specific limits to the range of pertinence of the categories of experience. The employment of reason beyond the domain of possible experience, that is to say, in relation to being in itself, gives rise to a "transcendental illusion." Phenomenology too sets out from the idea of a criterion of meaning specifying the range of pertinence of the concepts of the understanding, although it interprets the significance of this procedure differently from Kant. Heidegger, for example, not only identifies this legitimate range of the concepts with the limits of a finite subject, but he goes on to interpret the essence of being under the horizon of experience for such a subject. Apart from the structures of its disclosure to the finite subject, the idea of a being "in itself" is entirely meaningless. Modern phenomenology, like Marx, thus retains the Kantian idea of limiting the application of the categories to the possible experience of a finite subject, but it rejects as theological the postulated transcendence of being. Both thus arrive at what I will call the concept of a "finite horizon" of being and knowledge.

These clarifications and allusions may contribute to understanding Marx's intent in the *Manuscripts*, but it would be too much to say that Marx succeeds in presenting a satisfactory theory there. He circles around the concept of a finite horizon without achieving a clear statement of a new concept of objectivity defined in the domain of lived experience through a meta-theoretical revision. I believe that Lukács does finally accomplish this, independently of Marx's *Manuscripts* of course, but employing conceptual tools derived from the mature thought of Marx. It was Marx's later theory of ideology, with its implied assertion of the culturally immanent character of all human thought, which provided the basis for Lukács' theory.

BELIEVING AND DOING

As we have seen, Lukács formulates all epistemological questions in terms of the *consciousness of classes* rather than the *knowledge of individuals.* We usually conceive of the subject of truth as an individual possessed of science, and not as a social group caught in the illusions of everyday experience. Lukács, however, denies that *any* individual standpoint transcends the determination of some more general cultural perspective which it represents theoretically with more or less coherence and insight. On these terms, the validity of individual thought is to be measured ultimately by the limits of the thinker's culture.

I have argued above that Lukács explains cultural perspectives as the schemata of practical syntheses of reality; the synthetic function itself is attached to social classes. The effect of these assumptions is to enclose rationality without remainder in the embrace of culture, and culture in that of class practice. Reason, culture and practice are stacked like Chinese boxes, the one inside the other, with no way out. No personal discipline, no science, no wisdom can break this epistemological law. Lukács thus proposes an epistemology which is integrally cultural in character, which admits of no "outside" of culture from which reality could be viewed objectively, no privileged preserve of science on the margins of the world.

It bears emphasizing that this is not intended to be a deterministic thesis. Lukács does *not* believe all members of a given class achieve an understanding of the world corresponding with the limits of their "objectively possible" class consciousness. As individuals, they may fall far below this limit, or transcend it by adopting the class standpoint of another class in society. The point is that even in transcending one form of class determination the individual falls inevitably under another, and does not escape from consciousness into knowledge as the traditional philosophical view would have it.

So far Lukács' position appears to be merely relativistic, and this is indeed how it was understood by those who, like Karl Mannheim, attempted to elaborate a sociology of knowledge on the basis of his concept of false consciousness.[45] However, in postulating the intrinsic dependency of knowledge on consciousness, Lukács himself does not aim to deny the possibility of true knowledge. Rather, he insists that the historical involvement of the subject of knowledge is a necessary precondition for knowing, and not just a socially subjective barrier from which a "pure" science would have to abstract. This is a meta-theoretical reconstruction of the concept of knowledge *in* the relative, under a finite horizon, rather than a sceptical critique of human limits in the light of an unattainable eternal truth.

It should be recalled that Lukács' main target in these epistemological considerations is reified objectivism, and with it the idea that being in itself transcends the reach of practice. Relativism is not, he argues, a truly independent position, but a variant of the objectivist one. Both objectivism and relativism presuppose an "absolute" in the form of the "systematic locus" of thought as a supposed spectator on a reality in which it does not, in principle, participate. In the final analysis, Lukács claims, it matters little if, having presupposed the concept of thought as a pure logical space of representation, one accepts or denies the possibility of achieving truth on this basis; this very conception of theory is squarely situated under the horizon of the "absolute" in either case.

"This absolute," Lukács writes, "is nothing but the fixation in thought, the projection into myth of the intellectual failure to understand reality concretely as a historical process."[46] It is thus that culture as the repository of society's most general categories of thought and action, appears to transcend history and indeed all real connections with objects as an apparently eternal or transcendental system prior to the real process and founding for it. The absolute is this appearance of culture at the horizon of history as an unchanging essence which explains change. Lukács reverses this formula: culture does not transcend history and found it, but is rather a historical phenomenon to be grasped in its historical function. It is not in the transcendence of history that the truth is to be found,

but in the recognition of the historical character of all transcendence.

For Lukács society cannot be known in the absolute, but it
can indeed be known from within.[47] The subject of this
self-knowledge of society is the proletariat. What is the basis
for this unique epistemological qualification? It is not the
superior scientificity of the proletarian standpoint, as though
this class could cross the unbridgeable space between a reified
subject and object, thereby attaining the truth that escaped
the most conscientious efforts of earlier social classes. Nor is it
merely that the barrier of class interest does not stand between the proletariat and a truth that would lie evidently
before it. To understand Lukács' theory of proletarian true
consciousness, it is necessary to get to the root of his critique
of contemplative theory, for it is the practical role of the
proletariat which situates it in the truth rather than any
theoretical virtue.

Lukács traces the "fixation" of thought in a realm beyond
history to specific social causes. The absolute and its correlated concept of the relative appear in response to the untranscended immediacies of life in class society. Because of
the obstacles to conscious cooperation in this type of society,
whole domains of social reality confront the individuals as
alien powers over which they have no control. At the same
time, the dominant culture can only serve its historical function of justifying class rule insofar as this function remains
unconscious, insofar, therefore, as culture itself appears as a
repository of eternal truths. To this untransformed reality and
uncomprehended culture of class society, there corresponds
the illusion of a transhistorical, systematic locus of thought.

Lukács argues that the proletariat throws these immediacies into the movement of history and subjects them to
a practical mediation which decisively alters the position of
truth. Proletarian practice acts on the form of objectivity of its
objects; it consciously transforms culture and therefore reality
as well; and, as the expression of a cooperative and potentially

universal historical subject, this practice need not accept any merely given immediacy as its horizon.

As soon as mankind has clearly understood and hence *restructured* the foundations of its existence truth acquires a wholly novel aspect. When theory and practice are united it becomes possible to change reality and when this happens the absolute and its "relativistic" counterpart will have played their historical role for the last time. For as the result of these changes we shall see the disappearance of that reality which the absolute and the relative expressed in like manner.[48]

The idea of theory as observation of reality from a disincarnated "beyond" is overthrown, and theory brought under a finite horizon when it is finally located in a process of conscious cultural change.

Nietzsche claimed that truth was the last idol of a disenchanted world, the final form in which the eternal ripped the seamless web of time. Far more thoroughly than Nietzsche, Lukács proceeds to humanize truth itself, to make it enter into time as a real moment in the creation of history. For Lukács, there is no ontological barrier between perceiver and perceived, subject and object, form and content. Rather, the traditional, objectivist subject-object concept is itself a methodological illusion arising from the function of knowledge in the systems of practice of class rule. Where knowledge has a limited function on the margins of unconscious collective practices it cannot comprehend, there it will encounter its objects as transcendent, its principles as eternal. For Lukács, on the contrary, "reality" is a cultural product and not an objectivity which precedes culture and which would have to be perceived from a beyond of culture to be known in its truth. This reality produced in a cultural process can be known in the cultural forms of its production, where those cultural forms are themselves objects of conscious practice.

Difficult as it is to distinguish this position from a decisionistic or pragmatic theory of truth, it is necessary to attempt to do so. Such theories are close to Lukács' view in recognizing that believing is a form of doing, with real consequences in the world. But they focus on individual belief in particular "truths" for instrumental ends, and so arrive at an energetic faith which requires constant infusions of will power to be maintained in conflict with those stubborn realities that do not respond to a mere change in personal commitments. The problematic of the will in decisionism and pragmatism thus testifies to the transcendence of the real, which it is precisely Lukács' intention to overcome. Lukács is not concerned with the consequences of belief about particular matters, such as the existence of God, the destiny of nations, or even "every one of Marx's individual theses."[49] He does not argue, as William James might have, that the proletariat will acquire the capacity to rule if only it believes itself capable of doing so; after all, that might be mere wishful thinking, and, no matter how ambitious its beliefs, the proletariat might only be able to act under the horizon of capitalist society.

Rather, it is necessary to reverse the formula: it is because the proletariat *really* exists in a necessary tension with its own cultural signification in capitalism that it is capable of believing its condition can be improved through a radical cultural transformation in the course of which it would come to power. This is a matter which requires verification in the customary ways, on the basis of social theory and practice, and cannot be proven by an act of will or a criterion such as "success." The crucial question concerns whether the class is capable of initiating and sustaining such a cultural change, starting out from the tension between its social existence and potentialities, and its given cultural signification under capitalism. The theory of class consciousness yields an affirmative response to this question, arguing that the proletariat can (potentially) transform capitalist culture in the course of transforming what it itself is in society.

For Lukács ideas are acts, but they are *not* therefore

subject to an instrumental logic. The level at which believing is doing is simply inappropriate for such a reductive treatment. The kind of "belief" with which Lukács is concerned is situated not at the level of particular thought contents and ideas, but at the most general level of cultural forms. A change in culture is a change in social reality: this, rather than some merely pragmatic self-manipulation, is the principle of Lukács' historicism. In the case of the proletariat, Lukács conceives this change as a resynthesis of social reality, a mediation of its given reified form of objectivity. It is thus not this or that idea which is changed, but the "transcendental" condition of the objectivity of social objects in general, the forms in which they are socially produced as objects. It is only at this level of generality that theory and practice are "identical."

Particular beliefs falling under the horizon of the new culture in emergence may still be true or false as before, still require objective proof, and so on. But the new culture is a new production of social reality, not subject to such norms of proof because it is their horizon. It is not to be understood as a verifiable belief "about" social reality, but as a set of dispositions, practices, a mode of seeing and doing which is the very stuff of that reality. Nevertheless, unverifiable as it is, the new culture has a certain arguable truth value and therefore is not proposed for merely faithful adherence. Lukács asserts the epistemological superiority of the proletarian standpoint over that of the bourgeoisie on the basis of an immanent criterion that is hermeneutic in character; the dialectical standpoint of the proletariat arises from a mediation of reification, which it encompasses and transcends. Beyond some such immanent criterion, there is no conceivable way of comparing cultures as to their truth value.

Lukács' theory of the finite horizon is far more convincing than Marx's, and in it the concept of rationality is more successfully reconstructed. In Lukács' theory of the proletariat, conscious thought is no external spectator on reality, nor is it condemned merely to rationalize the results of class practices it cannot comprehend. Rather, as a necessary moment in the mediation of the given reified culture, thought is historically situated in a position from which history can be known in its truth. On this basis the concept of truth can be elucidated anew without reference to an absolute subject.

Could Lukács' theory of the finite horizon be used to complete Marx's theory of nature, resolving fundamental difficulties in the philosophy of praxis? Lukács himself draws back from applying it to the domain of nature and the natural sciences in which, he argues, there is no dialectic of subject and object, hence no conscious change in the form of objectivity. In what follows I will argue that Lukács reaches this conclusion because his conception of subject-object interaction is marred by certain traditional assumptions that make it impossible for him to apply it to nature. A theory of nature based on the concept of a finite horizon is possible, but only on the condition of first criticizing Lukács' understanding of subject-object identity.

8

Reconciliation with Nature

THE SYNTHESIS OF MARX AND LUKÁCS

In this concluding chapter, I will argue that neither the philosophy of praxis of Marx nor that of Lukács can stand alone, but that a synthesis of some of their major ideas can form the basis of a coherent position. In each case there are crucial difficulties that can be resolved by reference to the other. Lukács' overemphasis on the productive power of subjectivity can be corrected by reference to the Marxian reconciliation with nature in a participatory subject-object identity. Marx's lack of a coherent theory of rationality can be compensated by reference to Lukács' concepts of reification and mediation. The outcome of the comparison and critique of the two positions is thus a third formulation of the philosophy of praxis which takes into account their defects and accomplishments.

In briefest compass Lukács' philosophy of praxis may be summed up as a theory of subjectivity and a related theory of rationality. The theory of subjectivity is supposed to demonstrate the production of being as a whole, in its content and its form, its existence and its reality, by human subjects in the

240

course of history. This view might be described as "transcendental humanism," and indeed in its most extreme formulations it seems to transfer the creative power of the divinity to the human species. Lukács' saving inconsistency is his explicit recognition that finite human subjects cannot constitute nature as they have history. The problems that result from this inconsistency have already been discussed in detail above, but it is to Lukács' credit to have preferred these problems to a quasi-theological creationism.

Lukács' theory of rationality holds that the truth is a mediation of immediate appearances in a totality. In its main features this theory is derived from Hegel. It will be recalled that Hegel's dialectic of appearance transcends the immediacy of both formal-analytic law and its material substratum in experience by relating them in a concrete totality. Hegel does not return to the concrete of immediate experience, as demanded by romanticism and existentialism. The concrete to which Hegel refers is such by reason of its synthetic completeness, not its immediacy. Lukács' theory of rationality conforms to this requirement by integrating the dimension of law to history as a moment in the totality of social life. What Hegel calls the "law of appearance" is understood as the basis of a system of practice; as such this law enters into further real relations with practice in the course of historical development. Law does not transcend history, nor is it denied abstractly, but rather it is related to a process of cultural change. The historical totality is constituted in a practical mediation in which the truth is not only discovered but created through relating law to experience and transforming both.

There is a distinct tension between Lukács' theory of subjectivity and his theory of rationality. The theory of subjectivity seems to lead toward a utopian claim that reification can be wholly overcome in a future society in which the historical subject and object would be immediately one. Even allowing for the persistent reification of nature, as Lukács always does, this is a puzzling view, contradicting other important dimen-

242 Lukács, Marx and the Sources of Critical Theory

sions of the theory. Whether Lukács intended this theory of subjectivity to be taken to such an extreme, as his critics usually assume, or whether he intended to define it through other more realistic concepts he developed, it is fair to say that he left himself open to misinterpretation. At the limit, Lukács' position represents a definite regression from a Hegelian to a Fichtean stance in the domain of social theory. On these terms, one would have to imagine an identical subject-object the actions of which would have no unintended consequences and which would encounter no contingencies in its environment requiring it to adjust and transcend the given. With the complete abolition of reification, no law of appearance would arise from the subject's practice, which would, therefore, be able freely to create the (social) world according to its undetermined will.

In contrast with this bizarre implication of some formulations of the theory of subject-object identity, the theory of rationality has the proletariat constituting itself as a subject through an unsurpassable process of mediation which presupposes reification as its basis. Rationality is thus achieved not by ignoring appearance or creating a wholly new type of human condition in which appearance and reality immediately coincide, but through the perpetual mediation of the ever-new appearances in which reality comes to consciousness. The theory of rationality requires a subject-object identity which is intrinsically mediated, in which subjective and objective dimensions are united through an active process and not simply identified conceptually. Here reason arises from understanding, dialectics from analytic rationality, conscious action from a process in which unintended consequences and objective preconditions are integrated to the life of the subject. This mediated subject-object identity is not Fichtean, but has a properly Hegelian dialectical character.

This position is incompatible with any formulation of the critique of reification according to which reification characterizes only the bourgeois era. Given the internal link between reification and dialectics in the concept of mediation, it is impossible to eliminate the former without also eliminating the latter. Insofar as the truth is discovered in dialectics, reification is a necessary moment in the process of discovery. Reification is, in sum, not the "opposite" of dialectics, but a moment in it. What may nevertheless radically change in the course of history is the position of the reified moment in the totality to which it belongs. As István Mészáros writes, "Granting that it is unthinkable to supersede . . . all possible dangers and potentials of reification, is fully compatible with conceiving 'Aufhebung' as a succession of social enterprises of which the later is *less* . . . alienation-ridden than the preceding one."[1] Lukács himself says something like this in a passage which shows he was aware of the danger of a utopian interpretation of his theory:

At the same time it is clear that from the standpoint of the proletariat the empirically given reality of the objects does dissolve into processes and tendencies; this process is no single, unrepeatable tearing of the veil that masks the process but the unbroken alternation of ossification, contradiction and movement; and thus the proletariat represents the true reality, namely the tendencies of history awakening into consciousness.[2]

Lukács' dialectical conception of reification in his theory of rationality is incompatible with his creationist theory of subjectivity. Of the two, the former is by far the more important, especially since it provides the basis for an alternative interpretation of subject-object identity which can be employed to revise the philosophy of praxis. Marx's *Manuscripts* offer other elements for such a revision. It is true that at points the *Manuscripts* are at least as creationist as anything in Lukács, employing a concept of human labor which has more in common with Biblical Genesis than with anything that actually goes on in a factory or field. Yet there is also another tendency in Marx's text that emphasizes less the *creation* of nature *by* man than the *participation* of man *in* nature. In his discussion of human needs, Marx argues that the unity of man and nature rests on their mutual participation in each others' being, on what Ollman has called their "internal relation" to each other.

As I have shown, Marx's concept of the finite horizon is required to hold the participating moments of subjectivity and objectivity together in a totality that cannot be reduced to naturalism's abstract subject-object concept. But from this there arise other problems Marx cannot solve: as presented in the *Manuscripts,* Marx's concept of the finite horizon is incompatible with natural science. Thus while Marx's theory of subjectivity may well offer a viable alternative to Lukács' creationism, Marx himself developed this theory at the expense of the concept of truth, which ought to make room for the sciences, if not for them alone. The problems in Lukács and Marx are rigorously complementary; the solution may therefore consist in pulling together the most successful aspects of each theory. A synthesis of Marx's concept of participatory subject-object identity with Lukács' mediation theory of rationality constitutes a coherent and defensible version of the philosophy of praxis.

The critical test of such a synthesis is its ability to account for the relation of man and nature in a way which preserves both the truth of the sciences and the active powers of the human species. Lukács and the later Marx were wise to conclude that philosophy cannot legislate the truth of nature in competition with natural science. But is it necessary, in order to establish science in its legitimate epistemological rights, to accept a naturalistic ontology incompatible with the philosophy of praxis? I would like now to address this question in both its theoretical and practical dimensions.

META-THEORY OF SCIENCE AND TECHNOLOGY

Philosophy of praxis requires a meta-theory of science which affirms the priority of lived and living nature over its natural scientific construction, while also grasping the results of scientific research as moments in the disclosure of the truth of nature. There must be, then, a recognition of the quantitative, lawful dimension of nature which romanticism abstractly negates but which no Marxist theory can permit itself so roughly to dismiss. The corresponding theory of practice must project the possibility of a technical relation to nature which is not only destruction and transformation but also the "liberation" of nature, its release from human power simply to be what it is. At the same time, it must be shown that practical reconciliation with the givenness of inner and outer nature is a participatory mediation establishing subject-object identity in a noncreationist form. The few pages which follow will develop these themes on the basis of the synthesis of Marx and Lukács suggested above. These remarks are necessarily brief and inadequate, but they will have served their purpose if they breathe a little life into the philosophy of praxis which, I am convinced, is not yet the *"tote hund"* in the ideological zoo the major schools of contemporary Marxism take it to be.

In the Marxist tradition, variants of naturalism are the dominant alternative to philosophy of praxis. Naturalism assumes that the nature of natural science is more "real" than that of lived experience because it is more highly mediated and therefore richer in "truth." But the nature of natural science is also self-evidently an ideal theoretical construction; it abstracts from important dimensions of experience which are (currently) scientifically unproblematic, or incomprehensible or irrelevant to the scientist. These three categories cover a lot of territory. The nature of natural science is thus, as Hegel argues, a "law of appearance," significantly impoverished in comparison with the rich variety of immediate appearances of which it is the law. Yet, real as it is, lived nature is evidently lacking in "truth," in those larger interconnections and insights that make of science a deeper perception of reality than ordinary experience. These considerations suggest that neither scientific nor lived nature can stand alone as the whole. I will argue that the contradiction between the two "bifurcated" natures can be overcome, and that at the point at which the unity of nature is recomposed the antinomy of nature and history is also transcended.

It is Marx's historical theory of sensation which suggests a solution. As Marx explains it, "Industry is the actual historical relationship of nature, and thus of natural science, to man."[3] The maturation and humanization of the senses in the course of history is owing to the development of the objective human powers represented by technology. Hegel's critique of naive empiricism in the *Phenomenology of Mind* no doubt lies in the background of this conception of sense knowledge as a dimension of culture.[4] Unfortunately, Marx did not pursue the role of science in the process of mediation, for reasons that have been discussed above. But Lukács' dialectic of system and process, law of appearance and totality indicates a way of integrating the results of science to the Marxian theory of the senses in the general framework of a philosophy of praxis.

Marx's concept of the finite horizon is supposed to establish the ontological priority of living nature over the abstractly conceptualized nature of natural science. In the great struggle between Goethe and Newton, Marx chose the former. However, the priority Marx grants living nature is not in recognition of its immediacy. The nature of direct experience is no poetic schwärmerei, distinguished from the prose of equations and laboratory experiments by the absence of thought and reflection. Living nature is informed by science and technology, sensed and comprehended through forms of objectivity that are both social and scientific in character. Science participates in the education of the human senses by being integrated to everyday experience and conception as a dialectical moment in the perception of nature, infusing sensation with those larger interconnections and deeper conceptual insights that are its contribution to human experience. Science is thus integrated into living nature as a moment, while living nature is not merely immediate, but is always already culturally mediated.

The reified dimension of nature on which natural science is based is neither the whole of nature nor is it a mere illusion of alienated reason, as Marx seems to have believed in 1844. This dimension cannot be cancelled by a historical progress that would reveal the truth of nature as human labor. Yet the reification of nature can be comprehended as a dialectical moment of the process in which the senses, and with them living nature, have developed.

On this account, scientific laws are not immediately identical with the essence of what is, but are always subtly eccentric with respect to the real. It is this which makes possible their great simplicity, but also their inevitable transcendence by more perfected laws at a later stage. Throughout the course of scientific development, living nature too evolves under the impact of science, and contributes ever new material to the progress of research. It is on this basis that the progress of science occurs, drawing ever new resources from the in-exhaustible material of perceptual experience which it, in turn, enriches by its own development. Living nature thereby shares in truth to the degree that science informs it by shaping the schemata of perception.

At its most ambitious, philosophy of praxis demands the production of being by human subjects and the transcendence of reified law in free creation. What I am proposing here is the less ambitious but perhaps more believable claim that the nature of lived experience has the status of a primary reality in which both subject and object participate. The theory of the finite horizon argues that this primary reality cannot be further reduced, for example, to the physiologically inevitable illusions of the human animal. Living nature is, rather, a cultural phenomenom of a special sort, and as such the horizon of science and not its object. Science is not therefore to be compared with living nature as a new theory with an old and refuted one. The extraordinary privilege of living nature derives from the fact that it is not a theory at all, but a synthesis of theory and an infinitely rich "manifold" of experience to which science will always return.

In Lukács' theory of culture, the social totality contains a moment of system which stands in a determinate relation with the historical process of which it is the horizon. The systemic moment is not denied or reduced to the succession of process, nor *vice versa*, but rather these two dimensions of social life are dialectically interdependent. A similar dialectic of system and process can be applied to the theory of nature, in the framework of Marx's general approach to the senses. The laws of nature are not *aufgehoben* by a speculative mythology, but are brought into a real relation to the nature of experience as a quantitative, reified moment in the totality. Living nature is this totality, not because it is innocent of abstract lawfulness, but on the contrary, because it is a unity of law with its material substratum, a unity richer in both form and content than either science or sensation taken abstractly. Living nature is, in effect, a dimension of history and this explains why it is structured as a cultural phenomenon. Nature may not be "created" by human practice on the same terms as history, but its participation in a dialectic of system and process reveals its fundamentally historical character in another equally important way.

Living nature is also the reality to which science returns in its technological application.[5] The environmental movement has made us far more aware than were Marx and Lukács of the threat to sanity and survival implicit in the demand that nature be remade in the image of its human masters. We owe to the Frankfurt School some of the deepest reflections on the problem of practical reconciliation with nature; these philosophers anticipated current hopes and fears surprisingly early. The Frankfurt School lies on the nearer side of a demarcation line which separates the traditional rationalist productionism of Bacon and Descartes, of Marx and Lukács, from the present self-critical mood of serious contemporary rationalism. On this basis the Frankfurt School distinguished itself sharply from Lukács' early Marxism, rejecting the postulate of subject-object identity as vicious in its principle.

In the *Dialectic of Enlightenment,* Adorno and Horkheimer protest the untrammelled pursuit of power over nature, which they regard as the irrational core of identitarian rationalism.

In class history, the enmity of the self to sacrifice implied a sacrifice of the self, inasmuch as it was paid for by a denial of nature in man for the sake of domination over non-human nature and over other men. This very denial, the nucleus of all civilizing rationality, is the germ cell of a proliferating mythic irrationality: with the denial of nature in man not merely the *telos* of outward control of nature but the *telos* of man's own life is distorted and befogged. As soon as man discards his awareness that he himself is nature, all the aims for which he keeps himself alive—social progress, the intensification of all his material and spiritual powers, even consciousness itself—are nullified, and the enthronement of the means as an end, which under late capitalism is tantamount to open insanity, is already perceptible in the prehistory of subjectivity.[6]

The solution the authors propose is obscurely hinted at in scattered passages throughout the book. In one such passage, they remark: "By virtue of this remembrance [*eingedenken*] of nature in the subject, in whose fulfillment the unacknowledged truth of all culture lies hidden, enlightenment is universally opposed to domination."[7] And they go on to suggest that domination can only be dissolved when it is recognized as "unreconciled nature."[8] This unreconciled nature must not be conquered and absorbed but accepted through a process of reflection. It is such reflective acceptance of nature alone which really challenges power. "Dominant practice and its inescapable alternatives are not threatened by nature, which tends rather to coincide with them, but by the fact that nature is remembered [*erinnert*]."[9]

These strange passages are a critique of the ravages wrought by the "absolute subject" when it descends from its theoretical heaven to the practical transformation of the earth. The conquest of nature is inevitably also the conquest of man, insofar as human beings too belong to nature; the recognition of the "right" of nature to an independent life is therefore the recognition of that which in man *is* nature and must be so by the very finitude of the human being. Reconciliation with nature is also a necessary moment in the reconciliation of human beings with each other in which a socialist society would consist.

But it is important to note that this reconciliation concerns *"erinnert"* nature and not the nature of immediacy which, the authors argue, will always appear as a terrifying threat outside of poetry. Human beings are thus to be reconciled with a mediated nature, a nature transformed by technological conquest, scientific comprehension and human social development. The acceptance of this nature, or rather of that which in this nature is in need of acceptance, would be liberation from that struggle of modern times in which "nature tears itself apart."[10] Adorno and Horkheimer argue that this reconciliation begins with the theoretical recognition of nature's independence, the nonidentity of object and subject. But there is a certain ambiguity about this formulation, given the fact that "independent" nature is posited in its independence by a reflective subject on the basis of a historical and cultural development. This ambiguity becomes explicit in Marcuse's later discussion of the problem.

Adorno and Horkheimer hold back from the utopian task of describing a form of practice corresponding to the reconciliation with nature. They seem to see it only in negative terms, as a moment of relaxation in which enlightenment accepts finitude. Somewhat later, in the context of the utopian projection of the new left, Marcuse elaborated a positive theory of liberated technical practice. His advance over Adorno and Horkheimer consists in showing that reconciliation with nature is not merely a negative limit on human activity, but a new mode of activity in its own right.

Marcuse's essay on "Nature and Revolution" represents the furthest advance of the Frankfurt School in the direction of a Marxist theory of nature in socialist society. Marcuse argues that the capitalist view of nature as

value-free matter, material [there only] for the sake of domination is a *historical* a priori, pertaining to a specific form of society. A free society may well have a very different a priori and a very different object; the development of the scientific concepts may be grounded in an experience of nature as a totality of life to be protected and "cultivated," and technology would apply this science to the reconstruction of the environment of life.[11]

Marcuse goes on to suggest the possibility of a "liberation of nature" that would be "the recovery of the life-enhancing forces in nature, the sensuous aesthetic qualities which are foreign to a life wasted in unending competitive performance."[12] Marcuse thus foresees a reconciliation with nature through a new technical practice based on aesthetic forms of objectivity.

But Marcuse adds an important proviso to his theory of the liberation of nature.

Marx's notion of a human appropriation of nature retains something of the *hubris* of domination. "Appropriation," no matter how human, remains appropriation of a (living) object by a subject. It offends that which is essentially other than the appropriating subject, and which exists precisely as object in its own right—that is as subject! The latter may well be hostile to man, in which case the relation would be one of struggle; but the struggle may also subside and make room for peace, tranquillity, fulfillment. In this case, not appropriation but rather its negation would be the nonexploitative relation: surrender, "letting-be," acceptance. . . . But such surrender meets with the impenetrable resistance of matter; nature is not a manifestation of "spirit," but rather its essential *limit*.[13]

Marcuse here reaffirms the Frankfurt School's fundamental thesis of the nonidentity of man and nature, subject and object. But there is also a sense in which his theory is an affirmation of identity: not identity through the production of nature by human subjects in a mythologized process of objectification, but rather "identity" through participation in a larger whole. Here the Frankfurt School's insistence on nonidentity is superseded by a different kind of identity, the identity *of* nature *in* subject and object, which recognizes itself in reflection and aesthetic appreciation and so mediates itself in a positing that affirms rather than transforms what is. In this participatory identity, all creationist excesses of the Marxist theory of subjectivity have been laid to rest. It is no longer assumed that practice necessarily involves transformation in the strong and active sense Lukács and Marx sometimes give that term.

A PARABLE

Feuerbach long ago pointed out that theology lives on in philosophy far beyond its time. More recently, Ernst Bloch has shown that religion attempts to project utopian solutions to the socially insoluble problems of the day at the extreme edge of human subjective capacities. Marxism would be, on the terms of this theory, the secularization of religious utopia through the discovery of the way to a real resolution of the problems in social practice. In both Feuerbach and Bloch, the humanization or secularization of religion involves a critical appropriation of the hopes of the past in the context of a theory of finitude.

Philosophy of praxis begins with the attempt to carry out such a project not directly on the basis of a critique of religion, but indirectly, through a critique of religious survivals in pre-Marxist philosophical thought. In particular, the split between spirit and matter is discovered at the basis of the antinomy of subject and object, and the identity of the finite subject and object proposed as a basis for a thoroughgoing philosophical atheism, purged of theological conceptions. But we have seen that this enterprise is far more difficult than it seemed at first. Creationism still haunts the theory, and the Frankfurt School's critique of this theological residue seems to lead toward a contemplative affirmation of nature.

Philosophy of praxis is no abstract nature mysticism, but a concrete project for social change. Yet though it is no mysticism, it confirms the hypothesis of Feuerbach and Bloch. In the formulation I have given it, this philosophy is freed of certain theological postulates only to repeat others in a critical appropriation that ought to be acknowledged. The idea of letting be, or reconciliation as a positive mediation and a true positing is adumbrated in Jesus' parable of the lilies of the field. It is beautifully anticipated in a Buddhist tale which has a particular relevance to this discussion because it concerns a reconciled technology, the swords of the legendary maker Okazaki Masamune. This account is from Suzuki.

Masamune flourished in the latter part of the Kamakura era, and his works are uniformly prized by all the sword connoisseurs for their excellent qualities. As far as the edge of the blade is concerned, Masamune may not exceed Muramasa, one of his ablest disciples, but Masamune is said to have something morally inspiring that comes from his personality. The legend goes thus: When someone was trying to test the sharpness of a Muramasa, he placed it in a current of water and watched how it acted against the dead leaves flowing downstream. He saw that every leaf that met the blade was cut in twain. He then placed a Masamune, and he was surprised to find that the leaves avoided the blade. The Masamune was not bent on killing, it was more than a cutting implement, whereas the Muramasa could not go beyond cutting, there was nothing divinely inspiring in it. The Muramasa is terrible, the Masamune is humane. One is despotic and imperialistic, the other is superhuman, if we may use this form of expression.[14]

This tale is the mythological expression of the demand for a non-creationist concept of practice. The feeling that such a concept is self-contradictory only testifies to the persistent influence of the theological idea of creation. Behind this idea, in turn, stand the epistemological limits of class society. All human practice contains a nontransformative moment, a moment in which the letting be of what is establishes a horizon of transformation under which the active work of change goes on. Reification arises not from this moment of letting be *per se*, but from its systematic misconstruction in class society as an eternal law of nature beyond all mediation by the subject. Thus practice is narrowed to its transformative dimension, while the establishment of its horizon is conceptualized "contemplatively" as a reified objectivity opposed to man. Since practice cannot act on its horizon, the more vigorous its exertions the more effectively does it reproduce the very framework of assumptions within which it is condemned to operate. In the parable, the sword which cuts annihilates its object only to find another in the perpetual flow of the stream. Masamune's sword is the more powerful because it acts not on things—on leaves or men—but on the horizon of its own practice, the assumption that killing is an inevitable fate.

Can we find a model for such transcending practice outside the religious context of this tale? Marcuse seeks in the aesthetic dimension a new kind of unreified practice, for it is in that dimension that the nontransformative moment is most clearly a mediation, a positing that belongs essentially to practice itself as the basis for its more active side. For example, the architectural style which leaves trees standing is as much a mediation of nature as a different style which begins by levelling them. From an aesthetic standpoint, the living trees are as surely chosen and incorporated into the lives of human beings as if they had been bulldozed. What is more, the letting be of the trees shows respect not only for outer nature, but also for that which in human nature requires trees. It is as much nature in the subject as without which is mediated in this reconciliation; for, whatever human beings do to an

Other, they simulatenously do to themselves in another mode. That is, in effect, the defining trait of a finite being.

The concept of practice as transformation and the correlated concept of being as merely given immediacy preserve the creationist notions of theology they attempt to cancel. This is the fundamental flaw in the philosophies of practice of Marx and Lukács. While practice holds the place of the divinity in this new conception, the unreflected objectivity of nature bespeaks its degradation to mere matter. The outcome is incoherent: nature as immediacy calls forth the absolute subject, a secularized form of spirit, as its lord and master. But the postulate of the absolute subject devalues the sort of practice in which finite human beings can engage, giving rise to fundamental contradictions in the philosophy of praxis. The remarks above have attempted to unravel the tangled skein and to free philosophy of praxis from the burden of its creationist conception of subject and object.

Notes

(Throughout the footnotes, Georg Lukács, *History and Class Consciousness*, trans. by R. Livingstone (Cambridge: MIT, 1971) will be referred to as *"HCC."* All references are to this edition, but Livingstone's translation has sometimes been modified to approach literalness as nearly as possible.)

CHAPTER 1

1. The contrast between these two dimensions of the Marxian theory is usefully developed in relation to Lukács by Andrew Arato in "Lukács' Theory of Reification," *Telos*, no. 11 (1972), pp. 52–53. Cf. also, Stanley Moore, "Utopian Themes in Marx and Mao: A Critique for Modern Revisionists," *Monthly Review* 21, no. 2 (1969).

2. Important summaries of the debate are contained in: Ernest Mandel, *La Formation de la Pensée Economique de Karl Marx* (Paris: Maspero, 1967); Jürgen Habermas, *Theorie und Praxis* (Neuwied und Berlin: Luchterhand, 1967). Also interesting are: Herbert Marcuse, "The Foundations of Historical Materialism," in *Studies in Critical Theory*, trans. by J. de Bres, (Boston: Beacon, 1973), first published in 1932; Louis Althusser, "Sur le jeune Marx," in *Pour Marx* (Paris: Maspero, 1966); Bertell Ollman, *Alienation* (New York: Cambridge University, 1971); István Mészáros, *Marx's Theory of Alienation* (New York: Harper & Row, 1972).

3. Important discussions of the relation of the *Grundrisse* to *Capital* are: Roman Rosdolsky, *Zur Entstehungsgeschichte des Marxschen 'Kapital'* (Wien: Europa Verlag, 1968); Irving Fetscher, "The Young and the Old Marx," in Shlomo Avineri, ed., *Marx's Socialism* (New York: Lieber-Atherton, 1973); Ernst Mandel, *La Formation de la Pensée Economique de Karl Marx* (Paris: Maspero, 1967). The authors all agree that the early

concept of alienation in Marx is further developed in the concept of fetishism in *Capital*.

4. Mandel, *op. cit.*, p. 172.

5. *HCC*, p. xliv (emphasis omitted).

6. Marx, "Economic and Philosophical Manuscripts," *Karl Marx: Early Writings*, trans. and ed., by T. B. Bottomore (London: C. A. Watts, 1963), p. 217.

7. *HCC*, p. 197.

8. *HCC*, p. 144.

9. *HCC*, p. 145. For a further discussion of Lukács' concept of praxis, see Lucien Goldmann, *Lukács et Heidegger* (Paris: Denoël, 1973), pp. 103–105.

10. Herbert Marcuse, "The Foundations of Historical Materialism," *op. cit.*, p. 24. The translator has somewhat simplified the original. Cf. Herbert Marcuse "Neue Quellen zur Grundlegung des Historischen Materialismus," in *Der Deutsche künstlerroman, Frühe Aufsätze* (Frankfurt: Suhrkamp, 1979), p. 530–531.

11. Jürgen Habermas, *Knowledge and Human Interests*, trans. by J. Shapiro, (Boston: Beacon, 1971), p. 28.

12. Herbert Marcuse, *Reason and Revolution* (Boston: Beacon, 1964), p. 275.

13. *Ibid.*, p. 314.

14. *Ibid.*, p. 293. Clearly, Marcuse changed his position from that expressed in his 1932 essay, cited above.

15. Marx, "Economic and Philosophical Manuscripts," *op. cit.*, p. 155.

16. *Ibid.*, p. 157. In this, as in many other passages from the early Marx quoted here, italics have been left out for the sake of clarity.

17. One who sees Marx's *Manuscripts* as an ethical work is Eugene Kamenka. See his, *Marxism and Ethics* (New York: St. Martins, 1969). A contrary position is taken by Bertell Ollman, *op. cit.*, p. 47. Cf. Allen Wood, "The Marxian Critique of Justice," *Philosophy and Public Affairs* 1, no. 3 (Spring 1972). For an important discussion of the historical debate over Marxism and ethics, see "Y a-t-il une sociologie marxiste?" in Lucien Goldmann, *Recherches Dialectiques* (Paris: Gallimard, 1959).

18. Herbert Marcuse, *Reason and Revolution* (Boston: Beacon, 1964), p. 136.

19. Georg Lukács, "Moses Hess and the Problems of Idealistic Dialectics," in George Lukács, *Tactics and Ethics*, trans. by M. McColgan, ed. by R. Livingstone (New York: Harper & Row, 1975), p. 191.

20. Marx, "Letter to Ruge," L. Easton and K. Guddat, trans. and eds., *Writings of the Young Marx on Philosophy and Society* (New York: Doubleday, 1967), p. 213.

21. *Ibid.*, p. 213.

22. Frederick Engels, "Ludwig Feuerbach and the End of Classical German Philosophy," Marx and Engels, *Selected Works* (New York: International, 1968), pp. 596–597.

23. Marx, "On the Jewish Question," *op. cit.*, p. 50.

24. For a summary of the theory, see the appendix to Habermas' *Knowledge and Human Interests.*

25. Alfred North Whitehead, *Science in the Modern World* (New York: Mentor, 1948), p. 88.

26. Susan Buck-Morss, *The Origins of the Negative Dialectic* (New York: The Free Press, 1977), pp. 26–27.

27. Marx, "The Eighteenth Brumaire of Louis Bonaparte," Marx and Engels, *Selected Works* (New York: International, 1968), p. 121.

28. Herbert Marcuse, "Philosophy and Critical Theory," *Negations*, trans. by J. Shapiro (Boston: Beacon, 1968), p. 142.

29. Marx, "Theses on Feuerbach," L. Easton and K. Guddat, trans. and eds., *Writings of the Young Marx on Philosophy and Society* (New York: Doubleday, 1967), p. 402.

30. I owe many of the ideas in this section to Gerald Doppelt, who suggested that I include it.

31. Marx and Engels, *The Communist Manifesto* (New York: International, 1979), p. 29.

CHAPTER 2

1. John Locke, "An Essay Concerning the True Origin, Extent and End of Civil Government," in Ernest Barker, ed., *Social Contract* (New York: Oxford University, 1962), p. 133.

2. *Ibid.*, p. 15.

3. Jean-Jacques Rousseau, "The Social Contract," trans. by G. Hopkins, in Ernest Barker, ed., *Social Contract* (New York: Oxford University, 1962), p. 175.

4. Karl Marx, "Contribution to the Critique of Hegel's Philosophy of Right: Introduction," in T. B. Bottomore, trans. and ed., *Karl Marx: Early Writings* (London: C. A. Watts, 1963), p. 52.

5. *Ibid.*, p. 52.

6. Herbert Marcuse, "Philosophy and Critical Theory," in *Negations* trans. by J. Shapiro, (Boston: Beacon, 1968), p. 137.

7. Karl Marx, "Letter to Ruge," in Loyd Easton and Kurt Guddat, trans. and eds., *Writings of the Young Marx on Philosophy and Society* (New York: Doubleday & Co., 1967), p. 213.

8. Jean-Jacques Rousseau, *Du Contrat Social* (Paris: Gonthier, 1962), p. 247. Barker's edition has the tendentiously incorrect "to obey the laws laid

down by society is to be free." Cf. Ernest Barker, ed., *Social Contract* (New York: Oxford University, 1962), p. 186. For more on the relation of Rousseau and Kant, see Ernst Cassirer, *Rousseau, Kant and Goethe* (New York: Harper and Row, 1963).

9. Cf. Jeffrie G. Murphy, *Kant: The Philosophy of Right* (London: Macmillan, 1970), chapter III.

10. Karl Marx, "On the Jewish Question," in T. B. Bottomore, trans. and ed., *Karl Marx: Early Writings* (London: C. A. Watts, 1963), p. 13.

11. Karl Marx, "Letter to Ruge," *op. cit.*, p. 213.

12. This critique is basic to understanding the Marxian conception of socialism and socialist politics. Marx was aware of the Hegelian critique of Jacobin voluntarism and quite self-consciously worked toward a non-voluntaristic formulation of revolutionary theory. Marx believed political revolution to be through and through tied to class society because in it moral exigencies contrary to the "private" interests of the individuals are imposed by the state on a separate civil society of private owners. A revolution to abolish class society and private property would only reproduce these evils were it to attempt to impose a moral legislation in opposition to the perceived interests of the individuals. Rather, a socialist revolution against the very principle of class would necessarily have to be rooted in these interests; only on this condition would it overcome the antinomy of state and civil society, reason and need. Whatever the course of events in the existing communist countries, Marx at least was aware of the type of problems raised by conservative critics such as Leo Strauss or J. L. Talmon, who see in Marxism simply another version of Jacobin voluntarism. For more on Marx's approach, see especially his early essay, "Critical Notes on 'The King of Prussia and Social Reform' ", in L. Easton and K. Guddat, trans. and eds., *Writings of the Young Marx on Philosophy and Society* (New York: Doubleday, 1967). Cf. on Marx and Jacobinism, François Furet, *Penser la Revolution Française* (Paris: Gallimard, 1978).

13. Marx, "On the Jewish Question," *op. cit.*, p. 30.

14. *Ibid.*, p. 30.

15. *Ibid.*, p. 30.

16. *Ibid.*, p. 30.

17. *HCC*, p. 160.

18. *HCC*, p. 126.

19. Marx, "On the Jewish Question," *op. cit.*, p. 30.

20. *Ibid.*, p. 31.

21. Lucien Goldmann, "Philosophie et sociologie dans l'oeuvre du jeune Marx: Contribution à l'étude du problème," in *Marxisme et Sciences Humaines* (Paris: Gallimard, 1970), p. 148. For a recent reformulation of the problem, see Alvin Gouldner, *The Future of Intellectuals and the Rise of the New Class* (New York: The Seabury Press, 1979).

22. Karl Marx, "Contribution to the Critique of Hegel's Philosophy of Right: Introduction," in T. B. Bottomore, trans. and ed., *Karl Marx: Early Writings* (London: C. A. Watts, 1963), p. 53.

23. *Ibid.*, p. 52.

24. *Ibid.*, p. 58. For a fuller discussion of the relation of this early concept of the proletariat to Marx's later theory of class, see William Leiss, "Critical Theory and Its Future," *Political Theory* 2 (1974), part II.

25. Marx, "Contribution to the Critique of Hegel's Philosophy of Right: Introduction," *op. cit.*, p. 59.

26. *HCC*, p. 2.

27. Marx, "Contribution to the Critique of Hegel's Philosophy of Right: Introduction," *op. cit.*, p. 54.

28. Ludwig Feuerbach, *Principles of the Philosophy of the Future*, trans. by M. Vogel, (New York: Bobbs-Merrill, 1966), p. 5.

29. *Ibid.*, p. 70.

30. *Ibid.*, p. 58.

31. *Ibid.*, p. 67. For a useful discussion of the relation of Marx to Feuerbach, see Shlomo Avineri, "The Hegelian Origins of Marx's Political Thought," in S. Avineri, ed., *Marx' Socialism* (New York: Lieber-Atherton, 1972), pp. 3–4; passim.

32. Karl Marx, "Economic and Philosophic Manuscripts," in T. B. Bottomore, trans. and ed., *Karl Marx: Early Writings* (London: C. A. Watts, 1963), p. 163.

33. Marx, "Economic and Philosophical Manuscripts," *op. cit.*, p. 158.

34. *HCC*, p. 170. Cf. also Georg Lukács, "Moses Hess and the Problems of Idealist Dialectics," in Georg Lukács, *Tactics and Ethics*, trans. by M. McColgan, ed. by R. Livingstone (New York: Harper & Row, 1975), pp. 214–215.

35. Marx, "Economic and Philosophical Manuscripts," *op. cit.*, p. 197.

36. *Ibid.*, p. 203.

37. *Ibid.*, p. 203. Jean Hyppolite has written a famous defense of Hegel in response to such criticisms. See "Aliénation et objectivation," in Jean Hyppolite, *Etudes sur Marx et Hegel* (Paris: Marcel Rivière, 1965). For a response to Hyppolite, see István Mészáros, *Marx's Theory of Alienation* (New York: Harper and Row, 1972), pp. 242–245.

38. Karl Marx and Frederick Engels, *The Holy Family, or Critique of Critical Criticism*, trans. by R. Dixon and C. Dutte (Moscow: Progress, 1975), p. 70.

39. Marx, "Economic and Philosophical Manuscripts," *op. cit.*, p. 204.

40. *Ibid.*, p. 201.

41. *Ibid.*, p. 203.

42. *Ibid.*, p. 207.

43. *Ibid.*, p. 189.

44. Quoted in Bertell Ollman, *Alienation* (New York: Cambridge University, 1971), p. 275.
45. Marx, "Economic and Philosophical Manuscripts," *op. cit.*, pp. 126–127.
46. *Ibid.*, p. 208.
47. *Ibid.*, pp. 160–161.
48. *Ibid.*, p. 130.
49. The phrase is, of course, Hegel's. See, *Hegel's Philosophy of Right*, trans. by T. M. Knox (London: Oxford University, 1952), p. 12.
50. Marx, "Economic and Philosophical Manuscripts," *op. cit.*, p. 162. That the concept of reason is truly at issue in Marx seems to me to be a necessary implication of his discussion of the reform of the sciences. Cf. *Ibid.*, pp. 163–164. This aspect of his theory will be discussed at greater length in the conclusion of this book.

CHAPTER 3

1. George Lukács, "The Old Culture and the New Culture," trans. by P. Breines and S. Weber, *Telos*, no. 5 (1970), p. 21.
2. Edmund Husserl, *The Crisis of European Sciences and Transcendental Phenomenology*, trans. by D. Carr (Evanston: Northwestern Univ., 1970), p. 299.
3. The other major work of this tendency is Karl Korsch, *Marxismus und Philosophie* (Frankfurt: Europaische Verlagsanstalt, 1966), originally published in 1923, at the same time as Lukács' *History and Class Consciousness*. Korsch's book is available in a partial English translation under the title *Marxism and Philosophy*, trans. by F. Halliday (New York: Monthly Review, 1970).
4. Marx, *Capital*, vol. I, p. 105.
5. *Ibid.*, vol. I, p. 83.
6. *HCC*, p. 102.
7. For a discussion of the gap between Marx's critique of political economy and the revolutionary theory of socialism, cf., Stanley Moore, "Utopian Themes in Marx and Mao: A Critique for Modern Revisionists," *Monthly Review* 21, no. 2 (1969). Moore's argument is developed further in "Marx and Lenin as Historical Materialists," *Philosophy and Public Affairs* 4, no. 2 (1975).
8. *HCC*, p. 152.
9. *HCC*, pp. 184–185.
10. *HCC*, p. 231.
11. *HCC*, p. 102.
12. *HCC*, p. 179.

13. See, for example, John Horton, "The Dehumanization of Anomie and Alienation: A Problem in the Ideology of Sociology," *British Journal of Sociology* 15, no. 4 (1964), pp. 283–300. The best discussion I have seen is in an unpublished paper by David Harvey, Lyle Warner, Lawrence Smith and Ann Safford Harvey, "A Critical Analysis of Seeman's Concept of Alienation."

14. Peter Berger and Thomas Luckmann, *The Social Construction of Reality* (New York: Doubleday, 1966), p. 89.

15. An exhaustive survey of the various meanings of the concept of culture is provided by A. L. Kroeber and Clyde Kluckhohn, *Culture: A Critical Review of Concepts and Definitions* (New York: Vintage, 1963). They conclude that "most social scientists" would define culture as follows:

> Culture consists of patterns, explicit and implicit, of and for behavior acquired and transmitted by symbols, constituting the distinctive achievement of human groups, including their embodiments in artifacts; the essential core of culture consists of traditional (i.e., historically derived and selected) ideas and especially their attached values; culture systems may, on the one hand, be considered as products of action, on the other as conditioning elements of further action. (*Ibid.*, p. 357.)

David Kaplan and Robert Manners offer a broad survey of current thinking about culture in social science in *Culture Theory* (Englewood Cliffs: Prentice-Hall, 1972).

16. *HCC*, p. 203.

17. This, of course, places Lukács in diametrical opposition to any sort of functionalist social theory. For an interesting parallel critique of functionalism, cf. Alvin Gouldner, *The Coming Crisis of Western Sociology* (New York: Basic Books, 1970), pp. 219–220.

18. Max Weber, *On the Methodology of the Social Sciences*, trans. and ed. by E. Shils and H. Finch (Glencoe: The Free Press, 1949).

19. Maurice Merleau-Ponty, *Les Aventures de la Dialectique* (Paris: Gallimard, 1955), p. 31. Merleau-Ponty's book contains an important discussion of the relation of Weber to Lukács, particularly as concerns the problem of relativism.

20. For a further discussion of this distinction, see the conclusion of this book.

21. Hegel's *Phenomenology of Mind* might be interpreted as the first attempt to understand forms of rationality as cultural forms. The convergence of modern epistemology and social theory in recent years has renewed interest in this general problem area. Thomas Kuhn's work in the history of science, to give an example, invites cultural generalization.

Similarly, Paul Feyerabend's ever more radical critiques of positivism come
closer and closer to suggesting that the senses should be treated as cultural,
and not as biological organs of perception, a perspective which I will take up
in the conclusion to this book. From an entirely different angle, under the
influence of phenomenology, ethno-methodology in the social sciences has
developed a critique of the range and limits of various forms of rationality in
social life. (See, Harold Garfinkel, "The Rational Properties of Scientific and
Common-Sense Activities," in Anthony Giddens, ed., *Positivism and
Sociology* (London: Heineman, 1975).) Another convergent line of thought
has developed in France, around the work of Claude Lévi-Strauss, Michel
Foucault and Jacques Derrida, all of whom have discussed the forms of
rationality in cultural terms. (For a brilliant short statement of the problems
as they appear in France, see Jacques Derrida, "Structure, Sign, and Play
in the Discourses of the Human Sciences," Richard Macksey and Eugenio
Donato, eds., *The Structuralist Controversy* (Baltimore: Johns Hopkins,
1972).)

22. Gareth Stedman Jones, "The Marxism of the Early Lukács: An
Evaluation," *New Left Review*, no. 70 (1971), p. 44.

23. Lucio Colletti, *Il Marxismo e Hegel* (Bari: Laterza, 1969), p. 342.

24. Karl Marx, *A Contribution to the Critique of Political Economy*
(Chicago: Charles H. Kerr, 1904), p. 293. For a similar approach to the
interpretation of this passage, see Andrew Arato, "Lukács' Theory of
Reification," *Telos*, no. 11 (1972), pp. 31–32. A thorough discussion of
Marx's theory of appearance, from a somewhat different perspective, is to
be found in G. A. Cohen, "Karl Marx and the Withering Away of Social
Science," *Philosophy and Public Affairs* 1, 2 (1972).

25. Marx, *A Contribution of the Critique of Political Economy* (Chicago:
Charles H. Kerr, 1904), p. 302.

26. Hegel, *Science of Logic*, trans. by W. H. Johnston and L. G.
Struthers (London: Allen & Unwin, 1961), vol. II, p. 135.

27. *HCC*, p. 83.

28. Lukács, "Moses Hess and the Problems of Idealist Dialectics," in
Tactics and Ethics, ed. by R. Livingstone, trans. by M. McColgan (New
York: Harper and Row, 1975), p. 215.

29. *HCC*, p. 177.

CHAPTER 4

1. *HCC*, p. xiv.

2. Frederick Engels, "The Peasant Question in France and Germany,"
Marx and Engels, *Selected Works* (New York: International, 1969), p. 648.

3. *HCC*, pp. 110 and 187–188. It was Nietzsche who first attempted a

general critique of rationality as an expression of the will to power, identifying conceptual generality and hierarchy with corresponding social projects of control and domination. The Frankfurt School continues some aspects of this critique, which it enriches and concretizes in terms of the Lukácsian critique of reification.

4. Quoted by Lukács in *HCC*, p. 141. The passage is from *Die Differenz des Fichteschen und Schellingschen Systems*. In its entirety it reads: "The antitheses . . . which used to be expressed in terms of mind and matter, body and soul, faith and reason, freedom and necessity, etc., and were also prominent in a number of more restricted spheres and concentrated all human interests in themselves, became transformed as culture advanced into contrasts between reason and the senses, intelligence and nature and, in its most general form, between absolute subjectivity and absolute objectivity. To transcend such ossified antitheses is the sole concern of reason. This concern does not imply hostility to opposites and restrictions in general; for the necessary course of evolution is one factor of life which advances by opposites: and the totality of life, at its most intense is only possible as a new synthesis out of the most absolute separation."

5. *HCC*, p. 121.

6. *HCC*, p. 91.

7. *HCC*, p. 100.

8. *HCC*, p. 112.

9. *HCC*, p. 89.

10. *HCC*, p. 130. The implications of this Lukácsian concept of contemplation for the development of the Frankfurt School's theory of authority will be discussed in the next chapter.

11. *HCC*, p. 63.

12. *HCC*, p. 77. This dilemma Lukács has already treated at great length in *The Theory of the Novel* before becoming a Marxist. That early work, which contains Lukács' critique of romanticism and ethical idealism, concludes with a chapter on the "transcendence of social forms of life." The messianic-utopian stage in Lukács' thought lies here, in the idea of the creation of a new epic community through the dissolution of all social conventions and constraints in soul-to-soul encounters of the Dostoievskian type. Lukács' later idea of unity of theory and practice is an attempt to de-mythologize this early notion by supplying concrete mediations through which it could be realized. For more on Lukács' messianism, see Michael Löwy, *Pour une Sociologie des Intellectuels Révolutionnaires* (Paris: PUF, 1976).

13. *HCC*, p. 134.

14. *HCC*, p. 87.

15. *HCC*, p. 135.

16. For a sensible review of the position of the Frankfurt School, see William Leiss, *The Domination of Nature* (New York: Braziller, 1972), chapters 7 and 8. The appendix also summarizes and contributes to the debate over Marcuse's position on the ideological character of modern technology.

17. *HCC*, p. 129.

18. *HCC*, p. 112.

19. *HCC*, p. 128. Once again the parentage of Adorno and Horkheimer's *The Dialectic of Enlightenment* should be clear from its quite similar analysis of the contradictions of formal rationality and technological control.

20. Lucien Goldmann, *Mensch, Gemeinschaft und Welt in der Philosophie Immanuel Kants* (Zürich: Europa Verlag, 1945) and Georg Lukács, *The Young Hegel* (Cambridge: MIT, 1975).

21. *HCC*, p. 115.

22. *HCC*, p. 116.

23. *HCC*, p. 117.

24. *HCC*, p. 122.

25. *HCC*, p. 126.

26. *HCC*, p. 124.

27. *HCC*, p. 160. Implicit in this critique of Kantian moral idealism is a critique of political voluntarism in the left wing of the socialist movement. It is interesting that Lukács himself is generally perceived as a political voluntarist even though he elaborated the theoretical basis of a profound critique of that position. Lukács' own critique of sectarianism as a disguised ethical idealism is to be found in *HCC*, pp. 320–322 and 326–328. I have discussed this problem in Andrew Feenberg, "Lukács and the Critique of 'Orthodox' Marxism," *The Philosophical Forum* III, nos. 3–4 (1972), pp. 431–432. That same issue also contains a typical discussion of Lukács' purported sectarianism. Cf., Adam Schaff, "The Consciousness of a Class and Class Consciousness."

28. *HCC*, p. 134. This interpretation of Kant's ethics is of course alien to the concerns of recent Anglo-American analysis of Kant's thought. It is not, however, without precedent in earlier Kant-criticism. Cf., G.W.F. Hegel, *The Phenomenology of Mind*, trans., by J. B. Baillie (New York: Macmillan, 1961), pp. 615 ff.

29. *HCC*, p. 126.

30. *HCC*, p. 126.

31. *HCC*, p. 137.

32. *HCC*, p. 138. Kant defines the "intuitive understanding" as follows: "In fact our understanding has the property of proceeding in its cognition, e.g. of the cause of a product, from the analytical-universal (concepts) to the particular (given empirical intuition). Thus, as regards the manifold of the

latter, it determines nothing, but must await this determination by the judgment of the subsumption of the empirical intuition (if the object is a natural product) under the concept. We can, however, think an understanding which being not like ours, discursive, but intuitive proceeds from the synthetical-universal (the intuition of a whole as such) to the particular, i.e., from the whole to the parts. The contingency of the combination of the parts, in order that a definite form of the whole shall be possible, is not implied by such an understanding and its representation of the whole." Immanuel Kant, *Critique of Judgment*, trans. by H. H. Bernard (New York: Hafner, 1951), p. 255. The centrality Lukács attributes to the idea of an "intuitive understanding" in the development of classical German philosophy follows closely on Hegel's interpretation of the period. In *Glauben und Wissen*, Hegel even asserts that "*die Idee dieses urbildlichen, intuitiven Verstandes ist im Grunde durchaus nichts anders als dieselbe Idee der transzendentalen Einbildungskraft.*" G.W.F. Hegel, *Glauben und Wissen* (Hamburg: Felix Meiner, 1962), p. 33. This identification also underlies Lukács' interpretation of Fichte and Hegel. Among recent Kant scholars, those of the historical-ontological school seem to be closest to Lukács in emphasis. Cf. Heinz Heimsoeth, "Metaphysical Motives in the Development of Critical Idealism," Moltke Gram, ed., *Kant: Disputed Questions* (Chicago: Quadrangle, 1967). Heimsoeth writes, for example, that "It is a conviction of Kant's which endures to his last period, that complete and immediate knowledge is only present where the subject posits the object." *op. cit.*, p. 161.

33. *HCC*, p. 142.

34. The accuracy of this interpretation of Kant is not the issue here since this was in fact how Hegel understood critical philosophy. Cf. G. W. F. Hegel, *Glauben und Wissen* (Hamburg: Felix Meiner, 1962), pp. 20–21.

35. See Herbert Marcuse, *Hegels Ontologie* (Frankfurt: V. Klostermann, 1968), pp. 40–43 and especially pp. 133–134.

36. *HCC*, p. 155.

37. *HCC*, p. 147.

38. *HCC*, p. 17.

39. *HCC*, p. 18.

40. *HCC*, p. 201.

41. *HCC*, p. 155.

42. *HCC*, p. xxiii. For an evaluation of Lukács' self-criticism, see the concluding chapters of this book. Here it is necessary to point out the error of Lukács' assertion in this passage that Hegel rejected the postulate of subject-object identity, for Hegel did admit a mediated identity.

43. For a discussion of the historical background to Lukács' concept of

subject-object identity, see James Schmidt, "The Concrete Totality and Lukács' Concept of Proletarian *Bildung*," *Telos*, no. 24 (1975), pp. 2–40.

44. Max Horkheimer, "Traditional and Critical Theory," Max Horkheimer, *Critical Theory*, trans. by M. J. O'Connell (New York: Herder and Herder, 1972), p. 211. Subject-object identity in this sense is clearly quite different from the kind of identity rejected by the Frankfurt School. Cf. Max Horkheimer, *The Eclipse of Reason* (New York: Seabury, 1974), pp. 169–173. In that discussion, it can be seen that the Frankfurt School interprets subject-object identity entirely in terms of the relation of "spirit" to "nature," leaving out the interaction of theory and practice in history in which identity consists most importantly for Lukács. For a different view, cf. Martin Jay, "The Frankfurt School's Critique of Marxist Humanism," *Social Research* XXXIX: 2 (1972).

45. *HCC*, p. 21.

46. *HCC*, p. 163.

47. *HCC*, p. 185.

48. *HCC*, p. 187. To what extent does this treatment of the category of subjectivity answer objections to the use of that category formulated from a structuralist viewpoint? The structuralist critique of subjectivism and humanism began as a reaction to phenomenology and Sartreianism, doctrines interpreted to argue for the unbounded creative capacity of pure consciousness. The early formulations of the critique were scientistic and hence internal to the general antinomy of subjectivism/objectivism they attempted to transcend. (For an especially revealing example, see the November, 1963, issue of *Esprit*, containing a fascinating debate between Lévi-Strauss and several representatives of French phenomenology.) More recently, there has been a recognition in France that the simple "abolition" of the subject by a scientistic *coup de force* cannot resolve the specific problems posed by the study of society. The decisive question is not the ontological one of whether human subjectivity "exists" or whether it is a merely subjective illusion (of a "subject"?), but rather the methodological one of the position of subjectivity in a framework of structures and rules that it does not posit but which are—not so much determining for it as—constitutive of its very being. In different ways, Pierre Bourdieu and Michel Foucault have been attempting to think through the implications of this new position. A brief summary of Bourdieu's position and his relation to structuralism is contained in Pierre Bourdieu, "Structuralism and Theory of Sociological Knowledge," *Social Research* 35:4 (1968), especially pp. 703–706. Foucault summarizes his perspective somewhat paradoxically as follows: "The positivities that I have tried to establish must not be understood as a set of determinations imposed from the outside on the thought of

individuals, or inhabiting it from the inside, in advance as it were; they constitute rather the set of conditions in accordance with which a practice is exercised, in accordance with which that practice gives rise to partially or totally new statements, and in accordance with which it can be modified. These positivities are not so much limitations imposed on the initiative of subjects as the field in which that initiative is articulated (without, however, constituting its centre). . . . I have not denied—far from it—the possibility of changing discourse: I have deprived the sovereignty of the subject of the exclusive and instantaneous right to it." Michel Foucault, *The Archaeology of Knowledge*, A. M. Sheridan Smith, trans. (New York: Pantheon, 1972), pp. 208–209. Without claiming that Lukács (or Marx) anticipates the subtle and original modes of analysis elaborated by Bourdieu and Foucault, I think it can be shown that they are at least situated in neighboring conceptual fields, and that the critique of Marxist subjectivist-humanism elaborated in reaction to Sartre's *Critique* does not apply to their formulation of the Marxist theory of the subject.

CHAPTER 5

1. *HCC*, p. 52.

2. G. W. F. Hegel, *Hegel's Philosophy of Right*, trans. by T. M. Knox, (Oxford: Oxford University, 1971), p. 11.

3. Cf., for an example, Karl Kautsky, *The Dictatorship of the Proletariat*, trans. by H. J. Stenning (Ann Arbor: University of Michigan, 1964). For a detailed discussion of the problem of mechanical determinism in this period, see Lucio Colletti, "Bernstein and the Marxism of the Second International," Lucio Colletti, *From Rousseau to Lenin*, trans. by J. Merrington and J. White (New York: Monthly Review, 1972).

4. Marx and Engels, *The German Ideology* (New York: International, 1968), p. 14.

5. Engels, "Engels to J. Bloch," in Marx and Engels, *Selected Works* (New York: International, 1968), p. 693.

6. *Ibid.*, p. 692. Recently, Dissatisfaction among Marxists with mechanistic theory of ideology has been especially pronounced and fruitful in literary theory. See, for example, Raymond Williams, *Marxism and Literature* (Oxford: Oxford Univ., 1977).

7. *HCC*, pp. 201–202.

8. Cf. Shlomo Avineri, "Consciousness and History: *List der Vernunft* in Hegel and Marx," in Warren E. Steinkraus, ed., *New Studies in Hegel's Philosophy* (New York: Holt, Rhinehart and Winston, 1971).

9. Engels, "Engels to J. Bloch," *op. cit.*, p. 693.

10. Lucien Sebag, *Marxisme et Structuralisme* (Paris: Payot, 1964), p. 88.

11. Louis Althusser, *Réponse à John Lewis* (Paris: Maspero, 1973).

12. This way of posing the question suggests wider links between the early Marxist thought of Lukács and much recent social philosophy. For two particularly interesting reviews of various attempts to reconsider the nature of human subjectivity in the light of the social nature of man, see Richard J. Bernstein, *The Restructuring of Social and Political Theory* (Philadelphia: Univ. of Penn., 1978); and Mark Poster, *Existential Marxism in Postwar France* (Princeton: Princeton Univ., 1975), pp. 306–360. For a further development of this theme, see the next chapter of this book. In addition, the section of Chapter 7 entitled "Existential Marxism"—I owe the phrase to Poster—considers epistemological implications of this theme.

13. See Pierre Bourdieu, *Outline of a Theory of Practice*, R. Nice, trans. (New York: Cambridge, 1977), pp. 22–30.

14. Sebag, *op. cit.*, p. 88.

15. Martin Heidegger, *Being and Time*, J. Macquarrie and E. Robinson, trans. (New York: Harper and Row, 1962), p. 99.

16. Alfred Schutz, *The Phenomenology of the Social World*, trans. by G. Walsh and F. Lehnert (Evanston: Northwestern University, 1967), p. 42.

17. Lucien Goldmann, *Lukács et Heidegger* (Paris: Denoël, 1973), pp. 100–101.

18. Maurice Merleau-Ponty, *Les Aventures de la Dialectique* (Paris: Gallimard, 1955), p. 67.

19. Max Weber, *On the Methodology of the Social Sciences*, trans. and ed. by E. Shils and H. Finch (Glencoe: The Free Press, 1949), p. 42.

20. *HCC*, p. 51.

21. *HCC*, p. 51.

22. *HCC*, p. 51.

23. Max Weber, *op. cit.*, p. 92.

24. *Ibid.*, p. 92.

25. See Andrew Feenberg, "Lukács and the Critique of 'Orthodox' Marxism," *The Philosophical Forum* III: nos. 3–4 (1972), pp. 422–467.

26. Morris Watnick, "Relativism and Class Consciousness," in L. Labedz, ed., *Revisionism* (London: Allen and Unwin, 1962), p. 160.

27. James Miller, "Marxism and Subjectivity," *Telos*, no. 6 (1970), p. 180. For a thorough consideration of the arguments of Miller and others who see Lukács as already a proto-Stalinist in 1923, see Andrew Feenberg, *op. cit*; and Michael Löwy, *Pour une Sociologie des Intellectuels Révolutionnaires* (Paris: PUF, 1976), pp. 227–254.

28. *HCC*, pp. 51–52.

29. For Lukács' view as I interpret it, see Andrew Feenberg, *op. cit.* Cf. also essays by Lucien Goldmann and István Mészáros in *Aspects of History and Class Consciousness*, I. Mészáros, ed. (New York: Herder and Herder, 1972), especially pp. 75 and 100–102 in connection with themes developed here.

30. Antonio Gramsci, *The Modern Prince* (New York: International, 1959), pp. 113–114.

31. Georg Lukács, *Lenin: A Study on the Unity of his Thought*, N. Jacobs, trans. (London: New Left Books, 1974), p. 27 (trans. modified). This synthesis of Gramsci and Lukács parallels Lucien Goldmann's theory of the relation of artistic creation to social groups. Lucien Goldmann was probably the most influential interpreter of the early work of Lukács, especially in France. Without forming a school in the proper sense of the term, Merleau-Ponty, Lucien Sebag, Joseph Gabel and others in France developed a characteristic interpretation of *History and Class Consciousness* emphasizing the concept of practice, as I do in this chapter. Goldmann was the social theorist of the group who made the most impressive use of Lukács' categories, publishing a classic work of literary criticism based on Lukács' early theories and methods. See *Le Dieu Caché* (Paris: Gallimard, 1955). Goldmann's approach is summarized in a passage worth quoting to amplify what has already been said above concerning politics.

"In reality, the relation between the creative group and the work usually takes the following form: the group constitutes a process of structuration which gives rise in its members' consciousness to specific intellectual, practical and emotional tendencies in their attempt to elaborate a coherent response to the problems which are posed by their relations with nature and their inter-human relations. Exceptions apart, these tendencies remain, however, far from real coherence, to the extent that they are . . . counteracted in the individuals' consciousness by the effects of their membership in numerous other social groups.

"Thus the mental categories only exist in the group in the form of more or less approximately coherent tendencies which we have called worldviews, views which the group does not therefore create, but of which it elaborates . . . the constitutive elements and the energy that permits the unification of the latter. The great writer is precisely the exceptional individual who succeeds in creating in a certain domain, that of the literary . . . work, a coherent, or nearly rigorously coherent imaginary universe, the structure of which corresponds to that structure toward which the group as a whole tends . . .

"The considerable difference between the sociology of contents and structuralist sociology is apparent. The first sees in the work *a reflection of* collective consciousness, the second sees in it, on the contrary, one of the most important *constitutive elements* of that consciousness, the one which makes it possible for the members of the group to become consciousness of what they thought, felt and did, even without understanding its objective significance."

Lucien Goldmann, *Pour une Sociologie du Roman* (Paris: NRF, 1964), pp. 346–347 (my trans.). For an interpretation of Gramsci which shows the influence of Goldmann and Lukács, see Jean-Marc Piotte, *La Pensée Politique de Gramsci* (Paris: Anthropos, 1970).

32. Andrew Arato, "Lukács' Theory of Reification," *Telos*, no. 11 (1972), pp. 57–58.

33. The relevant passages in *HCC* are to be found on pp. 74–77, 164–165 and 180–181.

34. Marx, "The Eighteenth Brumaire of Louis Bonaparte," in Marx and Engels, *Selected Works* (New York: International, 1968), p. 121.

35. *HCC*, p. 186.

36. *HCC*, p. 164.

37. *HCC*, p. 149.

38. Cited in *HCC*, p. 149.

39. This aspect of Lukács' theory has a certain intuitive appeal, however, it is rather contradicted than otherwise by the most famous application of his own categories, Lucien Goldmann's study of Pascal and Racine. Cf. Lucien Goldmann, *Le Dieu Caché* (Paris: Gallimard, 1955). Goldmann has a marginal social class (the *noblesse de robe*) elaborating a coherent worldview.

40. *HCC*, p. 166.

41. *HCC*, p. 168.

42. Marx, *Capital*, trans. by S. Moore and E. Aveling (New York: Modern Library, 1906), vol. I, p. 20.

43. *HCC*, pp. 76–77.

44. Theodor Adorno, "Erpresste Versöhnung," *Noten Zur Literatur II* (Franfurt: Suhrkamp, 1961), p. 152.

45. Marx, *Capital* (Moscow: Progress, 1966), Vol. III, p. 831.

46. See Frederick Engels, *The Housing Question* (Moscow: Progress, 1970), pp. 22–24, 29, and 48. This is one of the clearest discussions of these matters in Marx and Engels, and it is particularly interesting in this context because of its explicit concern with authoritarianism in the lower classes.

47. Max Horkheimer, "Authority and the Family," in Max Horkheimer, *Critical Theory*, M. O'Connell, trans. (New York: Herder and Herder, 1972), p. 83.

48. *Ibid.*, p. 89.

49. Herbert Marcuse, "A Study on Authority," in Herbert Marcuse, *Studies in Critical Philosophy*, J. de Bres, trans. (Boston: Beacon, 1973), p. 133.

50. Stanely Aronowitz, *False Promises* (New York: McGraw Hill, 1973), p. 58. For another major attempt to revive the theory of proletarian class consciousness see Alexander Kluge and Oscar Negt, *Öffentlichkeit und Erfahrung. Zur Organisationsanalyse von bürgerlicher und proletarischer Öffentlichkeit* (Frankfurt: Suhrkamp, 1972).

51. *Ibid.*, p. 10.

52. *Ibid.*, p. 10.

53. There are of course also important differences in approach, Goldmann relying on a concept of homology to explain the relations between thought and action, while Aronowitz has a dynamic model of the relation which more closely resembles that of Lukács.

CHAPTER 6

1. Karl Marx, *The Poverty of Philosophy* (New York: International, 1963), p. 115.

2. Karl Marx, *Capital*, S. Moore and E. Aveling, trans. (New York: Modern Library, 1906), vol. I, pp. 15 and 23.

3. Pierre Bourdieu, *Outline of a Theory of Practice*, R. Nice, trans. (New York: Cambridge, 1977), p. 84.

4. Marx, *Capital*, op. cit., vol. I, p. 15.

5. *HCC*, p. 38.

6. *HCC*, p. 197. For more on the subject of what I have called the "non-moral" concept of the transition to socialism in Marxism, see Andrew Feenberg, "Transition or Convergence: Communism and the Paradox of Development," in Frederic J. Fleron, Jr., ed., *Technology and Communist Culture* (New York: Praeger, 1977), pp. 105–110.

7. Marx, "Economic and Philosophical Manuscripts," in *Karl Marx: Early Writings*, T. B. Bottomore, trans. and ed. (London: C. A. Watts, 1963), p. 162.

8. Max Weber, *On the Methodology of the Social Sciences*, E. Shils and H. Finch, eds. (Glencoe: The Free Press, 1949), p. 81.

9. *HCC*, p. 153.

10. Pierre Bourdieu, *Outline of a Theory of Practice*, R. Nice, trans. (Cambridge: Cambridge Univ., 1977), p. 9.

11. "The structures of intersubjectivity are just as constitutive for experiences and instrumental action as they are for attitudes and communicative

action. These same structures regulate, at the systems level, the control of outer and the integration of inner nature—that is, the process of adapting to society that, by virtue of the competencies of socially related individuals, operate through the peculiar media of utterances that admit of truth and norms that require justification." Jürgen Habermas, *Legitimation Crisis*, T. McCarthy, trans. (Boston: Beacon, 1975), pp. 10–11. It is true that Habermas formulates the relation of work to interaction in terms of a parallelism of relatively autonomous sub-systems, but passages such as the one cited here indicate that these are not equal in weight in the construction of social systems: the economy is no determining base, but rather a "limiting condition" for the elaboration of the socio-cultural system of meanings. For a sharp polemic against the Marxist theory of determination by the base, see Jean Baudrillard, *The Mirror of Production*, M. Poster, trans. (St. Louis: Telos, 1975).

12. Marshall Sahlins, *Culture and Practical Reason* (Chicago: Univ. of Chicago, 1976), pp. 164–165.

13. This is precisely the difficulty that has been raised for Winch's attempt to conceptualize social systems in terms of the rules to which their members are supposed to conform. See Peter Winch, *The Idea of a Social Science and Its Relation to Philosophy* (New York: Humanities, 1976). Cf. Ernest Gellner, "The New Idealism—Cause and Meaning in Social Science," in Anthony Giddens, ed., *Positivism and Sociology* (London: Heineman, 1975), especially p. 137.

14. Sahlins, *op. cit.*, p. 212.

15. Karl Marx and Frederick Engels, *The German Ideology* (New York: International, 1968), p. 7.

16. Marx, "Introduction to the Critique of Political Economy," in *A Contribution to the Critique of Political Economy*, N. I. Stone, trans. (Chicago: Charles Kerr, 1904), p. 280. (trans. modified.)

17. *HCC*, p. 326.

18. *HCC*, p. 183.

19. Antonio Gramsci, *The Modern Prince* (New York: International, 1959), p. 140.

20. *HCC*, p. 262.

21. For a discussion of Sartre's contribution, see Mark Poster, *Existential Marxism in Postwar France* (Princeton: Princeton Univ., 1975).

22. For a discussion of Baudrillard and several other French social theorists, see Robert D'Amico, "Desire and the Commodity Form," *Telos*, no. 35 (1978), pp. 88–122.

23. Bourdieu, *op. cit.*, p. 169.

24. *HCC*, p. 169.

CHAPTER 7

1. See John Hoffman, *Marxism and the Theory of Praxis* (New York: International, 1975). There are also several Althusserian critiques of Lukács in English which belong to the same general tendency. See Gareth Stedman Jones, "The Marxism of the Early Lukács: An Evaluation," *New Left Review* 70 (1971), pp. 27–64; and John Horton and Fari Filsoufi, "Left-Wing Communism: an Infantile Disorder in Theory and Method," *The Insurgent Sociologist* VII, no. 1 (1977). Both these articles make the mistake of identifying Lukács' turn to "orthodoxy" with the writing of his little book on *Lenin* in 1924, even though several major essays developing the viewpoint expressed in *History and Class Consciousness* are written in the years that follow. The question of *political* Leninism was simply not the touchstone of *philosophical* "orthodoxy" for Lukács these critics make it out to be.

2. Abram Deborin, "Lukács und seine Kritik des Marxismus," in Abram Deborin and Nikolai Bucharin, *Kontroversen über dialektischen und mechanistischen Materialismus* (Suhrkamp: Frankfurt, 1968), p. 192.

3. *Ibid.*, p. 192.

4. *Ibid.*, p. 214.

5. *Ibid.*, p. 218.

6. Maurice Merleau-Ponty, *Les Aventures de la Dialectique* (Paris: Gallimard, 1955), p. 66.

7. *HCC*, p. xxxvi.

8. For a balanced discussion of this commonplace charge, see Andrew Arato, "Lukacs' Theory of Reification," *Telos*, no. 11 (1972), pp. 42–43.

9. Alfred Schmidt, *The Concept of Nature in Marx*, B. Fowkes, trans. (London: New Left Books, 1971), p. 70. Jîndrich Zéleny carries the misunderstanding still further, writing that Lukács interprets Marx's first thesis on Feuerbach to call for "a reduction of all reality to practical human activity." See Jîndrich Zéleny, *Die Wissenschaftslogik und 'Das Kapital'* (Wien: Europa Verlag, 1968), p. 302.

10. *HCC*, p. xxiii.

11. *HCC*, p. 234. (my emphasis) Cf., Georg Lukács, *Geschichte und Klassenbewusstsein* (Neuwied und Berlin: Luchterhand, 1968), p. 410.

12. Andrew Arato argues for a similar conclusion in *op. cit.*, pp. 41–42.

13. *HCC*, p. 206.

14. *HCC*, p. 131.

15. *HCC*, p. 207.

16. See Lucio Colletti, *Il Marxismo e Hegel* (Bari: Laterza, 1969), pp. 317–356. This chapter is titled, significantly, "Da Bergson a Lukács."

17. *HCC*, p. 110.

18. *HCC*, p. 10. G. S. Jones quotes the second sentence of this passage

to prove Lukács' hostility to natural scientific method *in general*. (*op. cit.*, p. 20.) Such crudely selective use of quotations is evidently compatible with the "scientific" objectivity Jones boosts in his article!

19. *HCC*, p. 24.

20. *HCC*, p. 207.

21. For a sophisticated example of this approach, see Guiseppe Bedeschi, *Alienazione e Feticismo nel Pensiero di Marx* (Bari: Laterza, 1968), pp. 177–207.

22. *HCC*, p. 19.

23. *HCC*, p. 123.

24. Lucien Goldmann, *Sciences Humaines et Philosophie* (Paris: PUF, 1952), p. 17.

25. Alfred Schmidt, *op. cit.*, p. 79.

26. Karl Marx, "Economic and Philosophical Manuscripts," in *Karl Marx: Early Writings*, T. B. Bottomore, trans. and ed., (London: C. A. Watts, 1963), pp. 160–161.

27. *Ibid.*, p. 127.

28. *Ibid.*, p. 160.

29. *Ibid.*, p. 161.

30. *Ibid.*, p. 160.

31. *Ibid.*, p. 206.

32. *Ibid.*, p. 217.

33. *Ibid.*, p. 163. On the equivalence of idealism and materialism, cf. Robert Havemann, *Dialektik ohne Dogma?* (Hamburg: Rowohlt, 1964), pp. 27–32.

34. *Ibid.*, p. 164.

35. *Ibid.*, p. 164. Marx's discussion of the reform of science has divided commentators. For two different interpretations, cf. István Mészáros, *Marx's Theory of Alienation* (New York: Harper and Row, 1972), pp. 101–102; and Jean Hyppolite, *Études sur Marx et Hegel* (Paris: Marcel Rivière, 1965), pp. 112–113. Mészáros gives a common sense reading to Marx's text, which Hyppolite interprets literally as calling for the most radical transformation of natural science. Marx's critique of science has been renewed recently by Herbert Marcuse in *One-Dimensional Man* (Boston: Beacon, 1964), pp. 166 ff. Jurgen Habermas has written an important reply entitled "Technology and Science as 'Ideology' ", in Jürgen Habermas, *Toward a Rational Society*, J. Shapiro, trans. (Boston: Beacon, 1970), pp. 81–122.

36. *Ibid.*, p. 164.

37. Marx and Engels, *The German Ideology* (New York: International, 1947), pp. 36–37.

38. Ernst Bloch is the most famous example. For a discussion of the

difficulties arising from Bloch's position, see Alfred Schmidt, *op. cit.*, pp. 156–163.

39. Friedrich Nietzsche, "The Genealogy of Morals," in *The Birth of Tragedy and the Genealogy of Morals*, F. Golffing, trans. (New York: Doubleday, 1956), p. 255.

40. Marx, "Economic and Philosophical Manuscripts," *op. cit.*, p. 166. Cf. Jean-Francois Lyotard, "La place de l'aliénation dans le retournement marxiste," in Jean-Francois Lyotard, *Dérive à Partir de Marx et Freud* (Paris: UGE, 1973), pp. 112–115.

41. Cf., for example, Soren Kierkegaard, *Concluding Unscientific Postscript*, D. Swenson and W. Lowrie, trans. (Princeton: Princeton Univ., 1968), pp. 108–109. Like Marx, Kierkegaard objects to the act of abstraction in which the subject places itself outside of existence to interrogate existence. Marcel's position is less well known, but parallels this one. In his earliest writings, even before he knew of Kierkegaard, Marcel rejects the act of abstraction in which the subject conceives itself as an objective reality holding a real relation with the material substance of a body or an object of sensation. What can be so related, he asserts, is only the falsely objectified concept of the "mind," whereas in reality the subject as such disappears "behind" this objective misconstruction. It is significant that while Marcel rejects the totalizing and rationalistic aspect of Hegelianism as does Kierkegaard, he traces this particular argument back to Hegel. (See Gabriel Marcel, *Metaphysical Journal*, B. Wall, trans. (Chicago: Henry Regnery, 1952), pp. 102, and 332–339.) It is not clear to what text in Hegel Marcel refers, however, it may well be to the chapter on "Phrenology" in the *Phenomenology of Mind*. There Hegel attacks every form of objectivistic reduction of subjectivity, as epitomized in the absurd phrenological hypothesis which holds "the reality of self-consciousness to consist in the skull-bone." Hegel argues: "Brain-fibres and the like, looked at as forms of the being of mind, are already an imagined, a merely hypothetical actuality of mind—not its presented reality, not its felt, seen, in short not its true reality. If they are present to us, if they are seen, they are lifeless objects, and then no longer pass for the being of mind. . . . The principle involved in this idea is that reason claims to be all thinghood, even thinghood of a purely objective kind. It is this, however, *in conceptu:* or, only this notion is the truth of reason; and the purer the notion itself is, the more silly an idea does it become. . . ." In sum, the skull or brain, as the material reality of thought, exists as such only as an idea for thought; hence thought exists as material reality only insofar as that reality is a thought reality. The search for a material foundation for reason ends up "ingenuously" affirming a thought as reality. G.F.W. Hegel, *The Phenomenology of Mind*, J. B. Baille, trans. (London: Allen & Unwin, 1961), pp. 370–371. Like the hypothesis of the

creation of the universe, so in another way the reductionist hypothesis implies the existence of an absolute subject, beyond all but cognitive connection to existence.

42. Gabriel Marcel, "On the Ontological Mystery," Gabriel Marcel, *The Philosophy of Existentialism*, M. Harari, trans. (New York: Citadel, 1966), p. 19.

43. *Ibid.*, p. 18.

44. Martin Heidegger, *Being and Time*, J. Macquarrie and E. Robinson, trans. (New York: Harper & Row, 1962), p. 1.

45. For a discussion of the relation of Mannheim to Lukács, see Joseph Gabel, "Mannheim et le marxisme hongrois," in Joseph Gabel, *Idéologies* (Paris: Anthropos, 1974), pp. 255–278.

46. *HCC*, p. 187.

47. This is the thesis of Maurice Merleau-Ponty, *op. cit.*, pp. 43–45 and 63–64.

48. *HCC*, p. 189.

49. *HCC*, p. 1.

CHAPTER 8

1. István Mészáros, *op. cit.*, p. 249.

2. *HCC*, p. 199.

3. Marx, "Economic and Philosophical Manuscripts," *op. cit.*, p. 163.

4. See the chapter on "Sense Certainty" in Hegel, *op. cit.*, pp. 149–160. In reaction against the long dominant "logical empiricism," some contemporary epistemologists have rediscovered the basic insights of Kant and Hegel in this domain. Paul Feyerabend's critique of empiricism is particularly interesting. See Paul Feyerabend, "Problems of Empiricism," in Robert G. Colodny, ed., *Beyond the Edge of Certainty* (Englewood Cliffs: Prentice Hall, 1965), pp. 145–260; and Paul Feyerabend, *Against Method* (London: Verso, 1978), especially pp. 145–169. Feyerabend, Kuhn and the other critics of positivism in the fields of philosophy and history of science all emphasize the dialectical interaction of facts and theories, sense perceptions and conceptual frameworks. What is still missing from their account, however, is a larger cultural approach to the shifts in perceptions and paradigms they document. Perhaps their hesitation or inability to treat science as a cultural formation is due still to the heritage of positivism, its criteria of rationality, its impoverishment of historical and cultural thinking, and its attempt to autonomize science as a human activity supposedly independent of all others.

5. For a major recent study of theories about the relation of science,

278 Lukács, Marx and the Sources of Critical Theory

technology and domination, see Otto Ulrich, *Technik und Herrschaft* (Frankfurt: Suhrkamp, 1977).

6. Theodor Adorno and Max Horkheimer, *Dialectic of Enlightment*, J. Cumming, trans. (New York: Herder and Herder, 1972), p. 54.

7. *Ibid.*, p. 40. The German text is to be found in Adorno and Horkheimer, *Dialektik der Aufklärung* (Amsterdam: Querido Verlag, 1944, reprint n.d.), p. 55.

8. Adorno and Horkheimer, *Dialectic of Enlightenment, op. cit.*, p. 41. (In the German text, *op. cit.*, p. 55).

9. Adorno and Horkheimer, *Dialectic of Enlightenment, op. cit.*, p. 255. (In the German text, *op. cit.*, p. 305.)

10. Adorno and Horkheimer, *Dialectic of Enlightenment, op. cit.*, p. 253.

11. Herbert Marcuse, "Nature and Revolution," in Herbert Marcuse, *Counterrevolution and Revolt* (Boston: Beacon, 1972), p. 61.

12. *Ibid.*, p. 60. The concept of practice corresponding to such a "liberation of nature" is explained in Herbert Marcuse, *An Essay on Liberation* (Boston: Beacon, 1969), pp. 23–33.

13. Marcuse, "Nature and Revolution," *op. cit.*, pp. 68–69.

14. Daisetz T. Suzuki, "Zen and Swordsmanship I," in D. T. Suzuki, *Zen and Japanese Culture* (Princeton: Bollingen, 1959), pp. 91–92.

Index

279